They Laughed When I Sat Down

They Laughed

also by Frank Rowsome, Jr. TROLLEY CAR TREASURY

When I Sat Down

An *Informal History of Advertising*

in Words and Pictures

Frank Rowsome, Jr.

BONANZA BOOKS • NEW YORK

They Laughed When I Sat Down

Library of Congress Catalog Card Number: 59–14460

*This edition is published by Bonanza Books,
a division of Crown Publishers, Inc.,
by arrangement with McGraw Hill Book Company, Inc.*

Certain of the illustrations are supplied by courtesy of Procter and Gamble, Kellogg
Company, Ford Motor Company, *Advertising Age, Printers' Ink,* Curtis Publishing
Company, R. J. Reynolds Tobacco Company, and the Museum of the City of New York.

Acknowledgments

THIS book proposes neither to attack nor defend advertising. To assail an activity on which billions of dollars are spent annually would call, at the very least, for rolling up the polemic sleeves and spitting on the polemic hands; and to defend billions of dollars seems supererogatory, like being in favor of the west wind. Instead, the objective here is to examine informally how a single segment of the industry, magazine advertising, grew in America in the years between the Civil War and World War II. No oxen are gored, no monuments erected.

In one sense, however, the book *is* an impertinence. The notion that so huge and various a topic can be fairly covered in a single, liberally illustrated volume is cheeky. Almost every section wants, by the richness and variety of the material, to be a book in itself. A number of areas touched on—the flowering of patent medicines, the pioneering copywriters, the great growing days of the automobile—demand whole shelves of volumes. To pack it all between two covers is to ignore many beguiling byroads. Readers who care to explore them are directed first to a number of rewarding and entertaining books that this writer has gratefully drawn upon: E. S. Turner's *The Shocking History of Advertising*, James Playsted Wood's *The Story of Advertising*, and Frank Presbrey's *History and Development of Advertising*. A detailed (and hilarious) account of the original "They Laughed When I Sat Down" advertisement is included in John Caples' *Making Ads Pay*. Other books that touch on single aspects of the broad topic and that are both informative and entertaining include Jean Burton's *Lydia Pinkham Is Her Name*, Gerald Carson's *Cornflake Crusade*, and Earnest Elmo Calkins' engaging biography, *And Hearing Not*. Other fruitful areas for further exploration include the trade press—particularly *Printers' Ink* in the early days—and the memoirs of men like Rowell, Lasker, and Hopkins.

Dozens of people have cheerfully supplied the writer with facts, counsel, correction, and quantities of treasured old magazines. Among them, in alphabetical array, are Howard G. Allaway, Ava Armstrong, Earnest Elmo Calkins, John Caples, Nell Carson, Hugh Coryell, Ralph H. Flynn, Kendall Goodwyn, Godfrey Hammond, Howard C. Jensen, Frank Long, Nelson C. Metcalf, Everett Ortner, Eldridge Peterson, Ruth Smith, Robert P. Stevenson, John Sweet, Kenneth Swezey, and George Winoker. The only persons who have *not* been helpful, in fact, are the nameless past librarians who in years gone by instructed the bindery to cut off and discard advertising sections before binding magazine volumes.

Finally, particular thanks are owed to Roberta G. Marks for uncounted hours of red-eyed library labors. Miss Marks has been more than an expert researcher and library drudge; some sections of the book, including most of Chapter 4, were originally written by her.

Frank Rowsome, Jr.

Contents

They Laughed When I Sat Down

"Any fool can make soap. .

LEAFING through the pages of a sixty-year-old popular magazine can be a delightful experience. It is not so much the editorial contents—the earnest exposés of shame in high places or the sugar-glazed stories of thwarted love—as it is the old advertisements that enchant modern eyes. Those naive and touching ads seem to be windows opening directly on the time of our fathers, giving intriguing glimpses of the way people once lived, the bodily ailments that beset them, what they wore and ate and wanted. The catarrh and consumption cures, the horn phonographs and cast-iron stoves, the kerosene lamps and steel-wire bustles all tumble out together in a wonderful lack of sophistication.

In these old issues are reflected two very important historical phenomena. One is the popular magazine itself, product of growing American prosperity and the rise of a comfortable middle class. *McClure's, Munsey's, The Saturday Evening Post,* and *Ladies' Home Journal,* which suddenly came to success near the century's turn, are the direct forerunners of what we know now as The Mass Media. But more important, here is the birthplace of modern advertising. Here advertis-

2

on the Past

It takes a clever man to sell it.''

Thomas J. Barratt, of Pears' Soap

ing grew away from the simple announcements, posters, and signs — minor servants of trade — and became itself an alarmingly powerful method of merchandising.

These old advertisements are not, however, a completely accurate reflection of their time. They tend to disarm us by their ingenuousness and period charm — and because many of them are so engagingly awful. But it is doubtful if a picture showing a winsome child standing awestruck at father's feet, while mother, swelling like an hourglass, manipulated the controls of the Angelus Player-Piano, was ever exactly equivalent to reality. One peculiar characteristic of advertising is that it creates its own antibodies. One quickly learns, in reading the advertisements of one's own time, to build up automatically an immunity against their persuasions. It is no more logical to think Grandpa was regularly gulled by Old Sachem Bitters and Wigwam Tonic or Dr. Thacher's Electric Belt than to think that the typical American family now sit about the living room brandishing tall glasses of beer with expressions of simple-witted delight.

Nevertheless, magazine ads from about the turn of the century are particularly fascinating to modern eyes. Here are the beginnings of much that we know well. Automobiles ("Do you want a machine that has few parts, and all of them instantly accessible?"), electric lamps ("The most beautiful artificial light known!"), and washing machines ("Don't be a slave to your washtub!") have all made an appearance. Patent-medicine claims grow a little tamer, making less flagrant assaults on credulity. New brand-named soaps, cereals, and dentifrices begin to shoulder aside such mysterious nineteenth-century wares as "Dykes Beard Elixir" and the "Improved Home Turko-Russian Folding Bath Cabinet — Prevents Contracting Disease." Instead, we see Columbia (cylinder) records modestly described as

Clear   Rich
   Original   Entertaining
     Loud   Captivating
       Unrivaled   Outwearing
         Musical   Resonant
           Brilliant   Delightful
            Inspiring   Superior
              Attractive

3

And men still so conservative as to use a straight razor are promised "free shaves for 30 days to convince you beyond possible doubt that we mean exactly what we say and prove all we promise for the Gillette Safety Razor."

It is not just the products advertised that grow increasingly familiar after 1900. The ways in which they are presented also begin, though gropingly and uncertainly at first, to develop familiar patterns. Testimonials, present from the Paleozoic period of advertising, now come less from anonymous citizenry than from the famous and, by implication, more discriminating. The alarming possibility that one may smell bad is obliquely mentioned, beginning a motif that will echo like the horn of Roland for decades to come. Elaborate picture-frame settings, together with headlines and typefaces so splendid as to verge on illegibility, betray the presence of early art directors. Soaps and dentifrices let it be known that their use is a reliable route to romance; and the necessity of having *faith* in a cosmetic is suggested. The social utility of home machinery is underlined by a manufacturer who advertises in 1904: "You need an Edison Phonograph to entertain your friends. It is the only infallible amusement for every sort of visitor."

In those early days of the modern magazine it is still possible, of course, to find countless advertisers who have not gotten the word. Penny-pinching firms cling to the belief that since space costs money it should be thickly seeded with tiny type. In many ads, elaborate but unreadable structures of logic demonstrate conclusively that a failure to buy The Product is a surrender to unreason. Experiments, frequently disastrous, can be observed in whimsy, verse, allegory, and picturesque libels of competitors. Some advertisements, hopelessly unintelligible, suggest they were conceived in a blinding flash by the company owner himself and never submitted to tests more rigorous than approval by moist-palmed underlings.

As with any newly developing art, the boundaries of felicity are imperfectly mapped. Some meat packers, for instance, see no unwisdom in graphic illustrations of slaughtered animals.

The New 88 Note
ANGELUS PLAYER-PIANO

If you have ever spent the evening in the company of some well-skilled, versatile pianist you have experienced in part only the numberless delights which every evening await the owner of an *Angelus* Player-Piano. Many music lovers on first hearing the *Angelus* Player-Piano have expressed their absolute amazement that the music which it enables the player to produce is so much more artistic, so superior in every way to that which any other player-piano makes possible. This for one reason is because the *Angelus* Player-Piano only is equipped with

THE MELODANT

that wonderful device which picks out and emphasizes the melody notes in such splendid contrast to those of the accompaniment. Using the *Melodant* rolls tho *Augelus* player is enabled to bring out all the delicate beauties of the melody which, with the ordinary player-piano are usually lost in the maze of ornamentation which surrounds it. The *Melodant*, like the *Phrasing Lever*, the *Diaphragm Pneumatics* and the *Artistyle Music Rolls*, is a patented exclusive feature of the *Angelus*.

Hear the *Angelus* instruments before you purchase any other. The *Knabe-Angelus*, *Emerson-Angelus* and the *Angelus Player-Piano* in the U. S. The *Gourlay-Angelus* and *Angelus Player-Piano* in Canada

Write for our beautiful new booklet, and name of convenient dealer

THE WILCOX & WHITE CO.   *Business Established 1877*   **MERIDEN, CONN.**
Regent House,   Regent Street,   London.

Only twenty-odd years separated the ad above from that at left. But the difference is tremendous. Status symbolism and a hint of togetherness have already begun to rear their heads. That's a Phrasing Lever that Mom is working so feelingly on her player piano.

The enraptured creature at left, caught in the toils of corset boning, doesn't seem upset by her fix. Some grim details of what boning could really do, however, are hinted at in the ad below.

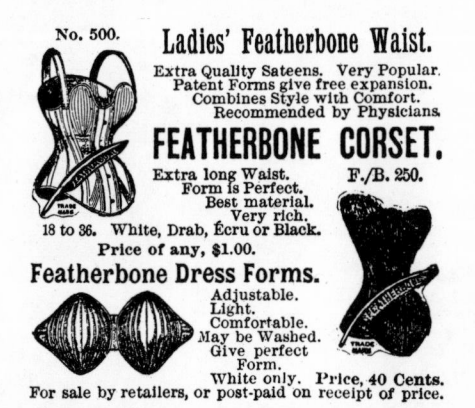

Often, too, there is a diffuseness of objective, a lack of the instinct for the jugular. An early Studebaker ad announced that the firm had excellent gasoline-propelled tonneau touring cars for sale. But if you felt that gasoline cars weren't right for you, it also offered an assortment of fine electric vehicles. And if by chance you were still adamant, there remained the firm's choice line of buggies and carriages.

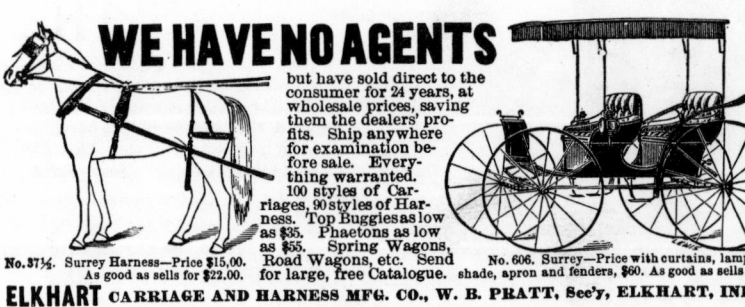

A tend-to-business salesmanship often turned up in tiny type. Those lines ("Surrey—Price with curtains, lamps, sunshade, apron, and fenders, $60. As good sells for $90") made it seem like a bargain for anybody's barn.

PORING over old magazines is more than just a trip to the attic of the American past. It is also an opportunity to examine the beginnings of today. Advertising, like the magazine itself, existed in this country before it became a republic. The first American magazine advertisement is believed to have been a tiny notice, soliciting the return of a runaway slave, in Benjamin Franklin's *General Magazine & Historical Chronicle* for May 10, 1741. Through most of the nineteenth century, however, advertising was a meek and docile handmaiden to commerce: "Fine laces and china, lately arrived by ship," and the like. Even during the prosperity following the Civil War, advertising amounted to a force no more meaningful than the plumes of vapor around Mt. Pelee before 1902.

Then, in a short generation bridging the turn of the century, came a violent eruption that still reverberates. It has reshaped the behavior of every American since, however willfully independent he may try to be.

Neither publishers nor advertisers kept adequate records in the early days—certainly nothing like the lush jungles of statistics surrounding the industry today. But the data that have been preserved indicate that magazines and advertising both had a phenomenally sudden growth. As late as the eighties there were only a handful of national magazines in this country. Most of them, like *Scribner's*, *Harper's*, and *Century*, were low-

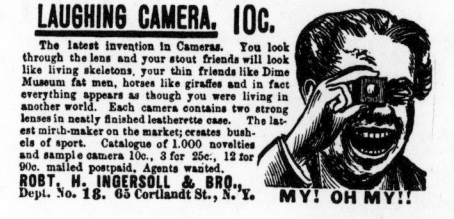

No. 2⅞.

$7.50

A persistent advertising problem has been finding an apt product name. This hair tonic sounded rather like a skin disease.

circulation periodicals edited specifically for an upper-class readership. Circulation rarely reached much over 100,000 per issue; such advertising as was carried was customarily walled off in a back section, to minimize annoyance to the fastidious reader.

But in the nineties the situation changed with giddy speed. *McClure's* shot from 8,000 circulation in 1893 to 250,000 in 1895; in the same period *Munsey's* rocketed from 40,000 to 500,000. Government figures revealed the startling fact that in 1900 the combined circulations of *McClure's*, *Munsey's*, *Cosmopolitan*, and the *Ladies' Home Journal* was 2,483,000 copies a month. And several years later the *Ladies' Home Journal*, which had had only a few thousand readers in the eighties, became the first U.S. magazine to exceed one million in circulation.

Advertising soared along with circulation, quickly breaking out of its quarantine sections in the back and diffusing through the editorial pages. Frank Munsey attracted many first-time magazine advertisers by announcing a rate of $1 per thousand circulation. *Harper's* unbent with the others, and discovered that it had carried a greater amount of advertising in 1900 than in the total of the previous twenty-two years.

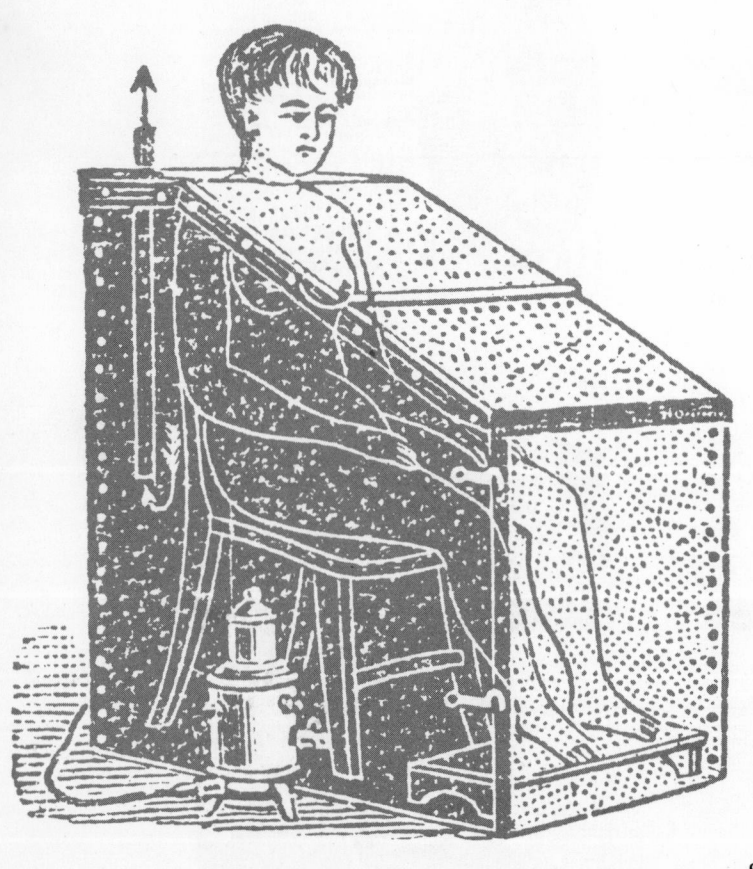

The lady mortifying her flesh at left is encased in an object called the Improved Home Turko-Russian Folding Bath Cabinet. One of its virtues was that "It Prevents Contracting Disease"—obviously an unpleasant ailment.

THE GEM PENCIL SHARPENER.

For Schools and Offices.

Sharpens both Lead and Slate Pencils.

GOULD & COOK, Manufacturers,
Leominster, Mass.
Send for Circular.

Small illustrations were found to be highly desirable in ads for products that might be strange to the viewer. This 1893 ad let the picture tell the story.

Why did it happen? The answers are interlocked. In one sense this was another historic combination of men and ideas at a point in time. Frank Munsey and S. S. McClure were both convinced that 10-cent magazines would have far greater potential circulations than did the established 35-cent "quality" periodicals, and this idea proved to be brilliantly right. An economic oddity of magazine publishing soon became evident: magazines could be sold at, or even below, the cost of their manufacture and still earn dazzling profits. (*McClure's* was netting $5,000 a month as early as 1896.) The money came, of course, from the advertising revenue that a large circulation attracted.

There were many other factors. In 1879 Congress had granted magazines the benefits of low-cost mailing privileges. Newsstands, the chief source of single-copy sales, grew considerably in numbers. The rural population also became newly accessible as R.F.D. routes increased from only 44 in 1897 to more than 25,000 in 1903. Most important of all, perhaps, was the spectacular climb of the national literacy rate with the spread of free and compulsory education, toward the end of the century.

Technical developments also helped. Newly perfected rotary presses were ten times faster than the old flat-bed ones, and the new photoengraving process not only permitted the easy reproduction of photographs but also eliminated the slow, costly step of cutting plates by hand in copper or wood.

Equally revolutionary new editorial skills appeared: men like McClure, George Horace Lori-

Unbridled, groundless claims of medical ads in the eighties seem more shocking now than they did then. After all, a nostrum might work; doctors didn't offer much better; and think of all the testimonials you could read.

mer, and Edward Bok developed the special knack of steering their magazines toward mass middle-class audiences. Just after the turn of the century the first magazine crusade—the muckraking exposés of business trusts and corrupt city governments—attracted hundreds of thousands of new readers to magazines.

Even more responsible for this explosive expansion of magazines and advertising were deep economic pressures. As the nineteenth century drew to a close, the country began to grow faster and faster in population and wealth. Except for the minor interlude of the war with Spain, there was peace in the land. The last frontiers were being settled; the West was won. A remarkable second industrial revolution was taking place in the factories: a host of new things could now be cranked out in seemingly unlimited volume—packaged foods and electric lights, phonographs and player pianos, mass-produced shoes, clothes, and furniture. Marketing all these new products was quite as important as manufacturing them. People had to be taught the pleasures of such new possessions as porcelain bathroom fixtures or bicycles.

The sudden national passion for bicycles is especially symptomatic, for it coincided almost precisely with the first great rush of national magazine advertising. Bicycle manufacturers, a highly competitive crew, broke trails that many others, notably the auto makers, would later follow.

The precursor of today's Grand Central Station was no mean shed, and it reflected none of Commodore Vanderbilt's "The public be damned!" viewpoint. The fine, bland arrogance of this copy, with its sidelong glances at lesser rivals, can be matched today in current airline ads, where the themes are parallel: the "perfection of modern facilities"; and safety, convenience, and luxury beyond belief. But the New York Central didn't offer nubile maidens serving free champagne.

Parker Pens

They're Good—

Made in many styles.

Smooth and easily they glide along— a pleasure to all who use them.

Sold and warranted by us and by more than 9000 of the best dealers.

See a section of our factory, Block 47, Varied Industries Building, World's Fair.

Free Accident Policy insuring against breakage of rubber parts.

No student's equipment complete without a Parker

LUCKY CURVE Fountain Pen.

Interesting—A Six-inch Aluminum Rule and Paper Cutter free to any intending purchaser of a Parker Pen who will write us to this effect, and send stamp for postage on ruler.

Let us send you our 20-page catalogue, "The Reason Why," and the name of a dealer where you can see the pen with the "Lucky Curve."

THE PARKER PEN CO. 34 Mill Street Janesville, Wis.

This plain but honest object is a 1904 fountain pen, innocent of the stylist's prettifying touch, as also is the copy. That squiggly border made someone happy.

The early, pre-craze cycle ads were directed toward mechanically minded readers and were soberly preoccupied with fine points of design. But as popular enthusiasm took hold and millions of Americans began to puff at the pedals, the ads changed in character. Pretty girls rather than tubular frames dominated the artwork, and the copy beneath forsook machinery for lyrical descriptions of effortless mobility. As Jerome K. Jerome observed, the ads suggested that "bicycling consisted of being wafted along by unseen heavenly powers." This was confirmed by another commentator on advertising, E. S. Turner: "The only persons shown straining at the pedals were those who bestrode machines of inferior make, or who were being pursued by bulls."

Another institution which generated much advertising, the inside bathroom, arrived late in this country. Built-in bathtubs were rare in the early part of the nineteenth century, and bathing was commonly managed in a portable tub in the kitchen. In the White House the first permanently installed bathtub showed up in 1850, during the presidency of Millard Fillmore. But high cost and the scarcity of indoor plumbing in general made spread of the custom slow. There was also considerable suspicion of bathing itself; frequent baths were widely supposed to lay one open to various diseases and general debilitation. Besides, wasn't there a link between bathing and deca-

"It's so Lovely I Just Can't Go to Bed."

a heating novelty is our....

Aluminum Oil Heater

Famous lost campaigns. Fifty years from now when our plastic bubble homes are run by uranium, present-day ads for lightbulbs and electric heaters may seem as quaint as these earnest efforts on behalf of kerosene appliances.

The Angle LAMP

A MODEL OF CONVENIENCE.

The only reason for the use of Gas and Electricity as lighting systems is their convenience and freedom from care. Kerosene oil gives a better, softer, pleasanter light than either, and is much less expensive. The Angle Lamp—the new method of burning oil—makes kerosene as convenient as gas or electricity; it actually costs less to burn than the troublesome old-fashioned lamp, and whether burned at full height or turned low there is

No Smoke, No Odor, Little Heat.

In fact, the Angle Lamp is the practical, economical, convenient method of burning which makes common kerosene oil the best and most satisfactory method of lighting city and country homes, stores, churches, factories, etc. We will gladly prove this to you by a **30 Days' Trial.**

Ask your dealer, but in the meantime **WRITE FOR CATALOG "D,"** showing 32 varieties from $1.80 up and full information about the only lamp that has ever been advertised. Please mention your dealer's name.

The Angle Mfg. Co., 78-80 Murray St., New York.

dence? Hadn't the Romans bathed incessantly during their celebrated Decline and Fall?

By the seventies, matters began to change. Bathing grew to be associated with the rich and refined and, before long, with the merely well-to-do and smart. By the eighties bathing was taken up with enthusiasm by the middle class, and advertising by Mott, Standard, Kohler, and Crane began to flower. Their ads featured not only great claw-footed iron tubs, but also ornately fauceted washbasins and flush toilets complete with richly varnished overhead tanks and artistic wrought-iron pull chains. Under the stimulus of advertising, having a fine bathroom grew to be a fashion, almost a fad. (There are marked parallels to the present rage for high fidelity: in each case costly new equipment was merchandised successfully to middle-class customers, who proved eager to buy shiny and mysterious objects which were not only pleasing in use but also testified to the taste and refinement of their buyers.) Though the iron foundrymen, brass-equipment manufacturers, and plumbers had no way of knowing it, they were

Triumph Pouring and Surging Washer.

building a demand for a whole new range of supplementary products in addition to their own wares. The lotions, potions, dentifrices, deodorants, razor blades, laxatives, toilet paper, and soaps that were to be consumed in this new domestic culture center were to amount to many billions of dollars; and all these in turn provoked ever-increasing programs of advertising. President Calvin Coolidge recognized this spiral of consumer demand when he told a convention of advertising men: "The uncivilized make little progress because they have few desires. The inhabitants of our country are stimulated to new wants in all directions."

By the turn of the century it had become evident that advertising — magazine advertising in particular — was the best way of reaching the large and growing middle class, a group for whom many products had a special symbolic value. For example, a rich man had always been able to buy a piano if he wanted one; so pianos had an associative link with the cultured rich. Advertising pointed out that pianos quite the equal of those

The eloquent headline and scene of domestic squalor below show a better grasp of advertising than S. C. Johnson's cataloguelike use of the same theme. But why the tot is enmeshed in the sewing machine is a mystery.

Mangles
Keep the Clothes White,
Save all the Fuel and 5-6 of the Labor,
Make the Servants Want to Stay.

Send for circulars and terms. Good agents wanted. Address,

S. C. JOHNSON
RACINE, WISCONSIN.

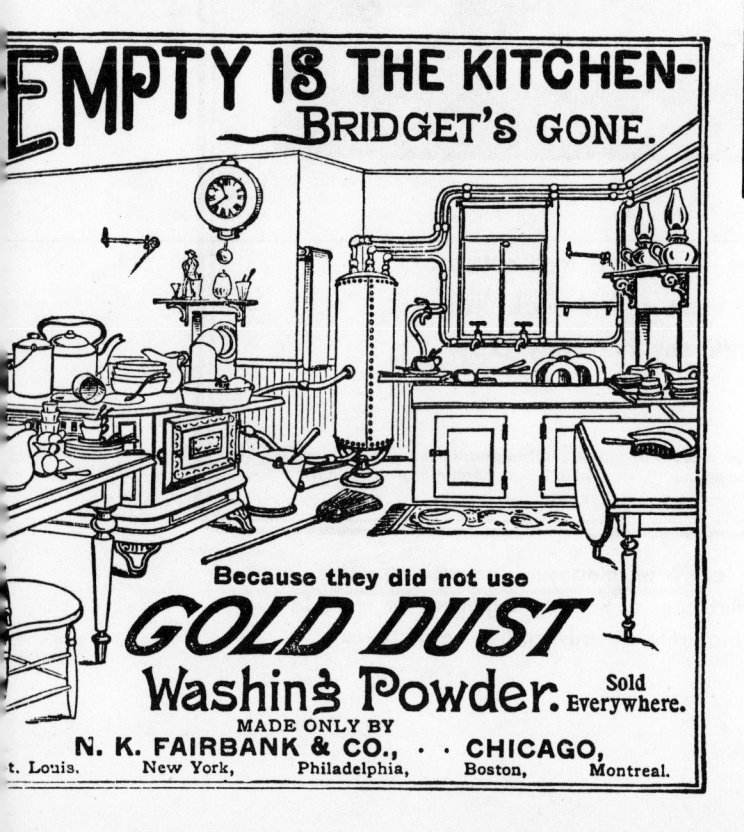

EMPTY IS THE KITCHEN-
BRIDGET'S GONE.

Because they did not use
GOLD DUST
Washing Powder. Sold Everywhere.
MADE ONLY BY
N. K. FAIRBANK & CO., · · CHICAGO,
t. Louis.   New York,   Philadelphia,   Boston,   Montreal.

The SINGER MAN'F'G Co.
SINGER

13

Linen is a more elegant material than cotton for summer dress. Linen will look like cotton if washed with any but Ivory Soap.

There is no "free" (uncombined) oil or alkali in **Ivory** Soap. The combination is complete. Containing no "free oil," it rinses perfectly. There being no "free alkali," it is harmless to color, skin or fabric. 99 44/100 per cent. pure. It floats.

Gracious living reared its sleek head early in magazine advertising. This larky scene of pat-ball is transmuted, by complex copy logic, into argument for Ivory Soap. The adjective "elegant" was aged prematurely by advertising copywriters.

14

hitherto owned only by the best people were now within reach of the moderately prosperous — and could even be had in self-playing models, in case nobody in the house was very good at lining out *The Lost Chord* or *The Rosary*. Piano ads frequently emphasized also the wholesome pleasures of family gatherings about the status symbol. This cozy image — which we now know as "togetherness" — has long shown peculiar power over potential customers, possibly because of its contrast with grumpy reality.

Even if symbols didn't exist naturally, advertising could often manufacture them. Vacuum cleaners had no natural associative tie with the

Clothing ads in the 1900s varied from the studied negligence of the Arrow Collar man to the anatomical improbabilities of corset models. Sometimes, as with Flexo Garters, the artist had trouble capturing the human form.

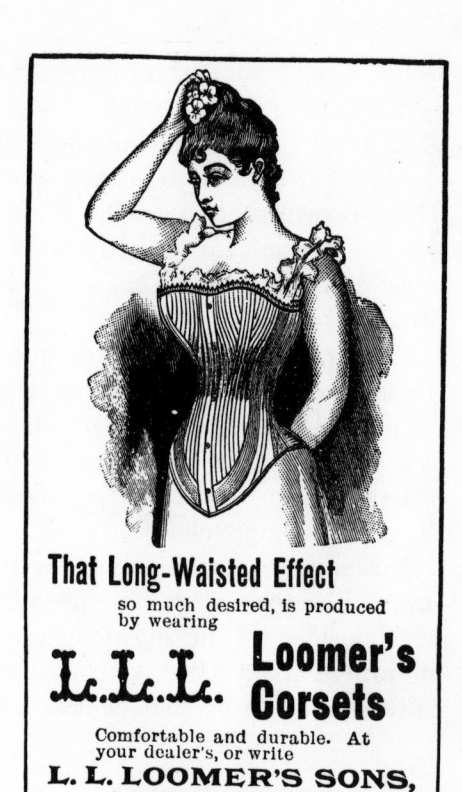

That Long-Waisted Effect
so much desired, is produced
by wearing
**L..L..L. Loomer's
Corsets**
Comfortable and durable. At
your dealer's, or write
L. L. LOOMER'S SONS,
Sole Mfrs., Bridgeport, Conn.
and Chicago, Ill.

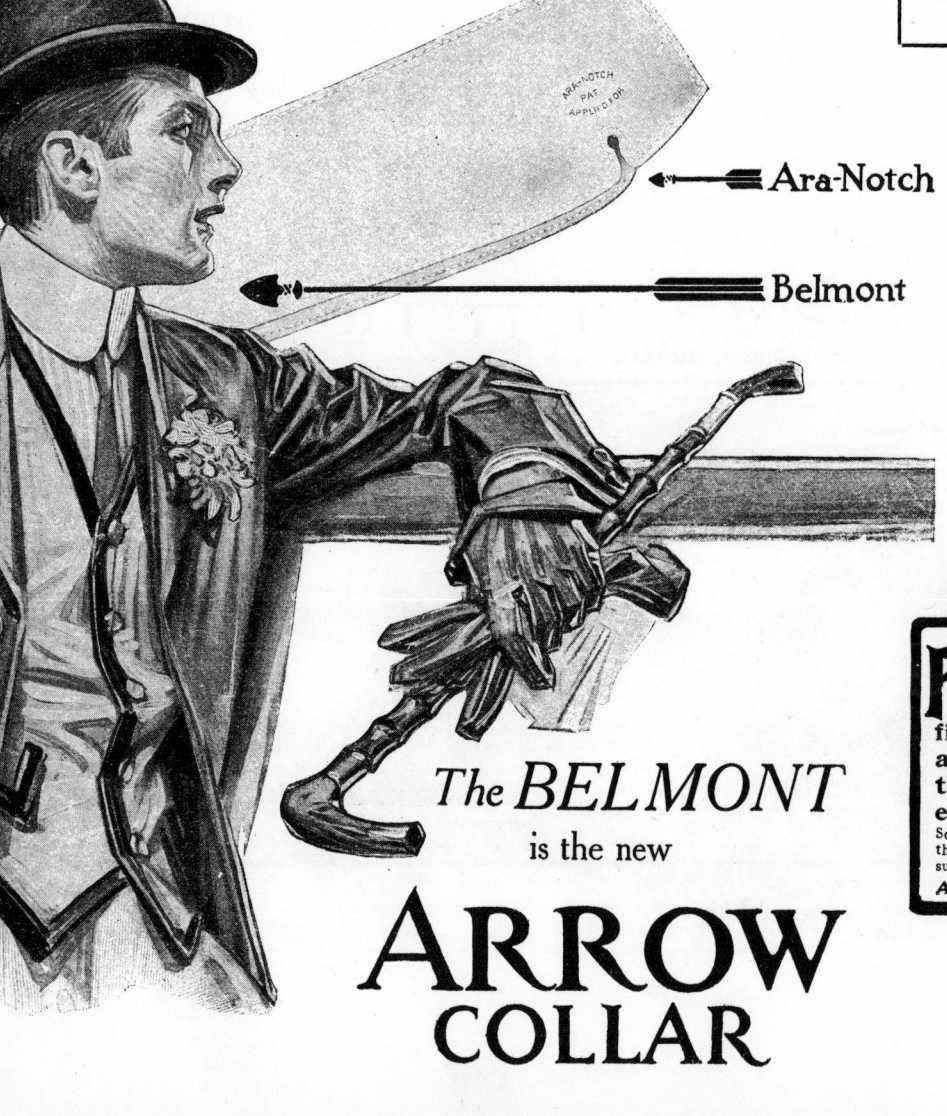

← ◄≡ Ara-Notch

← ◄≡ Belmont

The BELMONT
is the new

ARROW
COLLAR

MEN'S
Flexo Garters
fit perfectly, hug the limb comfort=
ably without binding, never let go of
the hose, never tear them, last longest, look neatest — are best garters.
Sold by all dealers. Insist on Flexo, and if the dealer hasn't
them, send us his name and 25c and we will see that you are
supplied. Flexo Garters in fine heavy ribbed silk elastic, 50c.
A. STEIN & CO.. 262 Fifth Ave.. Chicago

rich, whose homes were cleaned by platoons of servants. But it took no strain of logic to bridge the gap: buy a vacuum, the ads suggested, and enjoy the leisured ease of those with plenty of maids. Thus advertising took on the extra duty, beyond the description of new products, of explaining to a fast-expanding middle class the joys and rewards of possession.

There proved to be a new use for advertising in the mechanics of distributing The Product. A manufacturer could, if he wanted, use advertising as a weapon with which to prod sluggish retailers; or he could, by mail-order advertising, eliminate the dealer completely.

A classic early case in point was the inexpensive Ingersoll watch, which first appeared in 1892 and which in 1896 was ticking along at the disappointing rate of about 3,000 watches a year. The difficulty seemed to be that dealers weren't zealous

in pushing an item that retailed for only $1.50. Then the magazine *Cosmopolitan* persuaded the Ingersoll company to take a flier in national advertising. The very first ad, which cost Ingersoll $250, not only cleaned out many dealers' stocks completely but also sold 1,800 watches by mail.

This was an eye-opener that all magazine ad men began to use in their sales talks: use advertising to create a public demand, and you won't have to coax and cosset your dealers. Instead, the wretches will come begging for shipments with which to satisfy their eager customers.

Advertising solicitors did less talking about another new phenomenon: advertising had an eerie way of helping a competitor's sales, too. A lavish campaign for a particular brand of soup, soap, or tobacco had the effect of increasing total consumption of that commodity. This was mainly a reflection of the public's confusion about, or indifference to, competing brands. But it sometimes produced the anomalous result of unwilling advertisers being harried along the road to wealth by the exertions of their rivals.

The concept that advertising was something that might yield to rigorous scientific investigation was late in appearing, no doubt because it seemed an undignified, even raffish topic for scholarly

THE J. L. MOTT IRON WORKS,
84 to 90 BEEKMAN STREET, NEW YORK.   311 and 313 WABASH AVENUE, CHICAGO

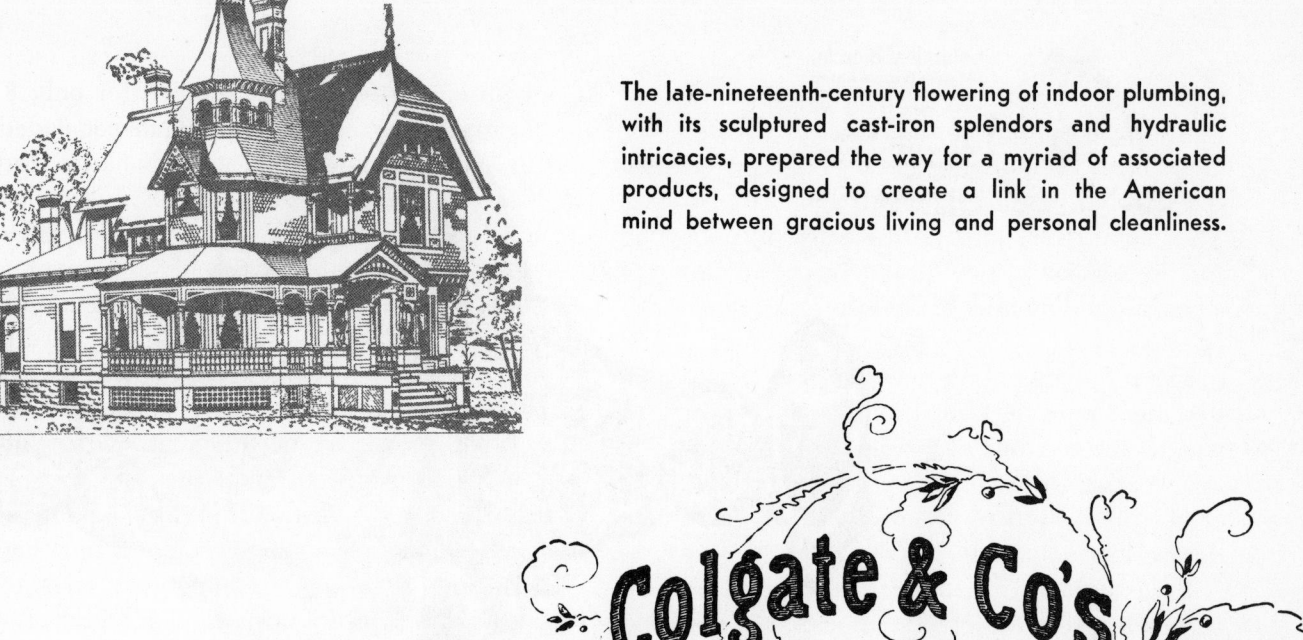

The late-nineteenth-century flowering of indoor plumbing, with its sculptured cast-iron splendors and hydraulic intricacies, prepared the way for a myriad of associated products, designed to create a link in the American mind between gracious living and personal cleanliness.

Colgate & Co's
CASHMERE BOUQUET
PERFUME
for the Handkerchief.

No luxury is so gratifying, harmless or inexpensive as this perfectly prepared perfume.

COLGATE & CO'S

name and trade mark on each bottle are a guaranty of excellence.

For the big-wheeled bonebreaker above, the copy was plain and terse; but when the bicycle fad was catching on, ads like the one below made light of the problems of learning to ride. Two aphorisms went with the ad at right: "A wheel is known by the company that makes it" and "Better pay for a name than pay for repairs."

Columbia Bicycles.

analysis. It was true that sound patent-medicine moguls, heavily dependent on advertising, did make comparative tests of new headlines and appeals. But such work was largely empirical, made without effort to create a generalized theory.

This began to change after 1902, the year that an earnest young scholar named Walter Dill Scott published in the *Atlantic Monthly* an article highly critical of advertising. His contention—later expanded into a book, *The Psychology of Advertising* — was that many ads violated basic precepts of psychology, and that if advertisers wanted to spend their money effectively, they'd better understand these precepts. Scott, a Ph.D. teaching at Northwestern University, cited as one of many examples the tendency for packers to show carcasses in illustration, noting that "it is conceivable that the sight of a dead carcass would whet the appetite of a hyena."

This tart-tongued scholar opened a Pandora's box of glittering new techniques for the youthful advertising industry: suggestion, imagery, associative ideas, and "the power of the direct com-

18

At the height of the bike craze, it was thought unnecessary for ads to argue or claim. It was often felt enough simply to summon up the idea of sporty and exhilarating fun a-wheel, preferably dressed to the nines.

mand." He also became an experimenter himself, busily testing batches of undergraduates for perception and recall of advertisements. His book, widely discussed in the trade, became almost a Bible for ambitious ad men. Scott went on to a distinguished career that in later years led to the presidency of Northwestern. Today his pre-Freudian ideas seem sound enough, if a little obvious and innocent. Such judgments do not, however, detract from his distinction as a dual pioneer — the first of the professors to admit advertising to the academic groves and the first of the parade of assured psychologist-shamans who have lately become such a noteworthy feature of the advertising trade.

EVEN today, with a perspective of more than a half century, the magazine and advertising explosion that began in the nineties seems to have had unfathomable consequences. For one thing, it is apparently still going on. There are reported to be 75 million habitual magazine readers in this country. About 46 different magazines have circulations of over a million, and one monster has more than 10 million readers. Magazine advertising has become an industry of staggering proportions. Single issues have often carried more than $2,000,000 worth of exhortations to buy. In one recent year advertisers spent an eye-popping $663,395,000 on magazine ads.

The giant dimensions of current advertising and the increasingly devious techniques at its disposal occasionally give alarm to thoughtful citizens. But while this anxiety seems at times all too reasonable, if we know where we have come from, how the main gambits of advertising have developed, and how time and familiarity have placed limits to the powers of even the most persuasive of them — at least some of those fears may be set at rest.

Chapter 2

The Age of

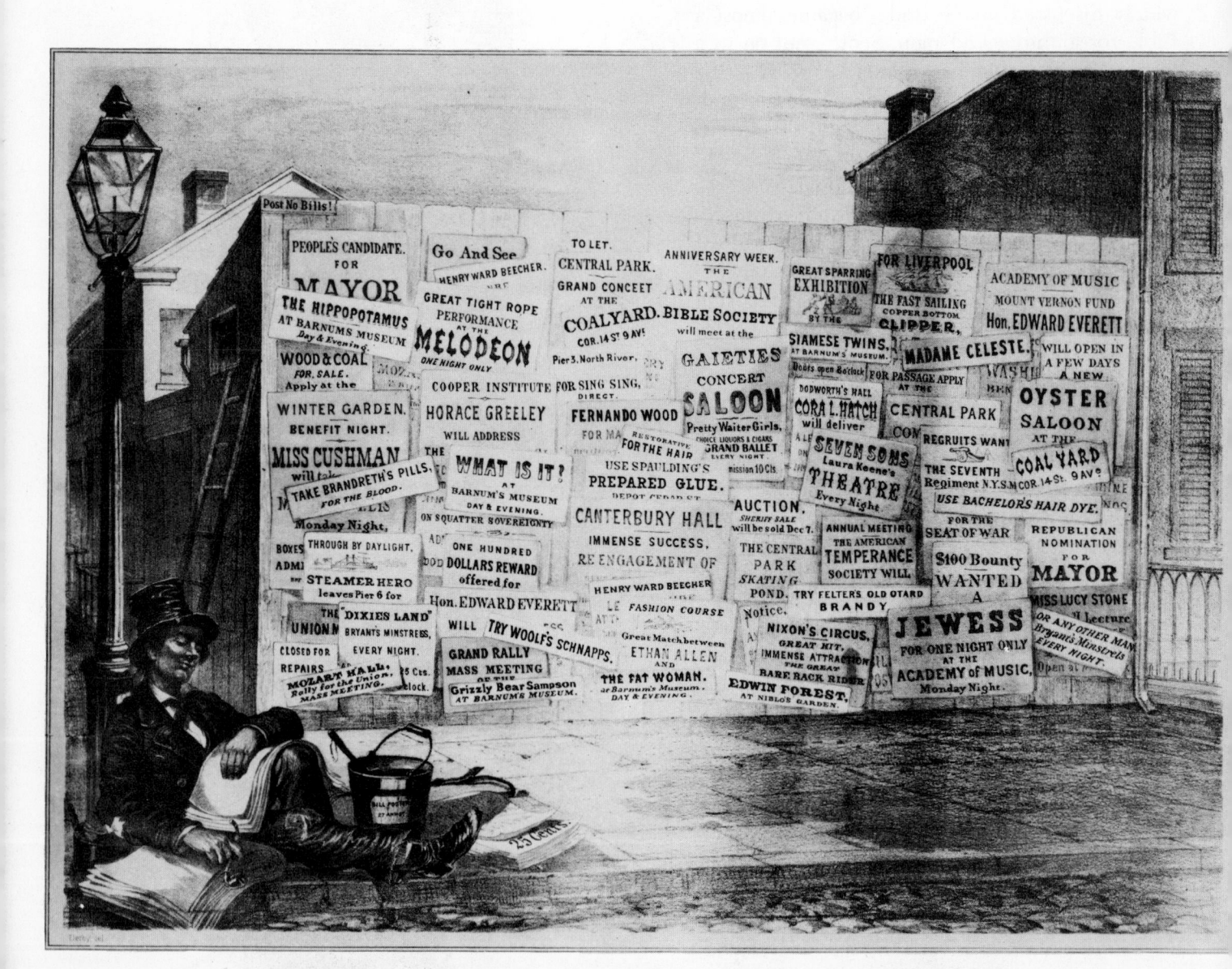

THE BILL-POSTERS DREAM
CROSS READINGS, TO BE READ DOWNWARDS
ROSS & TOUSEY GENL AGENTS 121 NASSAU ST NEW YORK

This print, from the sixties, reflects a form of humor then highly prized: ludicrous misreading of posters placed close together. Read downward, these common contemporary posters supplied several thigh-slappers. From The Museum of the City of New York.

Announcement

Advertising is like learning—a little is a dangerous thing. If a man has not the pluck to keep on advertising, all the money he has already spent is lost.　　　—Phineas T. Barnum

THE CHANGING social acceptance of men's occupations is not always noticed. It is proverbial that professional soldiers become heroes in war and bums in peace, but other occupations change, too. Doctors, for example, presently thought of as exceptionally dedicated and selfless (if, to be sure, uncommonly prosperous), were no such paragons during the nineteenth century. They were commonly thought of as faintly unrefined in their tastes and habits, with a tendency toward indelicacy that reflected their origins from leeches, pill rollers, and barbers. A similar though lesser sanctification has overtaken newspapermen; as late as fifty years ago they were admitted, if at all, via the servants' entrance. Nor has status always changed for the better; lesser varieties of nobility have clearly become scruffy, and clergymen no longer command the automatic, awestruck respect they once did when they were thought to have thunderbolts tucked in the clerical pockets.

No swing of the prestige pendulum has been more dramatic than that involving advertising men. Today they are at—or possibly even a little past—a peak of power and glory. Advertising is widely deemed an exciting and distinguished occupation. (Such nose-wrinking implicit in epithets like "expense-account princes" often has a detectable component of envy.) According to John McCarthy, a one-time advertising executive and alert observer of the profession, Madison Avenue has largely displaced Wall Street as the destination of eager lads bursting out of college

with shrill jets of ambition. To real-estate brokers, a newly tranferred advertising man is a treasure among prospects; to a newcomer to Exurbia, possession of a job with J. Walter Thompson, McCann-Erickson, or Young & Rubicam confers automatic status. Today advertising men are commonly held to be men of substance and influence who, along with engineers and not-too-pure scientists, are among the chief priests of our time.

It could not have been more different, say, seventy-five years ago. Any youth who voiced the ambition to go into advertising as a career would have had his forehead felt. Such few advertising men as existed then were hungry, rather furtive types known as newspaper agents. They were free-lance space brokers and had, in general, the standing presently given those engaged in the retailing of marijuana or dirty postcards. Volney B. Palmer, a busy Philadelphian who in 1841 founded what appears to have been the first United States advertising agency, found it necessary at first to sell real estate, coal, and firewood as well.

The dismal repute in which advertising men were held reflected the low state of the art itself in those early days. It was then commonly called "puffing," and was mainly employed in the promotion of patent medicines, soap, and dry goods. Its techniques were extremely primitive, consisting essentially of simple announcement of a product's availability, and amounting to little more than a printed equivalent of a sign or poster.

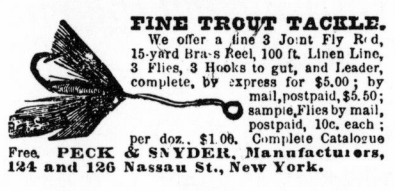

FINE TROUT TACKLE.
We offer a fine 3 Joint Fly Rod, 15-yard Brass Reel, 100 ft. Linen Line, 3 Flies, 3 Hooks to gut, and Leader, complete, by express for $5.00; by mail, postpaid, $5.50; sample, Flies by mail, postpaid, 10c. each; per doz., $1.00. Complete Catalogue Free. **PECK & SNYDER,** Manufacturers, 124 and 126 Nassau St., New York.

At first illustrations added but little to announcement ads. The message was still: We have it if you want it.

Newspaper and magazine publishers felt that at best it came close to violating the integrity of their journals, and they viewed it with a suspicion and dislike only slightly tempered by desire for the revenue it brought in. Merchants and manufacturers, finally, not only had to be persuaded that advertising was worth spending money on, but also that such open and brazen hawking of wares was not disreputable.

Indeed, one of the hardest tasks facing early advertising men was the campaign to gain acceptance of the all-important slogan, "It pays to advertise." Much effort and ingenuity were spent in this crucial promotion. British advertising agents, for instance, deriding the diffidence of those who refused to advertise, told the story of the old gentleman who was reduced by poverty to hawking goods on the streets. He refused to raise his voice above a whisper, and constantly muttered to himself, "I hope to goodness nobody hears me."

George P. Rowell, one of the pioneer advertising agents in this country, used a homely illustration with a similar theme: "The chap who could get all the business he wanted without advertising has been forced to advertise at last. The advertisement is headed 'Sheriff's Sale.'"

Testimonial success stories could also be unfolded before the wide eyes of prospects from an early date. A British pillmaker, Thomas Holloway, began in the mid-century years to spend amounts on advertising that were the wonder of his age. His advertising budgets grew from £5,000 a year in 1842 to a dizzy £45,000 a year by the sixties, and his profits rose in proportion. On this side of the Atlantic, Benjamin T Babbitt, a friend of P. T. Barnum, became the first soap millionaire, thanks to heavy, pyramided expenditure on advertising.

A self-assured young Englishman named Thomas J. Barratt made the most dramatic rise of all. He became a partner in a sleepy little firm manfacturing Pears' Soap. It spent £80 on advertising in 1865, the year Barratt became a partner. Within a decade he was spending more than £100,000 a year on advertising, and Pears' soap had become the most widely known commercial product in the world.

Some early campaigns were notable for instinctive use of effective advertising arts. Barratt, for example, though at work decades before Pavlov set his dogs a-drool, seems to have tried deliberately to condition the reflexes of mankind. Although he later used slogans and testimonials, it was by pure repetition of the product name that he made his mark. In much of Pears' advertising —in newspapers, magazines, posters, and billboards—Barratt showed no compulsion to explain or argue, amuse or frighten. For him it was enough to proclaim simply, "Pears' Soap." Endlessly repeated, these words were calculated to actuate a conditioning mechanism, until the idea of soap would immediately summon up the word Pears'. The two words didn't even have to be read; they need only be seen often enough to create this profitable conditioning. To critics of his advertising, complaining about the thousands of tiresome and seemingly useless signs—"But who on earth reads them?"—Barratt could look up from his sales figures and return an enigmatic smile.

But early advertising agents in general fought an uphill battle against the doubts of clients and the misgivings of publishers. The latter presented a constant and severe obstacle to the expansion of advertising. In fact, magazines and newspapers throughout most of the nineteenth century were far from eager to advertise, despite the money that advertising brought in. Publishers commonly believed that advertising was a marginal, not quite respectable business practice—a sign of commercial distress, something engaged in just as bankruptcy loomed.

Of the quality magazines which were predominant up until the end of the century, only one, the *Century*, openly invited advertising. The others simply tolerated it. A publication seldom actively sought ads. Instead, a prospective advertiser or his agent would appear at the magazine or newspaper offices, hat in hand, and would request permission to announce his wares. If there was space open in a forthcoming edition, and if the advertiser was prepared to pay in full in advance—a widespread requirement that reflected the general view that puffing was a shady pursuit—the ad might be allowed in. But *Harper's*, which took an especially stuffy attitude toward advertisers, once rejected $18,000 for twelve ads from a sewing-machine manufacturer, on the grounds that it preferred to advertise its own books on the page he coveted.

Nor was it possible to establish any fair or fixed rate for space. Not only were publishers fluid in their prices, they would brook no questions concerning circulation or readership. These were deemed a publisher's private business, no more to be pried into than his domestic arrangements. *Harper's* once refused to accept any ad brought in by one advertising agent after he had shown the impudence to inquire about the exact number of the magazine's readers.

Furthermore, the ordeal of the advertiser was not over when he was admitted to the sacred confines of the magazine pages. He was forced to comply with strict rules calculated to keep him from "defacing" the publication or "distracting" its readers. Magazines commonly segregated advertising in sections with no editorial matter, so that no reader might see advertisements unin-

tentionally. In newspapers the ads were less likely to be segregated, but the rules—pioneered by James Gordon Bennett's New York *Herald*—were even more stringent. Bennett allowed no illustrations, no headline type, nothing beyond a genteel, 8-point announcement that products were available for purchase. Even department stores trumpeting special sales were confined to the typographical whisper that is presently reserved for legal notices instructing the citizenry that bids on a garbage scow will be entertained, or cautioning mariners that certain buoys are due to be repainted.

Restrictions like these, as might be expected, stimulated artful evasion. Robert Bonner, proprietor of the New York *Ledger*, a weekly family paper of fiction and morally improving articles, waged celebrated battles with Bennett over how the *Ledger* might be advertised in the *Herald*.

Bonner had a deep faith in advertising, as a result of an accidental experience—one that has since come to be greatly cherished in advertising lore. In his first struggling days, with circulation shaky, Bonner had decided to try a little advertising. He wrote an eight-word announcement, "Read Mrs. Southworth's New Story in the Ledger," and sent it over to the *Herald*, marked "one line." But his handwriting was as illegible as Horace Greeley's, and the instructions were interpreted in the *Herald*'s composing room as

A mildly lunatic symbolism occurred in some early illustrated ads. This 1893 cut, from a Franklin typewriter ad, was somewhat far-fetched in its imagery.

"one page." So the line was set up and repeated down each column until it filled an entire newspaper page. When he saw the paper the next morning, Bonner was aghast; he didn't have enough in the bank to pay for so grandiose an ad. He scurried to the *Herald* office, but was too late—the steam presses had ground out the last edition. Bonner was in despair until the results of the ad began to come in. By afternoon the entire printing of his *Ledger* had been sold out, and later most of a second printing was snatched up. From then on Bonner was not only an enthusiast for advertising, but was also on the road to prosperity as a publisher.

But James Gordon Bennett was not entirely pleased, and a curious conflict with Bonner developed. Bennett thought that almost endless iteration might annoy readers, and made a rule that all advertisements must be changed daily. Bonner responded with a countering quibble: the ads would indeed be changed daily, but only in some trivial detail of punctuation or spelling. A number of other advertisers took up the challenge of the restrictive rules. One device, thought very daring at the time, was to let the small-type advertisement stand alone, surrounded by the conspicuous silence of a large white space. And ingenious ways to circumvent the no-big-type rule were devised. Masses of small letters were placed so as to form big ones. Sometimes adjacent space was bought so that words built up in this way could be splattered across several columns. But perhaps the most admired evasion of the

rules was the typesetting whimsy of arranging small letters in the shape of whatever was being advertised, such as a stove, an umbrella, or a bustle.

Newspaper publishers generally justified their regulations on grounds of the public good. It was said that large advertisers, if unrestricted, would unfairly dominate smaller rivals, and that unregulated advertising would be a club with which prosperous merchants could batter smaller competitors. This pious concern for the little fellow seems to have masked a more personal anxiety by publishers. If advertisers were given freedom to shout and clown and beat the drum loudly, might this not destroy the value of a paper? What reader would be able to keep his mind on the visually decorous news columns nearby, and who in such a din would trouble to read the editorials?

Gradually, however, the chafing rules broke down, as chafing rules have a way of doing. Department-store sales, announced in display type, were observed not to seduce readers away from

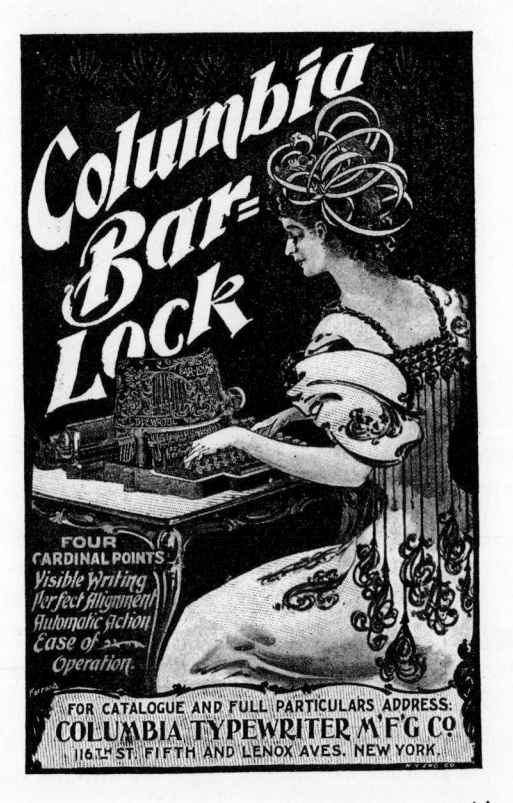

24

An ornament to any office, this typist had a problem with her hair. It could have been a ribbon or even snakes.

the news. (Actually, it would have required phenomenally powerful advertisements to have distracted readers from the HUSBAND SLAYS LOVER journalism that Bennett and Pulitzer, among others, were perfecting in the seventies.) More important, perhaps, was economic pressure; over the years advertising revenue crossed the divide between a pleasant by-product and a vital nourishment, and advertising became as necessary to magazines and newspapers as the publications were to advertising. And in the closing years of the century, with the arrival of mass magazines literally built on advertising, the shift became complete.

DURING the transitional period of the seventies and eighties, when the methods and results of advertising were still largely suspect, advertisers relied largely on the simple method of announcement, repeated as often as practicable, to bring their wares to the attention of the public. This was the method that Barratt used so effectively with Pears' Soap. But announcement and iteration were gradually discovered to have hampering limitations. They were slow and expensive, dependent as they were on the frequency rather than the quality of their appearance, and the results that they produced were often difficult to trace. They worked best, moreover, with familiar commodities that were in intermittent

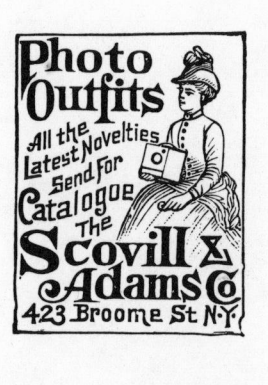

The symbolic illustration was always tempting. The Ivory ad at the left may have had its genesis in the cartoons of Thomas Nast. Above, a sample of pure announcement.

supply or had volatile prices. Very little benefit could be had from announcing the availability of something new or different; if the customer didn't know what the product was, he would hardly be stimulated by learning that he could buy it downtown. At length advertisers came to the conclusion that announcement wasn't enough, that further explanation was needed, and that brief and memorable phrases would greatly strengthen the bare proclamations of availability.

25

A kind of wild volubility overcame some advertisers. This hard-sell copy practically grabbed a reader by his lapels.

Pears' Soap

"MATCHLESS FOR THE COMPLEXION."

HONEST SOAP.

Cuteness dominated appropriateness, and no one was seriously troubled by the question as to whether what was good for monkeys and cats was just as good for people.

And so was born the fashion of slogans.

Much fumbling and misunderstanding attached themselves to the early use of slogans. Initial efforts were rather primitive, and inspiration was conspicuous by its absence, money often being fruitlessly spent to establish such highly forgettable epithets as "Guaranteed Invaluable"

and "The Best." But a few discerning advertisers recognized the two fundamental characteristics of an effective slogan. It was first a mnemonic device, to preserve an advertisement from the bleach of fading recollection. Secondly, it was an attention getter—a phrase that, given the right quirk of oddity, would get picked up and carried around by its reader as part of his mental impedimenta. A slogan invented by Barratt— "Good morning. Have you used Pears' Soap?"— proved to have just the right quirkiness to be highly successful.

Such also was the inspiration of Harley T. Procter, sales manager of a Cincinnati soap firm, whose creation of a name and two deathless slogans for one of the company's products catapulted it to fame and fortune. According to a Procter & Gamble chronicle, the creation of the product itself was accidental. One batch of experimental soap made in 1878 came out white, because it had been made without costly olive oil; and it floated, because a workman had forgotten to shut off the beaters while he was at lunch, causing more air than usual to be whipped into the mixture. The company called it White Soap (it was only one of twenty-four varieties the firm made then), and thought no more about it until Procter noted a number of reorders for "that soap that will float." It came to him that this product possessed special sales points. There was no need to fish for it in murky wash water, and its pallor could symbolize purity. He sent off samples to a testing laboratory and received back the pleasing and memorable statistic that White Soap was 99 and 44/100ths per cent pure. (Pure what was not specified.) Now all he needed was a catchy name, and this he found in church one Sunday morning in 1879. The reading was from the Forty-fifth Psalm: "All thy garments smell of myrrh, and aloes, and cassia, out of the ivory palaces, whereby they have made thee glad." Once "Ivory," "It floats," and "99 and 44/100ths per cent pure" were spread by liberal advertising, the great growing days for Procter & Gamble were at hand.

In time it grew clear that iteration coupled

Lovable animals at a stereopticon lecture once studied the glories of Ivory Soap in a full-page magazine ad. At left, a fine shrewdness by Procter & Gamble is reflected in the use of a miniature of The Product itself as a premium, to be worn on customers' watch chains.

with a memorable slogan or image was vastly more effective than just announcement alone. But difficulties were still encountered. The approach seemed to be suited only for widely distributed and broadly consumed commodities such as soap, tobacco, and the new packaged foodstuffs like flour and cocoa. It called for a distinctive touch, memorable and even lightly abrasive, that not every advertiser could manage. Finally, such advertising could not be timidly undertaken. Although this form of advertising had more impact than simple announcement, money still had to be spent, and spent lavishly, over a considerable period, before such a program would pay off. As the famous ad man Earnest Elmo Calkins put it:

An idea which is based on making a name or catchphrase a household word will never succeed unless the appropriation is a large one. There is a certain invisible line which no one yet has been able to find. To stop this side of it means failure. On the other side of it is success out of proportion to the amount of money spent. It is as if someone said that to spend one hundred thousand dollars in the United States would fail to make your idea a popular one, but by spending one hundred thousand and one dollars you could make your name or your idea a part of the vocabulary of the country, and get two or three hundred thousand dollars' worth of advertising additional which you did not get before. Just the particular point at which the tide turns and the public takes up your work and carries it on for you no one has been able to determine.

The beginning of the use of slogans is a milestone in the history of advertising, not so much because of the power added to the craft, but because such a development implied that there *was* a craft to advertising. Out of this period, in which advertising developed from simple announcement to more sophisticated forms, there also arose individual giants in the new field, men who did much to shape and alter its growth and form. The work of these men made the day of simple announcement seem quaint indeed.

Printers' Ink

George P. Rowell, who
thought advertising fun

Chapter 3 |

*The trade of advertising is now so near to per-
fection that it is not easy to propose any improvement. But as every art ought to be exercise
in true subordination to the publick good, I cannot but propose to these masters of the publick
ear, Whether they do not sometimes play too
wantonly with our passions?*

—Dr. Samuel Johnso

Printers' Ink

John E. Powers, the man who tried out honesty

Curtis Publishing Company

Cyrus H. K. Curtis, who advertised advertising

Great Ones

The incomparable showman, P. T. Barnum, disporting before the Prince of Wales at the London Olympia. Museum of the City of New York.

THE JUVENILE CAREER of a skinny, bright-eyed Yankee, born in 1810 and named Phineas Taylor Barnum, included these highlights: at twelve he was a house-to-house salesman of his grandfather's lottery tickets; at fifteen a clerk in his father's general store; at eighteen a bartender in the big city, and then, with the proceeds, proprietor of his own grocery store in Bethel, Connecticut; and at twenty-one, as a country newspaper editor, he was jailed for thirty days for picturesque libels of a deacon (he arranged to be greeted by a brass band the day the sentence was up). Destined to become a patron saint of advertising, Barnum was one of a little group of men whose ideas and enterprise permanently shaped the art.

Barnum himself later credited his service in the general store as being highly influential: "From six to twenty social, jolly, story-telling, joke-playing wags and wits, regular originals, would get together and spend stormy afternoons and evenings in relating anecdotes, describing their adventures, playing practical jokes on each other, and engaging in every project out of which a little fun could be extracted by village wits." It was an audience before which Barnum excelled. It was also essentially the same one that he played to, with immense success, for all his eighty-one-year life.

Several other experiences contributed to his education. He took an early flyer in promoting a patent medicine—a hair restorer—and was making a go of it when a partner decamped with the cash. (One of Barnum's chronic personal problems, curiously enough, was gullibility; he was repeatedly cheated.) He also spent some time as a free-lance writer of advertisements in New York. He specialized in patent medicines and theater handbills, discovering that they paired nicely. Barnum seems to have been the first man to load up theater ads with the lurid, pyramided adjectives and claims which up until then were the private preserve of the pillmakers.

His first triumph as a showman came at twenty-five when, for $1,000, half of it borrowed, he purchased the services of Joice Heth, a Negro woman of pronounced decrepitude. She was in fact toothless, blind, and partly paralyzed, but came with a document averring that she was 161 years old and had once been a slave owned by George Washington's father. Barnum coached her in remarks about how she well remembered her duties at diapering the infant Father of his Country. During the first six months that Barnum had Joice on exhibition, his gross receipts averaged $1,500 a week.

He regularly placed newspaper ads—spiced with pungent adjectives—to attract the populace

29

to this superannuated servant. These also gave him convenient access to editors—and it was in the editorial columns that he could plant and fertilize his most lush crops of advertising, in the form of publicity. "Of course I don't want you to publish a *thing*," he once assured an editor, "that is not of itself of *full interest* to your readers." He didn't bother to add that if nothing very interesting was on hand, he would invent it. Controversy, preferably in the form of outraged denunciation of his show, was a favorite gambit. When Joice Heth's receipts showed a slight downward curve, Barnum hastily wrote anonymous letters to the papers, denouncing her as "a humbug, a deception cleverly made of India rubber, whalebone, and hidden springs." Receipts soared as the customers flocked in, laden with preliminary indignation over so outrageous a fake.

When Barnum began to lavish his skills on advertising his American Museum in New York in 1842, it became evident that the only limits were the boundaries of human imagination. A violinist was only a fair attraction until Barnum had the billposters paste the posters upside down, conveying to a suggestible fraction of the public that this violinist played while standing on his head. General Tom Thumb—a young Connecticut midget who later became a rather worldly crony of Barnum—was an outstanding beneficiary of Barnum's genius for publicity. On his first European tour Barnum vainly tried to bring the General to the attention of the English royal court, but nothing happened until Barnum let it be known that he was shortly taking the General to Paris for a royal audience there. Not to be outdone by the French, Queen Victoria forthwith admitted the midget to several audiences—after which the tour became a commercial triumph. Barnum's sense of publicity sometimes took an oblique and rather devious form. In France he became convinced that the receipts of General Tom Thumb should be higher. He therefore concealed the midget for a time and circulated the rumor that the General had been kidnapped for her very own by a deranged noblewoman. Later, restored to public view, the General never drew better.

Barnum's list of firsts was impressive. He invented beauty contests and beautiful-baby contests—incidentally discovering the hazards of incurring the wrath of the mothers of losers. He discovered the powerful advertising appeal of importation, which was (and is) able to add magic enhancement to any product, but he used it so heavily that even in his own time it became a cliché: ". . . brought to you at great expense from beyond the sea." He explored the possibilities of a concealed take: staging a buffalo hunt and Wild West show across the river from New York in Hoboken, and, perplexingly, charging no admission whatever. But the event took place on a day when he had privately purchased all ferry receipts. They netted him $3,000.

Probably his most important contribution to advertising was the concept of the campaign. In Barnum's time advertising was simply a series of announcements, a process but not a progression. His acute sense of timing told him that this was wrong, that any promotion should have a carefully timed sequence, leading up to a crescendo of interlocked advertising and publicity. Once he bought a horse with a mildly freakish coat of hair. At first it appeared to have only modest exhibition possibilities. But he kept it hidden in the country for months, while he planted a series of newspaper reports, apparently trickling in from the frontier, that finally built up to a crashing climax—"Rare Opportunity to See the Amazing Woolly Horse, Lately Captured by Col. Fremont in the Wilds of the Rocky Mts!!!!" Another historic build-up campaign was the one staged for Jenny Lind in 1850. It converted her, in the months before her arrival in this country, from a relatively unknown soprano to the toast of America, greeted by ecstatic thousands who vied to draw her carriage.

It is in the ripe prose of his posters that Barnum comes most vividly alive today. No small, tame man could possibly call a horse act "rushing, blazing, sulphureous." From The Museum of the City of New York.

A MIGHTY MIRROR OF DEPARTED AGES

◆ MAGNIFICENT REVIVAL AND MOST GLORIOUS PRESENTATION OF ◆

P. T. BARNUM'S

❧ GREAT ROMAN HIPPODROME ❧

AFTER AN UNBROKEN NIGHT OF TWENTY CENTURIES

THE RESPLENDENT SUN OF IMPERIAL

ROMAN PASTIMES

REAPPEARS, to Dazzle and Electrify the Western World with All the Luster of the Great

COLISEUM'S PROUDEST DAYS

and THE OLYMPIAN TRIUMPHS OF THE HEROIC AGES.

THE RUSHING CHARIOT RIVALRIES,
DAUNTLESS EQUESTRIAN STRUGGLES,
HERCULEAN GAMES OF 2,000 YEARS AGO.

And also introducing in the **Most Famous Racing Circuit of the World.**

Caravans of Giant Coursing Elephants and Camels

Great Stables of ARABIAN, EUROPEAN and AMERICAN THOROUGH-
BREDS, A Colossal Company of CHAMPION MALE and FEMALE

EQUESTRIANS, ATHLETES AND PEDESTRIANS

Scores of Indomitable Lady Charioteers, Most Noted Jockeys, Steeple-
Chase Celebrities, and Bareback Champions, in a Stupendous
Programme of Thrilling Deeds.

JUMBO AS NATURAL AS LIFE

COURIER CO.

Herds of Huge Trained Wild Beasts in the Most Famous of Arenas

PRODIGIOUS HIPPODROMATIC PROCESSIONS,

PAGEANTS AND GORGEOUS SPECTACLES

4- Horse Lady Roman Chariot Races. Elephant Races. Roman Two-
Horse Standing Races. Hurdle Races, with Male and Female Jockeys
Grand Steeple Chase. Camel Races. Liberty Races. Race Horse
against Man. Lilliputian Pony and Monkey Races. Mustang Mule
and Donkey Races. Ostrich Races. Sack Races. Wheelbarrow Races.
Go-as-you-please Races, Arabian, English and American Thorough-
bred Races. Female Pedestrian Races. Bovine Races. Free-for-all,
Uproariously Ludicrous Obstacle Races, for Substantial Purses and Valuable
Prizes. Breezy. Bold. Thrilling

WILD WEST ILLUSTRATIONS

Of the Deeds, Dangers and Pastimes of the Boundless Plains, Including

THE MURDEROUS ATTACK ON THE OVERLAND MAIL COACH

The Savage Surprise by genuine Sioux and Pawnee Indian Warriors. The
Pursuit. Ferocious Onset. Brave Defense. Heading Charge and Rescued
by genuine Mounted Cowboys, Trappers, Scouts and Troopers.

*A Rushing, Blazing, Sulphureous, Living Reflex of
Remorseless Border Warfare.*

A PRINCELY FORTUNE IN REGAL WARDROBE

Lavish Decoration, and Classicly Correct Armor and Costumes.

A STUPENDOUS MIRROR OF DEPARTED EMPIRES

A Boundless Feast of Sensation, Excitement and Fun for the Million both Rich and Poor, Old
and Young, which we alone possess the popularity, capital, facilities and experience to successfull
and satisfactorily provide. **THE ONE AND ONLY ILLUSTRIOUS UNION OF**

PAST AND PRESENT NOBLE PASTIMES

THE MOST REFINED AND EXHILARATING ENTERTAINMENT, UPON
THE MOST MAGNIFICENT AND PERFECT SCALE.

The Crowning Effort of the Giant of Wonderland

☞ ALL WITHOUT EXTRA CHARGE

Though, in its Supremely Splendid Self, alone worth many times the One
Price of Admission to all the Thousand Wonders of The United Greatest
Shows on Earth.

★ A RIVALRY OF NATIONS IN EARTH'S GREATEST AMPHITHEATER. ★

Barnum was a public figure for fifty-six years, becoming in his later years as much an attraction in his own right as Jumbo, the Siamese Twins, or Jo-Jo the Dog-faced Boy. He wrote his autobiography early and revised it almost every year thereafter; more than half a million copies were sold. Many thousands were bought by ambitious young men seeking his secrets of success. Wrote Frank Presbrey, an advertising man turned historian: "Barnum's influence on advertising, publicity, and marketing was immense. It was visible in the brass bands used to publicize department-store sales, and in the trick-copy ads of the Seventies and Eighties. Many used Barnum's methods with little modification. It took a long time to discover that playing a practical joke on a man and giving him a full quarter or dollar's worth of fun in the performance was something different from mixing foolery with an article to be purchased in a serious mood."

It took more than a long time. Advertising has never wholly lost an echo of the brass band, the thundering adjectives of the circus posters, and the strident spiel of the freak-show barker.

THE DISTINCTION, if that is the term, of being the inventor of the advertising agency must be shared by several men. One of the earliest known agents was the Philadelphian Volney B. Palmer, who divided his time in 1841 between selling ads and firewood. Then in New York in the early forties there was John L. Hooper, an advertising solicitor for Horace Greeley's New York *Tribune*. Whenever he sold an ad in the *Tribune*, Hooper noted, his customers were likely to ask him to put it in the other papers too, and he was always willing to oblige. But Greeley frowned on this amiability, for it graveled him to steer any revenue toward his rivals. So Hooper set out as a free-lance advertising agent, with his office in his hat. He won a fine local reputation because he always paid the newspapers himself and then collected from his advertisers—unlike Palmer, who took no responsibility for collections.

Neither of these pioneers, however, really began the process that has led, a century later, to

Barnum hated white space, feeling that no ad or poster gave him his money's worth until he packed in something for everyone.

such corporate phenomena as J. Walter Thompson, N. W. Ayer, and Batten, Barton, Durstine & Osborn. This honor must be chiefly reserved for a jaunty Bostonian, George P. Rowell, whose compulsive urge to make a fortune was tempered by a teacherish tendency to tell everyone else how to do it too.

In 1865 Rowell gave up his job as an advertising solicitor for the Boston *Post*, and, with $1,000 savings, founded an advertising agency. He was a young man bubbling with bright ideas. Advertising was at that time commercially untidy to the point of chaos. Newspaper circulations were unverifiable except insofar as publishers' claims established the extreme upper limits. Announced advertising rates were what publishers thought it would be nice to get for their space; the rate card bore only a remote relationship to

"Select List"

Geo. P. Rowell & Co.'s Select List of Local Newspapers.

Many persons suppose this list to be composed of CHEAP, low-priced newspapers. The fact is quite otherwise. The catalogue states exactly what the papers are. When the name of a paper is printed in FULL FACE TYPE it is in every instance the BEST. When printed in CAPITALS, it is the ONLY paper in the place. The list gives the population of every town and the circulation of every paper. IT IS NOT A CO-OPERATIVE LIST. **IT IS NOT A CHEAP LIST.** At the foot of the Catalogue for each State the important towns which are not covered by the lists are enumerated. **IT IS AN HONEST LIST.**

An old advertiser writes: "I prefer the LOCAL LIST for the reason that, while but few persons in any particular town subscribe for a class medium (or large city weekly), nine out of ten subscribe for their local paper, and the ten'h one borrows it from his neighbor."

An advertiser, who spends upwards of $5,000 a year, and who invested less than $350 of it in this List, writes: "Your Select Local List paid me better last year THAN ALL THE OTHER ADVERTISING I DID."

The rates charged for advertising are barely one-fifth the publishers' schedule. The price for single States ranges from $2 to $80. The price for one inch one month in the entire list is $650. The regular rates of the papers for the same space and time are $3,083.16. The list includes 977 newspapers, of which 193 are issued DAILY and 784 WEEKLY. They are located in 807 different cities and towns, of which 28 are State capitals, 371 places of over 5,000 population, and 483 County Seats.

For copy of List and other information, address

GEO. P. ROWELL & CO.
Newspaper Advertising Bureau,
10 Spruce St., New York.

Rowell advertised himself, not hesitating to use business copy in a general magazine. *Leslie's*, 1880.

what the space could be bought for. Commissions to an agent varied from a frosty nothing from prosperous big-city papers to a pathetic 75 per cent offered by the hard-pressed proprietors of small weeklies. (A small weekly paper tended to value its space according to the remoteness of its deadline—higher if the deadline was a few days off and other ads optimistically expected, and very low on press day, when the proprietor became frightened that not only would his space fail to earn revenue, but that he might have to fill it with expensively composed editorial matter.) The situation was further complicated by the fact that only a few advertisers, notably the patent-medicine moguls, could afford to engage in the intensive circulation-estimating and rate-haggling necessary for getting value for the money spent on advertising.

Rowell came onto the scene with what amounted to a package service. He made up a list of 100 newspapers and attached realistic circulation estimates. He assured prospective clients that if they advertised on this exclusive Rowell list, their money would be efficiently spent. And so perhaps it was, at least comparatively. But the alert young freebooter had not neglected himself. Of the papers on this list, only a very few insisted on little or no commission; the vast bulk were papers willing to give Rowell as much as a 75 per cent rake-off. He had been able to use two powerful levers in dickering with publishers. One was a promise of continued and regular patronage if he was given a high commission. The second was an offer of cash payments, less a 3 per cent discount. Cash was a powerful lure to many a small publisher, especially in rural areas, since his subscription revenues were often in the form of eggs, vegetables, and hay. The gloriously profitable possibilities of Rowell's bright idea were reflected in his very first month's business: a billing of $2,000 to advertisers, and payments of $600 to papers.

Rowell's next inspiration was a logical extension: he became a space wholesaler. He contracted to buy newspaper space in bulk, and then retailed pieces of it to advertisers. This too was highly successful, for it brought in many new, first-time advertisers attracted by his appeal: "An inch of space in 100 newspapers a month for $100." Soon Rowell was prospering greatly. He enlarged his agency, moved it to New York, and later bought out John Hooper, whose agency had long outgrown his hat. Rowell began to offer a variety of special state and regional lists. They were all composed on the same principle: a very few of the important but stiff-necked papers, and a large number of those that gave big commissions.

Rowell was too buoyant a person to hold his tongue about his gold strike. Quickly he found himself surrounded by competitors, each offering similar selected lists. As competition tightened, Rowell wrestled with his conscience over the varying commissions and finally scrapped the system he had invented. He decided to charge advertisers a flat 25 per cent commission, and to pass on all savings to them. There had been uncertainty in the early days as to whom the agent really represented—the advertiser, the publication, or simply himself. In 1875 Rowell announced a new policy: he proposed to take advertisers into his confidence, to function literally as their agent, and to take a set recompense for his services. It was a big step forward for the regularization of agencies, though not, perhaps, for Rowell's personal fortune.

A crucial part of the list system had been Rowell's canny estimates of actual newspaper circulations. These he gave away as early as 1869 with the publication of the first edition of *Rowell's American Newspaper Directory*, a massive compilation of data about 5,411 papers. Its publication brought loud complaints—from competing agents, who felt that he was disclosing professional secrets that might help advertisers to place their own ads, and from some publishers whose circulation claims were pruned down drastically. But the squawks didn't bother Rowell; he felt that advertising was too important—and, probably, too much fun—to be choked into a private guild.

Soon he began putting out a house organ, the *American Newspaper Reporter*, that was supposed to plug the Rowell agency, but that usually assumed the grander task of plugging advertising generally, and of telling the world how George P. Rowell felt it should be handled:

Come right down with the facts, boldly, firmly, unflinchingly. Say directly what it is, what it has done, what it will do. Leave out all ifs. Do not claim too much, but what you do claim must be without the smallest shadow of weakness. Do not say "We are convinced that," "We believe that," or "Ours is among the best," or "Equal to any," or "Surpassed by none." Say flatly "the best," or say nothing. Do not refer to rivals. Ignore every person, place, or thing except yourself, your address, and your article.

This pedagogical bent led Rowell in 1888 to found a weekly magazine, *Printers' Ink*. It grew to be not only a semiofficial spokesman for United States advertising, but also—because it specialized in how-to articles on techniques—a kind of graduate school for advertising men. Its influence under John Irving Romer (to whom Rowell sold it in 1908) continued and spread. In a notable truth-in-advertising campaign begun in 1911, *Printers' Ink* began plugging for state laws to make deceptive advertising illegal, and the laws then widely adopted are still known as the "Printers' Ink statutes."

From its founding until the nineties, when it was overtaken by N. W. Ayer, Rowell's agency was the biggest and best-known in the country, and this, in combination with the platform provided by *Printers' Ink*, made the old gentleman the dean of American advertising. He was not the sole inventor, of course, of the agency idea. Others were being founded in the same period, notably Ayer in 1869 and Carlton & Smith in 1864 —the latter to be taken over and renamed a little later by a bearded visionary named James Walter Thompson. But Rowell, with his enthusiasm for ideas, advertising, and money, was the most dominant and engaging of the founding fathers.

UNLIKE their modern counterparts, geared to provide clients with services ranging from sonnet

COASTING—

is the term given by bicycle riders to their practice of taking the feet from the pedals and allowing the machine to run with the momentum acquired from previous effort.

This is the season when many business men are tempted to try "coasting" with their Newspaper Advertising.

The newspapers themselves however do not "coast." They are regularly issued, and regularly read, and the advertisers who have learned that

Keeping Everlastingly At It Brings Success

are regularly represented therein. They would no more "coast" with their advertising than with their employees, or any other every-day business necessity.

Coasting is a down-grade exercise. Success is an up-hill station. We have been there ourselves. We have gone there with many successful Newspaper Advertisers. We will be glad to start with you.

Correspondence solicited.

N. W. AYER & SON,
Newspaper Advertising Agents,
Philadelphia.

From earliest days, N. W. Ayer was a dignified, earnest agency. The solemn slogan about Keeping Everlastingly At It is still a local credo. From *Harper's*, 1893.

LIFE FORCE

The essence of life is force. The measure of force we call vitality. If this is lacking, there is loss of flesh, lack of resistive power, a tendency to catch disease easily, especially a tendency to Consumption. For low vitality nothing is better than *Scott's Emulsion.* It supplies force by furnishing the nourishing, strengthening elements of food in an easily digested form; when ordinary food is of no avail, *Scott's Emulsion* will supply the body with all the vital elements of life.

If that label is not on the bottle it is **not**

SCOTT'S EMULSION

Let us send you a book about it, *free*

50 Cents and $1.00, all Druggists

SCOTT & BOWNE, Chemists, New York

Powers' extraordinary prose was marked by declarative sentences, forcefulness, and a faintly communicated irritability at the necessity for writing it at all.

writing to psychiatry, the first advertising agencies were simply space buyers. What was *said* in an advertisement was not felt to be an agent's concern. A client should write his own ad; he knew the product best, and it was, after all, his money. If he was unskilled with words, let him hire some ink-stained wretch to hone his phrases.

This curious viewpoint, which survived until competition among agencies became more intense, produced an interesting group of free-lance ad writers, often called "literary men." Some were journalists like Henry J. Raymond, the founder of *The New York Times,* who like Barnum nourished himself in a lean period by writing patent-medicine copy. Some were authentic literary types who needed the money; Bret Harte wrote in praise of Sapolio just as, more than a half-century before, Lord Byron had crafted verses to order for Warren's Shoe Blacking. Some were professional personalities like Elbert Hubbard, who wrote ineffable sincerities about Gillette razors, Knox hats, and Steinway pianos. Many "literary men" were professional writers with little public reputation but considerable standing in advertising circles: men such as Nathaniel C. Fowler, Manly Gillam, Charles Austin Bates, and John E. Powers. Of them all, Powers was the most influential on the future course of copywriting.

Powers wrote in a style of lucid simplicity that stood out sharply from the embellished prose of his time. As early as 1886 businessmen were pleased to pay $100 a day for the use of his pen, and a generation of copywriters followed along earnestly in his footsteps.

The following ad, run in newspapers in 1881 for Wanamaker's department store, shows Powers's lean prose at work. It was set at his insistence in 12-point Caslon Old Style type—a large and legible face, used at a time when almost all ads were in tiny agate type.

The writer has had his eyes mended with a pair of glasses. Ink is blacker than it was; letters are bigger and plainer; and the words spring right out of the paper. The world is probably better than most of us see it. A little irregularity in the eyes upsets the balance of things. We sell glasses to restore the sight. Let any reader who is aware of a want of sharpness ask our spectacle man to quiz him, take the measure of his eyes, and show what help there is for them. He may find that seeing is very different from what he thought.

Powers had been a salesman before he became a copywriter—a subscription agent for the *Nation,* and a distributor of sewing machines. He turned to advertising when he was selling sewing machines in England; and a whole series of unconventional stunts—including the use of a traditional Christmas pantomime as a kind of singing commercial for sewing machines—had distracted the British public into buying sewing machines by the shipload, and had given the young man a reputation as a supersalesman.

Back in this country Powers wrote advertisements for Lord & Taylor, the New York department store, and here his peculiarly effective prose style took shape. As Earnest Elmo Calkins, later a famous copywriter, noted: "There is no training school for the advertising man equal to the department store. He writes about nearly every article of human consumption, and he has some testimony each day as to whether his advertising has pulled. I could look around the store each morning and tell which ads had succeeded and which had failed." In Powers's case this training paid off; for John Wanamaker promptly lured him away at a better salary.

Powers worked for Wanamaker for six years, with such outstanding success that a school of Powers imitators began to form. Among the "literary men" the term "Powersism" became lingo for a pithy, faintly sententious phrase or paragraph. Short sentences and a homemade King James Version style began to turn up in many ads. He became so much the fashion that even an anti-Powers school of thought appeared. It held that his copy, though pleasing, was theoretically unsound: "A lack of ability to long concentrate the attention, and a disinclination to concentrated mental effort, is a distinctively American trait. It makes people eschew large amounts of type, lengthy explanations of the relative merits of wares, and everything that necessitates more than brief attention." This dissident opinion, directed more toward ad length than prose style, grew into a doctrine of "two-word copy"—e.g., Use Sapolio, Eat H-O. It did not succeed in masking the fact that Powers's ads had a remarkable effectiveness. The reasons were for a time mysterious.

Powers contended that there was nothing puzzling about his technique. It was simply a matter of "saying the right thing to the right people in an acceptable way." Good copywriting was a combination of selling sense and writing ability. Exaggeration was a fatal blunder. Powers wrote naturally in terse, Baconian sentences, and these shone forth in a day when the characteristic diction was a lacy filigree of dependent clauses. He insisted on tidiness of layout, used only very brief headlines (three words at most, preferably fewer), and whenever possible specified 12-point Caslon Old Style type. It grew to be a kind of fetish with him. E. S. Turner wrote that "rivals who imitated his makeup were said to have found great initial difficulty in telling a lie in Caslon Old Style."

For the true secret of Powers's success did not lie in short sentences or clean layouts or Caslon Old Style. The story is told of him that a merchant sought his aid, complaining that business was terrible. Was there anything new that the great man could suggest? "Yes," Powers replied. "Let's try honesty."

Powers was rigidly, almost fanatically truthful in all his work. He made John Wanamaker very uneasy by his tendency to use in advertisements the exact remarks that store section managers confided to him. "We have a lot of rotten [raincoats] that we want to get rid of" or "[The neckties] are not as good as they look, but they're good enough—25¢." Such unexampled frankness startled customers and usually sold out the goods promptly. But it was a continuing source of anxiety for management, which passed the word to section men to be *very* careful about what they said to Powers. In 1886, after Powers advertised that part of a stock of American-made hats had

been fitted with British labels to see which would sell the better, Wanamaker fired him.

He became a free-lance "literary man." It was estimated that his fees exceeded $10,000 a year— then an unprecedented sum for a copywriter. By 1890 his clients included Scott's Emulsion, Beecham's Pills, Carter's Little Liver Pills, Macbeth Lamp Chimneys, and Murphy's Varnish. To each of them Powers explained what would later become an advertising truism; that it was important to study the product carefully, because an approach that worked fine for one mightn't work at all for another.

He confounded belittling critics by displaying virtuosity with both tersely epigrammatic and long-copy ads:

> Nobody else apparently dares put his name on his lamp chimneys.
>
> Macbeth

Or:

> I make bad chimneys, too. But I don't put my name on them.
>
> Macbeth

And for Murphy's Varnish:

> In a board walk the largest item of expense is the lumber; in a splendid violin the least item of expense is the lumber. In a plain wall the stone is the chief cost; in a piece of classic statuary the cost of the stone is hardly reckoned.
>
> This principle, in a certain degree, applies to the making of a fine varnish. We do not pretend that we put from three to five dollars' worth of material into each liquid gallon; but we do put in the scientific knowledge and expert skill and the long-continued care which no ordinary varnish contains.
>
> If you wish to get rich music or a treasure of the sculptor's art or a job of varnishing that will be satisfactory, you must pay for something else than raw material.

In his later years John E. Powers assumed the mien of a rather testy Old Testament prophet. It was, perhaps, his privilege, for his influence on advertising was very great. He had been one of the first to insist on clean, legible layouts, one of the first to demonstrate that honesty had a way

When Powers let fly in Caslon Old Style, the impact was stunning. These ads, appearing in the nineties, were far ahead of their time.

of communicating itself, one of the first to note that exaggeration weakened rather than strengthened. But his greatest contribution by far was the matter that had eluded analysis earlier in his career: he had invented a whole new rationale of advertising, to reinforce the older ones of repetition and slogans. This was the concept of "reason-why" copy—the idea that an advertisement should devote itself to showing why it was in a reader's self-interest to buy The Product.

Reason-why was a concept that was to preoccupy advertising men for the next thirty years, that was to elevate copywriters to new status, and that was to give ground only when advertising discovered the hidden powers of hope and fear.

PROBABLY the most glittering success story in American magazine publishing—at least until the emergence of such new-model heroic figures as Henry Luce and DeWitt Wallace—is that of Cyrus H. K. Curtis. It reads today, with an eerie air of nature imitating art, as if it were designed for serialization in early issues of *The Saturday Evening Post*.

Curtis, a short but enterprising tyke from a genteelly poor family in Portland, Maine, had troubles as a newspaper boy. The other kids tended to beat him up whenever he appeared on their established routes. So at twelve he worked out the maneuver that would be useful to him for the rest of his life: he hunted for an untapped market. In this case it. turned out to be the soldiers on a nearby harbor fort; they were eager for news (it was 1862) and had no daily papers. He persuaded the paper's circulation manager to advance him one day's credit. Then, toting his bundle, he evaded the paper boys lying in wait for him, arrived at the fort by sailboat, and sold all the papers in minutes, despite a surcharge of two cents apiece for extra service.

Curtis was one of many nineteenth-century youngsters who were fascinated by the little printing presses offered for sale in such places as the pages of *Youth's Companion*. At thirteen he set out to be a boy publisher. (He was in good company: Hawthorne, Edison, Josephus Daniels, Albert Lasker, and Frank Munsey were a few of the many who had put out juvenile papers.) By sixteen Curtis had driven up the circulation of his *Young American* to 400 copies a week—with a weekly gross of $8 on a capital investment of $200 in printing equipment. Then came the Portland Fire of 1866, which destroyed his press. He quit school to become a dry-goods clerk.

The Horatio Alger themes recurred during this industrious young man's career. A dry-goods salesman in Boston at nineteen, he found that he didn't need a full hour to eat his lunch, and became a newspaper ad solicitor in the unoccupied interval. This proved so promising that he tried to quit the dry-goods job, but his boss argued that he had a moral duty to stay at least a year. Polite as well as industrious, he finished out the year and then became a full-time ad salesman.

In the early seventies he started his first adult publishing venture, a little magazine called the *People's Ledger*. It used elderly or secondhand fiction, the rerun rights to which were usually purchased for five dollars a story, and it provided only a precarious living. (Incidentally, the Curtis Publishing Company might have developed in Boston except for casual circumstance: Curtis and his young wife Louisa went off to see the Centennial Exposition of 1876, and while in Philadelphia Curtis discovered that he could get his *Ledger* printed a shade more cheaply there.) He sold the magazine in 1878, made another try at selling ads, and, in 1879, took the step that was to lead to glory.

It didn't seem, at first, like much of a step. With one partner and $2,000 borrowed from his brother-in-law, he founded a four-page farm weekly, the *Tribune and Farmer*. He worked feverishly at selling ads, peddling subscriptions, editing the paper, and sparring with his partner, who proved a rather thorny personality. Before long the weekly began to show a small profit, though it betrayed no high prospects.

One of the four pages of the *Tribune and Farmer* was intended to provide moral and improving reading matter for farm women. Curtis, overworked and not really an editor anyway, pasted it together in a harried hour each week, mainly from stale clippings and "exchanges." Once Louisa gently derided the page, and Curtis snapped, "If you think you can do any better, do it!" Under Louisa's guidance, the page soon grew to be the most popular part of the paper. In 1883 Curtis decided it could stand as a separate supplement. He ordered an artist to produce a cover, headlined the "Ladies' Journal." The artist, not at all good with words, trotted back bearing a cover with "Home" inserted in it. The Curtises concluded to leave it in rather than remake the cover.

With Louisa's editing, the *Ladies' Home Journal* became an immediate hit. She held to a note of freshness and practicality, in a day when other women's magazines were drenched with a fusty sanctimony established decades before by *Godey's Lady's Book*. In less than a year circulation climbed to 25,000, and Curtis's partner began rumbling about the amount of time devoted to this supplement. So the partnership was dissolved, the partner keeping the *Tribune and Farmer*. Shortly thereafter, it expired. Cyrus and Louisa kept the *Journal*, which throve.

Curtis had by this time a highly developed view of the potentialities of advertising. In particular, he was preoccupied by the then new idea of advertising an advertising medium itself. In 1885 he applied to the N. W. Ayer agency for a $400 credit, to be spent plugging the *Journal*. They called him in for a conference. "We don't think you have any resources to amount to much," Curtis was told, "but we'll take a chance on you. If you make good, all right; if you don't, $400 won't break us." It was the beginning of a close relationship between the agency and the publishing house. Soon Curtis was spending large sums through Ayer to advertise his magazines, and Ayer itself was placing much general advertising in them.

That this was more than mutual back-scratching was suggested by several later incidents. One occurred when Francis Wayland Ayer endorsed a Curtis note to a paper company for $100,000— on the proviso that the endorsement be concealed from Curtis. Another came when Curtis, wanting the services of a gifted copywriter who did not work for Ayer, made a peculiar deal: he bought the copy himself and gave it to Ayer, so that the agency could retain his account.

Louisa retired from editing in 1889, by which time the *Journal* circulation had climbed to an exhilarating 443,000. Edward W. Bok, her successor (and son-in-law), was mildly eccentric, but displayed the same sure and gifted touch. He printed what would come to be called "service" articles—how to bring up babies, how to decorate homes, how to manage on a budget. He ran numerous campaigns—vigorous attacks on patent medicines, public drinking cups, bird-decimating

40

It was a fusty and outdated competitor that Louisa Curtis faced with her fresh new ideas. Once a fine periodical, *Godey's* was gradually running downhill.

JUNE.

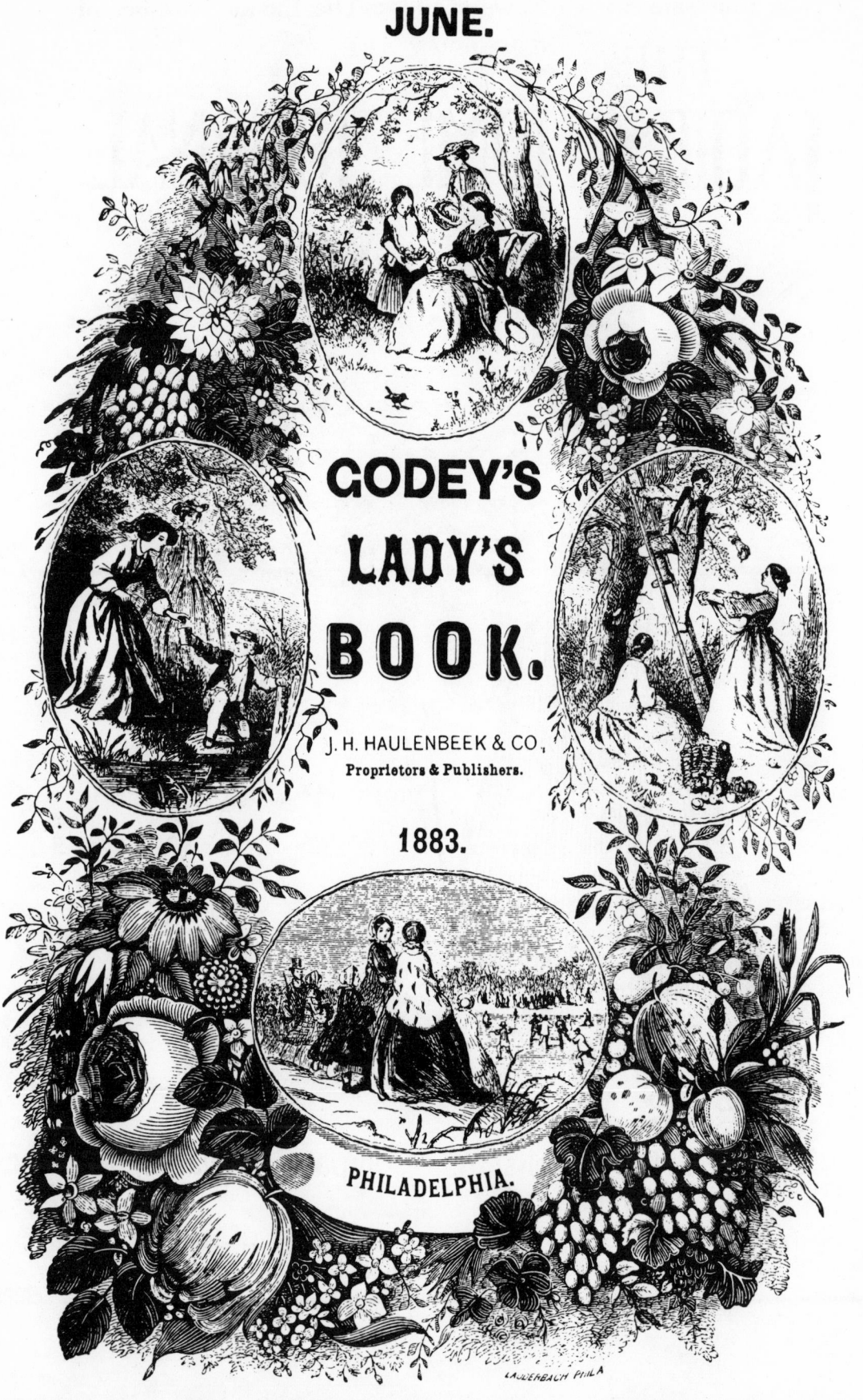

GODEY'S LADY'S BOOK.

J. H. HAULENBEEK & CO,
Proprietors & Publishers.

1883.

PHILADELPHIA.

Publication Office, 1006 Chestnut Street, Philadelphia, Pa.

Curtis was so convinced a believer that he didn't hesitate to advertise his
magazine in others. This was a *Harper's* ad drawn by Charles Dana Gibson.

feathered hats, venereal diseases. Always he served up an artful blend of fiction and regular features, the latter including a personal-problem answer column that drew letters so intimate that Bok hastily arranged to have them read by female eyes alone.

Curtis for his part was doing his job equally well. In the nineties he was spending as much as $200,000 a year on promoting the *Journal* as an advertising medium, which made him one of the country's larger advertisers. In 1893 he made the courageous decision to exclude patent medicines, at the cost of a drop in revenue. But within a couple of years the *Journal* was quite as profitable as before and proudly announced the largest magazine circulation in America.

Despite the success of the *Journal*, Curtis met with general skepticism when, in 1897, he spent $1,000 for a wheezy, broken-down old weekly called *The Saturday Evening Post*. What brought the reaction was not the purchase, which he could well afford, but the grandiose announcement that it was to be "pushed into a circulation exceeding that of any weekly in the United States." The *Post* had a spotty past, a part-time editor who got $10 for his weekly chore of pasting up reprint material, and 2,231 subscribers, none noticeably loyal. When it learned of Curtis's plans to resuscitate this moribund object, *Printers' Ink* observed waspishly that he seemed determined to "blow in all the profits of the *Journal* on an impossible venture."

For several years this pessimism seemed warranted. At first the *Post* grew only slowly, in spite of the large sums that Curtis pumped into promoting it. A total of $1,250,000 was injected into the old weekly before it began to move under its own power. Then, of course, it turned into a fantastic success. Curtis's central idea—a mass magazine built around telling, in fiction and fact, romantic stories about business—turned out to be sound and wonderfully timed. By 1907 circulation was 726,000 and ad revenue $1.2 million; a little more than a decade later, circulation was an unprecedented 2,000,000, with ad revenues of $25 million.

During the last decades of his life (he died in

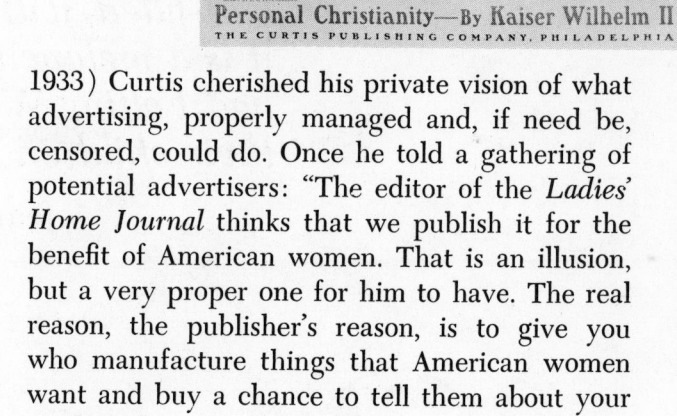

1933) Curtis cherished his private vision of what advertising, properly managed and, if need be, censored, could do. Once he told a gathering of potential advertisers: "The editor of the *Ladies' Home Journal* thinks that we publish it for the benefit of American women. That is an illusion, but a very proper one for him to have. The real reason, the publisher's reason, is to give you who manufacture things that American women want and buy a chance to tell them about your products."

Curtis had one important advantage over the ordinary run of visionaries: he was, in his time and place, thoroughly right. He foresaw great tidal currents a decade before most men did, and he was willing to bet enormous sums on the accuracy of his foresight. Yet he was also blessedly lacking, even in later years of wealth and deference, in that tendency toward omniscience that so often envelops the highly successful. He showed great skill at handling his editors—an exacting test for publishers—and left them alone except when it was necessary to help repel outraged individuals bent on opening the editorial veins. A short, bearded man with a big cigar, Cyrus H. K. Curtis normally said little and listened a lot. He was bored by such extracurricular activities as European travels, except for that one moment each week when he got a cable reporting how much advertising *The Saturday Evening Post* had closed with. When asked for the secret of his success, he had a one-word explanation: "Advertising!"

Chapter 4 | Shake Well

In the pages of old magazines and newspapers, half-filled with patent-medicine advertisements, it is a melancholy picture that unfolds. The women had Falling Wombs, the men had Failing Powers; their children were afflicted with Worms.

—Jean Burton, *Lydia Pinkham Is Her Name*

PATENT MEDICINE was a rich and voluptuous Jezebel that taught advertising to put away its childish things and seek out its full powers. The liaison between the two was, in fact, one of the ripest in commercial history. Both had had relatively staid existences before their nineteenth-century juncture, but after they had met and interacted, neither was ever the same again. Selling patent medicines taught advertising dozens of effective new techniques (notably, powerful mixtures of suggestion, testimony, and faith), together with a certain tough-minded practicality (Well, how many bottles of The Product will it move?) that advertising has never forgotten.

The affair raged with increasing passion and profit up to the passage of the first Federal Food and Drug Act in 1906. Then, slowly, it began to wane. The liaison is not over even yet, of course, as anyone able to focus an eye upon television can testify. But advertising today, orotund and graying at the temples, often bends upon patent-medicine accounts the same uneasy regard that might be given the appearance of a blowsy ex-mistress, rouged and dyed and fraught with potential embarrassments.

Before Using

In the decades following the Civil War, however, patent medicine was more than advertising's queen—it was the principal support of *all* magazines and newspapers. The tonics, laxatives, and cancer cures of the time were quite as important as automobile, appliance, and food accounts together are today. The ads possessed, moreover, a social acceptability that they lack now. Such respectable periodicals as the religious weeklies, of which there were more than four hundred in America in 1870, gladly opened their pages to patent-medicine advertising, and were mainly supported by it. So fastidious a magazine as the *Atlantic Monthly* carried in 1868 notices for Dr. J. W. Poland's "Humor Doctor, an Invaluable Medicine for Purefying the Blood." The *Atlantic* also happily sold a back-cover half-page to Turner's "Tic Doloreux or Universal Neuralgia Pill, the Undoubted Cure for All Excruciating Ills."

The official history of N. W. Ayer & Son, one of the oldest and most distinguished advertising agencies, describes the situation in these terms:

The backbone of the typical advertising agency's business in the 19th Century was patent medicine,

and the Ayer firm was no exception. It advertised sure cures for cancer, for consumption, for fits, for stuttering. It advertised "Compound Oxygen," which cured almost every human ailment; Kennedy's Ivory Tooth Cement, which made "Everyone his own dentist!"; and "Dr. Case's Liver Remedy and Blood Purifier," which would supplant the doctor entirely. Other aids to good living included liver and stomach pads, worm destroyers, cough remedies, antibilious bitters, and cures for gout, rheumatism, deafness, ague, neuralgia, and rupture. [There was also] the Pino-Palmine mattress which introduced "into every home, wherever situated, the VERY AROMA WHICH MEDICATES AND TONES THE FLORIDA AIR . . ."

[There] was a great variety of fantastic concoctions, some of them without any great physiological effect, others definitely harmful, and perhaps the majority composed largely of alcohol, designed to lull pain by intoxication or satisfy the cravings of "teetotalers."

No one, at that time, attempted to check such enterprises. Laissez-faire, expressed or implied, was the watchword. It would never have occurred to the businessman of the day—even a sincerely religious one—to introduce into his business activities a social point of view. Nor did it occur to an agent that he

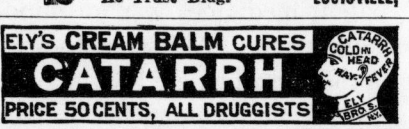
45

was in any way concerned with the merit of the things advertised, any more than a railroad was concerned with the commodities it carried, or a bank with the source of the money deposited.

The term "patent medicine," incidentally, is a misnomer. Few of these products were actually patented. Not many makers would willingly have disclosed the ingredients of their brews; and certainly few would have wanted to release them to the public domain at the end of the patent period. Most were simply secret-formula proprietaries, usually with their labels trademarked, after such protection against infringement became available in the seventies.

9   83

THERE IS NO beginning to the history of patent medicines. Secret healing potions are as old as man. The earliest Mediterranean cultures had a strange faith in the curative power of aloes; Nineveh and Tyre had a number of favorite nostrums; Egyptians were pushovers for dried mummy and newt's eye. The notion that secrecy and supernaturalism should not cloak drugs is a very recent concept; for millenniums men believed otherwise. Many common products first came into fashion through their alleged healing powers. Coffee, tea, and tobacco all appeared in Europe as privately imported wonder drugs. Nor, in the past, was there any snobbery in high places about such nostrums. Queen Elizabeth sold a state monopoly in patent medicines; George III gave a testimonial for Ching's Patent Worm Lozenges. Addison observed sardonically in the *Tatler* that selling patent medicines was an important function of advertising: "A Use of these Writings is to inform the World where they may be furnished with almost every Thing that is Necessary for Life. If a Man has Pains in his Head, Cholicks

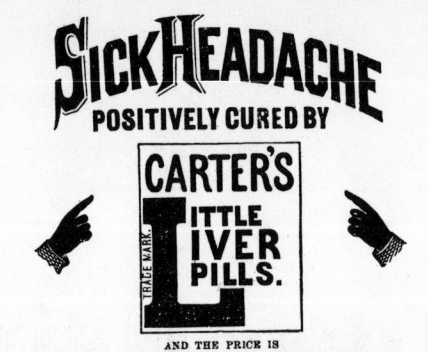
in his Bowels, or Spots on his Cloathes, he may here meet with proper Cures and Remedies." And Benjamin Franklin, always an alert entrepreneur and ornament to his times, owned several proprietaries, including "Seneka Rattlesnake Root, Complete with Directions for Use in the Pleurisy."

In the early part of the nineteenth century it seemed as if the patent-medicine trade in the United States could scarcely grow larger. Actually, the success of the pioneers merely testified to the size of the lode lying close beneath the surface. Dr. Benjamin Brandreth began in 1835 to sell pills that were to make his name world-famous. By the 1840s Dr. James C. Ayer, destined to become the Henry Ford of patent medicines, was starting on the career that would earn him $20 million. Dr. Jayne of Philadelphia, snubbed by his profession after he had begun to manufacture his Expectorant and other secret-formula medicines (one of which could "snatch the tender infant from an early grave"), soothed his injured feelings by building himself a house with solid-silver doorknobs.

But all this was as nothing compared to the patent-medicine boom after the Civil War. There were a number of causes, aside from the growing capacities of advertising. Many thousands of returning soldiers suffered from aches and pains. They had experienced both the rigors of war and those of army rations, at that time so dietetically barbarous as to constitute training for a lifetime of dyspepsia. Another cause of the boom was the hordes of new settlers who, cutting adrift from their old homes, pushed Westward toward sparsely populated and doctorless territory. When a forehanded man took his family to

BUFFALO LITHIA SPRING No. 2

NATURE'S GREAT SPECIFIC FOR DYSPEPSIA AND GOUT.

Photograph of Dolly Shelton, an old colored woman, taken Jan'y 10, 1889, in her 96th year.

At Eighty years of age bedridden from Dyspepsia and Gout. She was miraculously restored by this Water.

Her case stated by Dr. James Shelton, residing near the Buffalo Springs :

"Dolly Shelton, formerly a family servant, resides a mile from BUFFALO SPRINGS. When about eighty years of age, she was bedridden, a sufferer from ATONIC DYSPEPSIA and RHEUMATIC GOUT. I advisved remedies in the case as palliatives merely, not regarding her recovery as among possibilities. While she was in this condition, a Spring was discovered at Buffalo, now known as Spring No. 2. Without suggestion, she at once commenced the use of it, and in a few months (I advised her only at long intervals, not feeling that I could be of service to her), I found, to my great astonishment, that it was proving highly beneficial. There was marked Improvement of the DIGESTION, and also of the GOUTY SYMPTOMS. Under continued use of the water, there was continued improvement until she was able to substitute a diet of *meat* and *vegetables* for bread and milk, boiled rice and corn meal, mush, &c,, and there was also entire disappearance of the GOUTY AFFECTION. At the same time there was a gradual increase of flesh and nervous vigor until she could walk, without unusual fatigue, several miles at a time over the surrounding hills. She is now living, and certainly not under ninety-five years of age. She claims to be a hundred; would weigh I suppose, two hundred; is in good general health, and walks without difficulty about her house, yard and garden, having had no return of DYSPEPSIA or GOUT."

February 1, 1889.

For sale by leading druggists everywhere.

THOMAS F. GOODE, Proprietor,

Testimonials with good credibility and a strong before-and-after theme were invaluable. This gem, high in human interest, characterized both the doctor and patient.

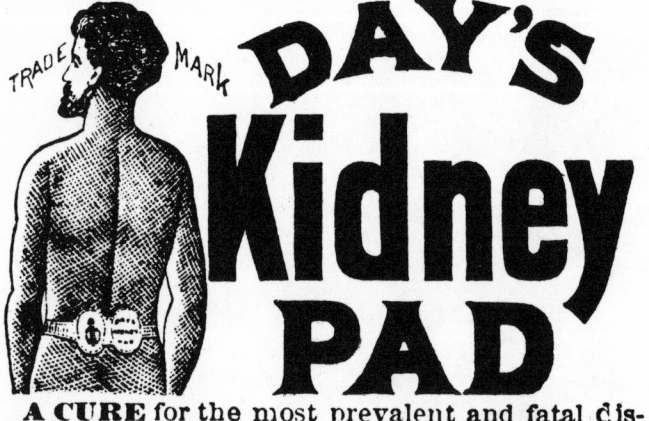

DAY'S Kidney PAD

TRADE MARK

A CURE for the most prevalent and fatal diseases that afflict mankind **FOUND AT LAST.** Internal medicines never did nor never can cure **KIDNEY DISEASE. STOP IT NOW;** apply Day's Kidney Pad **AT ONCE,** and be cured of all affections of the **Kidneys, Bladder and Urinary Organs.** It is the only treatment that will cure **NERVOUS AND PHYSICAL DEBILITY,** and that distressing complaint, **"BACK ACHE."** It will annually save many times its cost in medicines and plasters, which at best give but temporary relief. Sold by Druggists or sent by mail on receipt of price, **$2.** Our book, "How a Life Was Saved," giving a history of this new discovery and a large record of most remarkable cures, sent free. Write for it.

Patent-medicine advertising wasn't restricted to pills and potions; it was also fine for selling electro-mechanical curatives. The copy with the ad below asserted that "Genuine Dr. Scott's Electric Goods . . . are permanently charged, wonderfully efficacious."

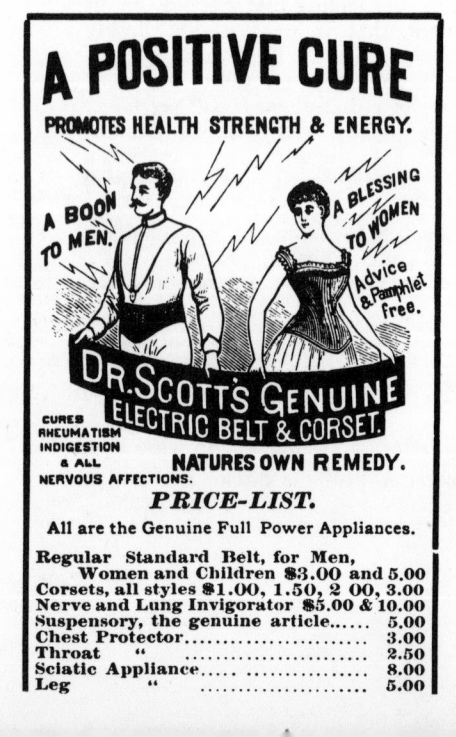

A POSITIVE CURE
PROMOTES HEALTH STRENGTH & ENERGY.

A BOON TO MEN.   A BLESSING TO WOMEN

Advice & Pamphlet Free.

DR. SCOTT'S GENUINE ELECTRIC BELT & CORSET.
CURES RHEUMATISM INDIGESTION & ALL NERVOUS AFFECTIONS.   **NATURES OWN REMEDY.**

PRICE-LIST.
All are the Genuine Full Power Appliances.

Regular Standard Belt, for Men,
   Women and Children $3.00 and 5.00
Corsets, all styles $1.00, 1.50, 2.00, 3.00
Nerve and Lung Invigorator $5.00 & 10.00
Suspensory, the genuine article...... 5.00
Chest Protector....................... 3.00
Throat   " 2.50
Sciatic Appliance.....   .... 8.00
Leg   " 5.00

a country where there was no physician within a hundred miles, he laid in a chest stocked with such favorites as Mandrake Pills, Pulmonic Syrup, Radway's Ready Relief, Piso's Cure for Consumption, Dr. Pierce's Golden Medical Discovery, Mrs. Winslow's Soothing Syrup, and Dr. Olcott's Pain Paint or Pain Annihilator.

The medical profession, though the logical foe of the patent-medicine man, was in no position to do battle against the enthusiasm for self-medication. For one thing, the supply of physicians was too small and too unevenly distributed. For another, such doctors as there were couldn't be compared with today's toters of antibiotics. The profession was technically primitive; anesthesia was rare, antisepsis even rarer, calomel the almost universal prescription, and mortality from a dozen common diseases appallingly high. The profession was also riven with internal problems of heresy, quackery, and imperfect training. As late as 1870 the dean of the Harvard Medical School explained the absence of written examinations on the grounds that too few of the candidates for graduation could write well enough to make such a test fair.

And patent medicines prospered for another reason: they often worked. If a person suffered from a self-limiting or psychosomatic illness, if he believed the medicine could help him, and if it contained enough alcohol or cocaine to induce a sense of well-being, he could easily become a contented customer. In combination, alcohol and faith could work miracles.

ADVERTISING for a patent medicine was, as late as the seventies, an empirical art: if it got sales it was good. St. Joseph's Oil, a rheumatism ointment, used what might be described as the conditioned-reflex approach. The firm, founded on borrowed money just after the Civil War, grew quickly to the point where its proprietor, Charles A. Vogeler, was able to appropriate $600,000 a year for advertising. Although he made heavy use of newspapers and magazines, his particular enthusiasm was for outdoor advertising, then mainly barn and fence-post signs.

48

He once bought a big Mississippi steamboat, ostensibly for delivery of the remedy up and down the river but actually because it could be made into a giant traveling billboard bearing the words ST. JOSEPH'S OIL in letters so enormous that they could be read miles away from the bank. Vogeler once had the same three words painted hugely on a rock at Niagara Falls, where they became a conspicuous part of the natural scene. Only after he had milked the resultant public protest for the fullest possible publicity did he consent to paint the sign out (amid further bursts of publicity).

This Barnumesque technique did not win the praise of the master himself. In his *Humbugs of the World*, Barnum wrote: "Any man with a beautiful wife or daughter would probably feel it disagreeable if he should find branded across her smooth white forehead, or on her snowy shoulders in blue and red letters, such a phrase as this: 'Try the Jigamaree Bitters!' And it is about as nauseous to find 'Bitters' or 'Worm Syrup' daubed upon the landscape as it would be upon the lady's brow."

But as a general rule Vogeler patterned himself less on Barnum than on Thomas Barratt of Pears' Soap. "We want to associate the words 'St. Joseph's Oil' and 'rheumatism' so thoroughly in the minds of every man and woman in the United States," his advertising manager once confided, "that at the first twinge they have, they will think of St. Joseph's Oil."

This differed sharply from the approach used by Warner's Safe Kidney and Liver Cure, which in the 1870s pioneered the effective new technique of the bogus news story. The headline, calculated to catch the most jaded eye, was set in standard headline type, and presented complete with subheads and a news lead. HOW A LIFE WAS SAVED! a typical headline might shrill, followed by an excited narrative of how James J. McGonigle, say, the sole support of his wife and eight children, was suddenly struck down by dangerous disease. Attended and despaired of by the best physicians, he was *in extremis*—and was snatched from the brink by last-minute applications of

Warner's Safe Kidney and Liver Cure. Such decoy ads, far from producing reader resentment, were vastly effective at the time, as testified to both by the success of Warner's Cure and by the appearance of hordes of imitators. It was a time, remote from later canons of propriety, when good-natured chicanery was expected and even appreciated. And the masquerade ad, wearing the false whiskers of a news story, article, or even short story, has had a place ever since.

Another contribution by patent medicine to advertising lore came with the discovery of the special power of a cryptic and technical-sounding name. The outstanding early example of this was something called Drake's Plantation Bitters. This did not sell well until its advertising and label were changed to feature the letters "S. T. 1860 X." Business picked up noticeably, and Drake and his partner made a point of refusing to explain what the mysterious notation meant. Instead, they shrewdly nurtured public discussion of the mystery. One word-of-mouth theory was that it was a kind of anagram for the proud boast: Started Trade in 1860 with $10. George P. Rowell, the early advertising agent, became so fascinated by the cryptogram that he was unwilling to accept Drake's professional confidence that the letters had no meaning whatever and were used simply to attract attention. Instead, Rowell plugged away at transposition ciphers. Once he thought he had it cracked: the clue came from his knowledge that Plantation Bitters was simply rebottled Santa Cruz rum. Rowell noted that if for 1, 8, 6, 0 one substituted C, R, O, I the cryptogram then spelled St. Croix, a notable rum port. He rushed triumphant to Drake, who complimented his ingenuity but insisted that the only function of the marking was to keep customers wondering and remembering.

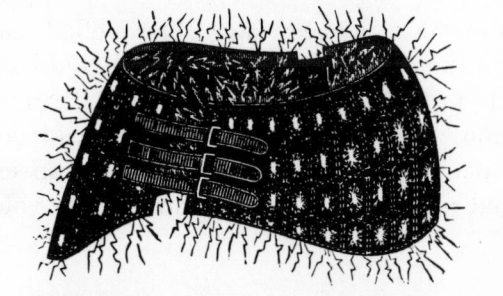

THE ABOVE CUT ILLUSTRATES OUR MAGNETIC Belt. One of the grandest appliances ever made for Lame Back, Weakness of Spine and any diseases of the Kidneys. This belt will give relief in Five Minutes, and has never failed to cure Lame Back!

49

PAINSFOE
THE HOUSEHOLD REMEDY FOR PAIN.

Drawings didn't have to be good to be graphic. The contorted face of this tyke, squalling so miserably, nearly sent a man straight out to the druggist.

From his vantage as an advertising agent, Rowell concluded that the patent-medicine business was too promising to pass by. He sought out a medical student at a New York hospital and urged him to brew up something useful. According to Rowell's memoirs, the lad returned shortly with a "liquid having a soothing effect on the stomach. And no matter what ails a man, it is either as a result of stomach difficulty or it will, to some extent, induce such a difficulty." Even a man who splits his toe with an ax, the medical student lectured Rowell, will feel pain not only in the injured member but in the stomach as well—and there this medicine will act as a soother and sweetener.

The prospect delighted Rowell, for he had already noted that the stomach was the happiest hunting ground for successful proprietaries. A cold cure that he knew of had been a flop until it was readvertised as a stomachic, after which it did nicely. But as he studied the bottle, Rowell felt that "it almost made me sick at the stomach to look at it. . . . A dirty brick-colored sediment formed in the bottom, and the upper part remained muddy and unpleasing to the eye." When sniffed, the remedy gave off a malodorous reek of brewed rhubarb, imperfectly disguised with peppermint. Rowell was about to abandon the venture ("it looked nasty; it smelled nasty") when the student explained that it could also be made in tablet form, thus avoiding its more obnoxious aspects. In planning his advertising campaign, Rowell took counsel from an experienced medicine man: "You must write your advertisements to catch damned fools—not college professors. Then you'll catch as many college professors as you will any other sort." During the first year on the market the rhubarb pills moved very slowly. But under Rowell's intensive nurture business picked up to modest success, and for one short period the Tabules were selling at a rate of 10,000 nickel packages a day.

Rowell's little flier in medicine was trivial compared to the giants in the field. There was Seth W. Fowle's mint, known to the public as Dr. Wistar's Balsam of Wild Cherry. There was Dr. S. Andral Kilmer's famous Swamp Root, so intensively advertised that Dr. Kilmer was better known to farmers and backwoods people, it was said, than the President of the United States. There was Hostetter & Smith's Stomach Bitters, so solidly established that no retailer was permitted to order less than fifty dozen bottles at a crack. (And so popular that Hostetter reportedly left an estate of $18 million.) There was Dr. Joseph H. Schenk's Sea-Weed Tonic, which was brewed for the first time in a back-yard barrel but which prospered until it built a mansion on a 300-acre estate, with a gleaming yacht swinging at anchor nearby. There was Buchu, the most glorious fluid extract of the many in the armory of Dr. Henry T. Helmbold, the "Prince of Druggists." The Prince's proud question, based on an annual advertising appropriation of more than a quarter of a million dollars as early as 1869, was "Who has not heard of Buchu?" (Not many, apparently; more than three million bottles were shipped that year.)

Some remedies grew to industrial proportions. One was Lydia E. Pinkham's Vegetable Compound, a specific for female disorders that was launched commercially in 1875. Mrs. Pinkham, a matron of Lynn, Massachusetts, with a large family, an impecunious husband, and pronounced feminist tendencies, had been cooking up her compound for years as a kind of free service to ailing females in the neighborhood. In the hard times after the Panic of 1873, with her family in straits, she and several of her enterprising sons set about peddling it.

The Compound was a combination of six Indian herbs—including two described in an old pharmacopoeia that the Pinkhams owned as Aletris, or True Unicorn, and Asclepias, or Pleurisy Root—conveyed in a vehicle of 18 per cent alcohol. It did not find a ready market at first. The Pinkham sons spent several lean years in trying to press it on druggists, many of whom were skeptical about the profit possibilities of female disorders. By 1880, when the little family enterprise was just beginning to prosper beyond the kitchen-table stage, Lydia took a decisive step. She resolutely poured every cent of earnings that could be spared into intensive advertising, and she showed a fine instinct for copywriting: "A sure cure for Prolapsus Uteri, or Falling of the Womb . . . a great help in pregnancy, it relieves pain during labor . . . second to no remedy that has ever been before the public." So powerful did this advertising prove to be that soon no Pinkham need ever be needy again.

Mrs. Pinkham's instincts were infallible. She solicited letters from ailing women: "Lydia Pinkham in her laboratory at Lynn is able to do more for women than any physician in America. Any woman is responsible for her own suffering if she will not take the trouble to write Mrs. Pinkham for advice." Letters came in by the thousands, and she replied with pamphlets of sound hygienic counsel and good words for the Compound, and also with terse but understanding personal notes. She selected the best letters sent to her as testimonials. Her ads spoke directly to lonely or anxious women, using the language of helpful but no-nonsense sisterhood. When Mrs. Pinkham died in 1883 there was a question as to how her place could possibly be filled in the highly profitable business. But by a stroke of good fortune, a Boston advertising man named James T. Wetheral turned up with the almost miraculous ability of writing ads that sounded, in their sympathetic, just-us-girls way, precisely as if they had been dictated by Lydia herself.

Analytical businessmen in the big patent-medicine firms discovered that good testimonials were almost priceless. They were readable; they

WOMAN CAN SYMPATHIZE WITH WOMAN.

HEALTH OF WOMAN IS THE HOPE OF THE RACE.

Yours for Health—
Lydia E. Pinkham

LYDIA E. PINKHAM'S
VEGETABLE COMPOUND.

A Sure Cure for all FEMALE WEAK-NESSES, Including Leucorrhœa, Irregular and Painful Menstruation, Inflammation and Ulceration of the Womb, Flooding, PRO-LAPSUS UTERI, &c.

Quite the most remarkable thing about Lydia Pinkham was her intuitive feeling for undiscovered advertising principles. This ad, from the eighties, is notable for the early use of art that showed, not the product, but a confidence-building image. It was enhanced by the two overlines, both aimed like a rifle at the lonely, ailing women who were her prospects. Her suggestion that men just didn't understand was inspired.

Get Plump!

LORING'S Fat-Ten-U and Corpula Foods Make the Thin Plump and Comely and impart Vim to the Debilitated — They Cool the Blood and Prevent Unpleasant Perspiration

These foods cure nerve and brain exhaustion, which you know as general debility or nervous prostration. They make pale folks pink and thin folks plump and weak folks well and despairing folks happy. Women have learned that they more than take the place of all female remedies and regulators. They will make you young all your life. You know it is better to be a young old man or woman than a prematurely old young man or woman

The portrait above is that of Mrs. Sara Montgomery Wade, Vincennes Avenue, Chicago, who writes: "In six weeks Loring's Fat-Ten-U and Corpula Foods increased my weight 32 pounds, gave me new womanly vigor and developed me finely. They should be used in hot weather, as they keep you cool and make you well."

No "tonics," "nervines," "sarsaparillas" or other medicines are necessary when Fat-Ten-U and Corpula are used. Corpula, $1.00 a bottle. Fat-Ten-U, $1 and $2 a bottle. Send for a free copy of "How to Get Plump and Rosy" and instructions for improving the bust and form.

A Month's Treatment, $2.00

Write to our Chicago Medical Department about your thinness or about any other medical question. Our physicians will advise you free of charge.

Send letters and mail, express or C. O. D. orders to Loring & Co., Proprietors. To insure prompt reply, mention Department as below. Use only the nearest address:

LORING & CO. DEPT. 119.

No. 42 West 22d Street, New York City.
No. 8 Hamilton Place, Boston, Mass.
No. 115 State Street, Chicago, Ill.

added a note of seemingly independent confirmation; they nurtured that seed of faith required of the ideal patent-medicine customer. They led to the persuasive conclusion: Goodness, if the remedy really helped these poor people, it certainly ought to help me. Finally, the testimonial led with inexorable logic into what was proving to be patent medicine's most potent copy theme, the before-and-after-taking demonstration. Before-and-after, buttressed by drawings and testimonials, could sell The Product in carload lots.

There seems to have been some traffic among manufacturers in the names and addresses of reliable testifiers. There was definite trade in lists of buyers, who were of course prime prospects for the heavy purchase of different remedies. Dr. S. B. Hartman's Peruna found it profitable to use testifiers by mail as well as by published ads. Peruna paid a selected list of enthusiastic testifiers twenty-five cents for each letter of independent confirmation mailed out. One of his company's form letters read:

As you are aware, we have your testimonial to our remedy. It has been some time since we have heard from you and so we thought it best to make inquiries as to your present state of health and whether you still occasionally make use of Peruna. We also want to make sure we have your present street address correctly, and that you are making favorable answers to such letters of inquiry which your testimonial may occasion. Remember that we allow 25 cents for each letter of inquiry. You have only to send the letter you receive, together with a copy of your reply to the same, and we will forward you 25 cents for each pair of letters.

We hope you are still a friend of Peruna and that our continued use of your testimonial will be agreeable to you. We are enclosing stamped letter for reply.

Very sincerely yours,
The Peruna Drug Manufacturing Company

The dean of the medicine men was Dr. James C. Ayer. By 1871, after thirty exciting years in the business, he was a multimillionaire with a line of more than a dozen popular remedies, led by Ayer's Cherry Pectoral, Ayer's Sarsaparilla, and Ayer's Cathartic Pills. That was the year that the

Presumably the customer could alternate between Fat-Ten-U and Obesity Pills until a happy equilibrium was reached.

little Massachusetts town of Groton Junction decided to rename itself after its most distinguished citizen (it has been known as Ayer ever since). The operation was a big one: rows of pill machines, big batch mixers, arrays of bottling machines, a small paper mill for the production of anticounterfeit labels. Running at capacity, the factory could turn out 630,000 doses a day. Once 25 million advertising almanacs were given away; each year advertising contracts were signed with 1,900 newspapers. "Our annual issue of pamphlets," said Dr. Ayer in a speech during the ceremonial renaming of the town, "if laid solid upon each other, would make a pile eight and one quarter miles high. If laid end to end, they would extend for 1,894 miles." The old doctor concluded his speech with a summary of the patent-medicine rationale: with people spreading thinly across the land, with doctors scarce and often untrained, home remedies should be kept close at hand by one and all.

What kind of man was this patent-medicine titan? It is difficult to penetrate the dense cloud of gentility emitted by Ayer's official biographer, though several inferences suggest themselves. One is that for all the money and local homage, he may have felt a faint defensiveness about his business. His biographer is delicately reticent about the sources of Ayer wealth. The flannel mills in Lowell and the real-estate and lumber holdings in Florida are freely discussed—but it is not until the rites for renaming the town are mentioned that the biographer can bring himself to speak of Cathartic Pills. One other glimpse slips through the fog of propriety: a fleeting image of a tough, sardonic old man, so deeply amused by the moral dilemmas of others that he stage-managed a few himself as practical jokes. Once when the town church took up a subscription for a new set of bells, Ayer graciously told the committee that waited upon him that he would be delighted to contribute the money for one large bell by himself, the F bell. As the committee beamed, the old doctor added soberly that of course it would have to have the words CATHARTIC PILLS and CHERRY PECTORAL cast around its rim.

This poker-faced proviso was too much for the committee; they retired in confusion and held meetings. "Bells were meant to chime the praises of Almighty God, not the merits of patent medicines," declaimed one member. A deputation was sent back to Ayer with tactfully phrased demurral. Ayer was adamant: no words, no bell.

After weeks of disputatious meetings, the committee came reluctantly to the view that an F bell with advertising on it was better than no F bell at all. When word of this victory of practicality over principle was brought to the old man, he announced with hearty guffaws that he had been expecting this conclusion—but that actually his F bell would be wholly free of words. He could have added that he had too high an opinion of the value of advertising to wish it hidden in a steeple.

Ayer's newspaper contracts, like those of other big concerns, were shrewdly drawn to enforce editorial support against anti-patent-medicine legislation. Two typical clauses ran:

It is agreed in case any law or laws are enacted, either state or national, harmful to the interests of the J. C. Ayer Company, that this contract may be cancelled by them from date of such enactment, and the insertions made paid for pro-rata with the contract price.

It is agreed that the J. C. Ayer Company may cancel this contract, pro-rata, in case advertisements are published in this paper in which products are offered with a view to substitution or other harmful motive; also in case any matter otherwise detrimental to the J. C. Ayer Company's interest is permitted to appear in the reading columns or elsewhere in this paper.

Thus most newspapers were forced to work for patent-medicine interests. Whenever a threatening reform measure was introduced in a State Legislature, the companies would dispatch telegrams to publishers recommending that the papers work to shelve the measure, lest the company be forced to discontinue advertising. Since the revenue at stake was very large, this was a strangle hold that few papers had the courage to break. It was estimated that during the nineties the newspapers of the country received much more revenue from patent medicines than did the proprietors of the medicines. *Collier's* once commented invidiously that "Mr. Hearst's papers alone reap a harvest of more than half a million dollars per annum from this source."

Reform, nonetheless, grew increasingly hard to put down.

OFTEN a collision can be seen coming before the instant of impact. This was true of the patent-medicine business in the nineties, then on an intersecting course with newer conditions and standards in American life. In the face of attack new justifications for the industry were created. One was the doctrine of *caveat emptor,* as in James Gordon Bennett's celebrated rejoinder when reproached for the advertising he ran: "Business is business, money is money; we permit no blockhead to interfere with our business." Another defense was counterattack: why should meddling laws peck away at the proud enterprises that are dedicated to that finest of human activities, solacing the sick? Still a third response, favored by many advertising men, was mock-psychological: the public, as Barnum demonstrated, *likes* to be slightly humbugged.

Effective reform, when it came, arose not from the newspapers but from magazines. The first big step came in 1892, when Cyrus H. K. Curtis announced that the *Ladies' Home Journal* would henceforth accept no more "medical advertising." This was courageous, for the *Journal* had been a favorite of the medicine men; and it was important, because it was just then drawing ahead of the *Youth's Companion's* 650,000 circulation to become the biggest United States magazine. The *Journal's* advertising revenue took a nose dive in 1893, and it was later estimated by its editor, Edward Bok, that the excluded ads would have brought the magazine about $300,000 a year. Following the *Journal's* example, a few other magazines began to exclude or censor ads; and a few resolute newspapers, notably *The New York Times* after Adolph Ochs gained control in 1896, also began to refuse nostrum copy.

With a stubborn instinct for self-destruction, the patent-medicine industry responded with increasingly flagrant claims. Restoratives of lost manhood, pills for gonorrhea and syphilis, and a white powder named Antidipso that a wife could slip furtively into her drunken husband's coffee all began to blossom fetidly on newspaper advertising pages. "As competition increased," wrote Frank Presbrey, "advertisers found it necessary to make claims stronger than those made by rivals. Extravagance in assertion finally became a game in which the public appeared to be regarded as onlookers who would cheer the biggest liar or the funniest clown—and then rush in and buy his product." Lists of diseases that could be cured by proprietaries grew longer, and advertising writers discovered the heady possibilities of inventing new diseases, including Sparks Before the Eyes, Ear Throb, Dragging Sensation in the Groin, and, as a special appeal to the suggestible, Creeping Numbness.

The second major blow against patent medicines also came from the *Ladies' Home Journal.* Noting the huge readership that S. S. McClure

Patent-medicine techniques, adapted to the sale of other products, usually betrayed their origin. The cosmetic below used a switch on before-and-after; the unfortunate "living example" here was only half repaired. On the facing page: a fruity experiment in sale by pure suggestion.

The noble, knowing savage was only part of the sales pitch
for this stomachic of the sixties. The fine print beneath
also carried a glowing testimonial from a Yale professor.

Old Sachem Bitters and Wigwam Tonic.

THESE delicious and far-famed Bitters are recommend
ed by the *first Physicians of the country*, on account of
their *PURITY AND GREAT MEDICINAL VIRTUE*

had drawn with exposés of trusts and grafting, Bok hired a young law-school graduate named Mark Sullivan to collect all evidence damning patent medicines that he could find. In 1904 the *Journal* began to print chemical analyses of many secret preparations. Some were shown to be real painkillers in the most terminal sense of the word. Those partial to several catarrh cures realized why it was difficult to stop taking the stuff: cocaine was an important ingredient. Soothing syrups for infants contained heavy doses of morphine. Stomach bitters were shown to be mainly cheap rum or brandy, or simply alcohol and colored water.

Lydia Pinkham's Vegetable Compound was a particular target for the *Journal*, but here the objection was aimed more at the advertising than the product. Modest women learned to their horror that ads urging them to confide in Mrs. Pinkham neglected to state that Mrs. P. had been in her grave for twenty-two years. The *Journal* documented this fact with a photo of her tombstone. The magazine even suggested that these womanly confidences were in all likelihood a source of coarse male hilarity in the Pinkham offices—after which the names and addresses of their writers were sold to mailing-list firms at a nickel apiece.

In 1905 *Collier's* jumped on the band wagon with telling effect. Samuel Hopkins Adams wrote a blistering series of pieces called "The Great American Fraud." He told his readers that they were fools if they used worthless preparations, and even bigger fools for paying extravagant prices for them. As one example he cited Peruna. This could be made at home, said Adams, "by mixing half a pint of 180-proof cologne spirits [a commercial term for potable alcohol] with a pint and a half of water, adding thereto a little cubebs for flavor and a little burnt sugar for color." If bought as Peruna the cost was a dollar a bottle; made at home, about eighteen cents. Adams cited estimates that Americans were drinking more alcohol in patent medicines than in all licensed beer, liquor, and wine sold in the country. It was already common knowledge that the Bureau of Indian Affairs had had to prohibit the sale of Peruna on the reservations: like firewater, it made the Indians act up.

The exposés had a powerful impact on the public. When Mark Sullivan dredged up more material than the *Journal* could use, *Collier's* presented it in still another series, this one on how medicine men coerced newspapers and State Legislatures. (About this time the bloodied medicine men came groggily to the counterattack. Some publishers, they alleged, were using a blackmailing argument: feed us fat advertising contracts or we'll exposé you out of business.) Also about this time the N. W. Ayer agency, which was close to Cyrus Curtis, announced a policy of refusing all patent-medicine business. Mr. Ayer (no relation to Dr. James C.), observing that he had already dropped two lucrative accounts, one of them Dr. Williams's Pink Pills for Pale People, put his decision this way: "It reached the point where it became necessary to make or fake miracles." And in December, 1905, the American Medical Association, no mean combatant in a street fight but one hitherto strangely silent, suddenly spat on its hands and plunged into battle.

What was heralded as victory came in June of 1906 with the passage of the first Pure Food and Drug Act. (It was spoken of, in conjunction with state laws, as the "Wiley Laws," after the crusading Dr. H. W. Wiley.) The law was not a tight one, but it was a beginning. Misrepresentation, especially in claiming cures, was prohibited. Ingredients like morphine, cocaine, and alcohol had to be identified on the label and strength specified. A few patent-medicine makers, dazed or incredulous, simply ignored the law and continued to put out their old products. But when arrests, convictions, and fines resulted, it became obvious to all that the wild and woolly days were over.

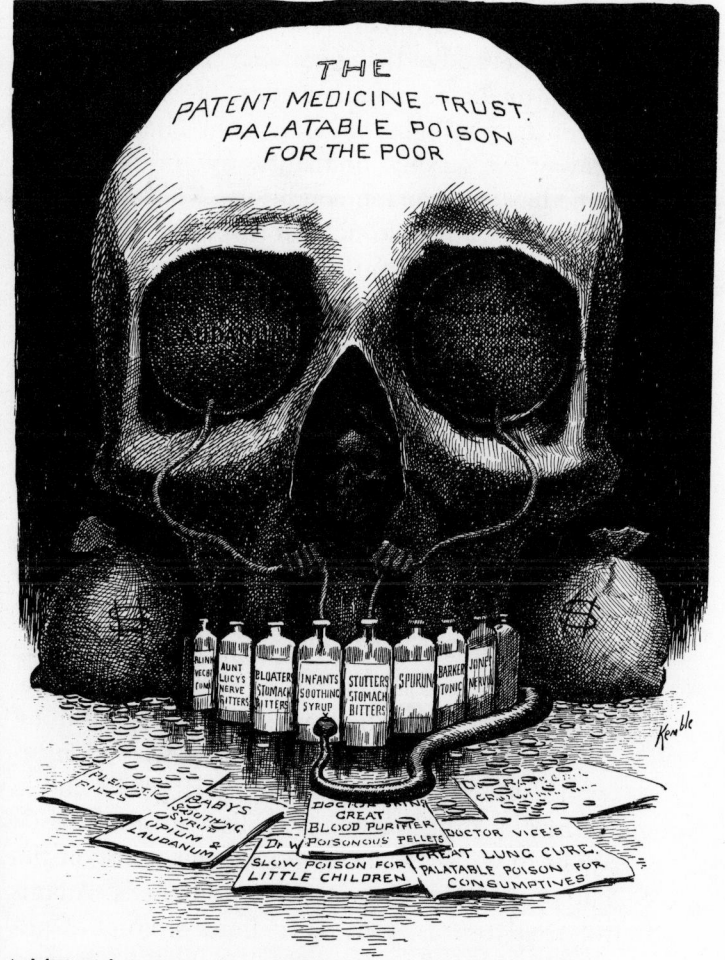

Additional impact was added to the furious magazine crusade against patent medicines by cartoons like this one, drawn by E. W. Kemble for *Collier's*. The dim lettering on the casks in the eye sockets reads "Laudanum" and "Cheap Poisonous Alcohol." A second skull lurks within.

ADVERTISING MEN who know about it have not always felt easy about this early dalliance with Jezebel. Partly this has come from an awareness of how deeply their occupation was involved. Advertising was not just an adjunct; it was part owner. The biggest agencies of the day, including Lord & Thomas in Chicago, the Rowell Agency in New York, and Pettengill & Company in Boston, were among those that had bought into patent-medicine firms. This was thought to be doubly shrewd: insurance against the loss of a valuable account, and an often profitable investment. Many more agencies stumbled into part ownership of patent-medicine firms the way N. W. Ayer did—by accepting shares for unpaid bills, in preference to payment in pills or sarsaparilla.

Advertising's semiofficial interpretation of the patent-medicine epoch was presented in 1929 by Frank Presbrey. He deplored the "disesteem" that patent medicines gave advertising. He noted that in the nineteenth century the advent of the middleman between maker and buyer brought about a kind of insulation that encouraged shabby ethics. Besides, it was Barnum's day, a time of cheerful chicanery, summed up in the old folk story about the grocer who called down to his son to sand the sugar, water the vinegar, put pebbles in the beans, and then come up to evening prayer. Finally, Presbrey noted, "patent medicine's big successes revealed the immense possibilities of selling through print."

A less equivocal defense was offered years ago by Claude C. Hopkins, one of the most brilliant copywriters advertising has ever had. Speaking of patent-medicine manufacturers, he said: "I have never known higher-minded men. They felt that they were serving humanity by offering good remedies for common conditions. They were aiding those who could not afford physicians. There was much reason in their arguments. And I still believe those medicine makers did far more good than harm. But medical sciences advanced. We came to realize that ailing people should have a diagnosis. The real trouble should be located instead of quelling symptoms."

Hopkins's testimony should perhaps be read in the light of his record with a germicide called Liquozone. It had been almost out of business when Hopkins—who believed that it had saved his daughter's life—began writing its simple, sincere, plausible ads. In the next year Liquozone shot up to a dazzling net of $1.8 million. Soon, with factories building overseas and ads running in seventeen languages, Liquozone was a worldwide success that was earning Hopkins and a partner a large fortune. (It also inspired H. G. Wells to write *Tono-Bungay*, a rich satire on the patent-medicine business.) In *Collier's* Adams referred to it as "that marvellous product of advertising and effrontery." And at Lord & Thomas, the agency where Hopkins was a shining star among the copywriters, his envious colleagues referred to it as "99 per cent Lake Michigan, flavored with medicament."

In his defense of the medicine men, Hopkins pointed out that they did much to train advertising people for the great days ahead. "A patent medicine was inherently worthless until a demand was created for it. It offered the supreme test of a man's skill. The greatest advertising men of my day were schooled in the medicine field."

Here Hopkins was right. By tracing the effects of ads on sales, nostrum advertisers were able to uncover a large body of technical advertising lore. They learned such new things as the effect of an ad's position on its pulling power. They traced variations caused by season, weather, news, and a publication's personality. They discovered and measured the extra effectiveness of magazine covers. They explored the potency of testimonials and the before-and-after gambit. An uncounted number of attention-getting devices were thought up and tried out, and the best identified. Pioneering study went into headlines, typefaces, ornaments, layouts, and illustration. The extra value of illustration was revealed in the regular use of Mrs. Pinkham's matronly features or Pain Paint's evil imps, busy with their augers on the neuralgic head. And copywriting in particular benefited from the discoveries of the patent-medicine epoch—notably such revelations as the leverage of fear, hope, and suggestion.

It remained, in the fullness of time, for at least one old patent medicine to find unexpected defense. In the reforming climate of the recent past, Lydia E. Pinkham's Vegetable Compound came under sharp Federal fire for its advertising claims. But then, to the astonishment of the government's analytical chemists, the quaint old remedy was found to provide its users with mild estrogen therapy. This was despite the fact that estrogens and their effect on female functioning had been totally unknown in the days when Mrs. P. was brewing her Compound in the kitchen. On further analysis the source of the estrogens was identified: the two old Indian herbs that she had always popped in—Asclepias or Pleurisy Root, and Aletris or True Unicorn.

Chapter 5

The Cereal

NOWHERE were the almost frightening potentialities of advertising better demonstrated than in the sudden, gold-rush growth of the breakfast-food business. Prepared cereals were comparatively rare at breakfast before the closing years of the last century; fried salt pork, and fried meal, mush, or hominy were the typical (and leaden) start to each day. But as early as 1910, thanks to volleys of inspired advertising, the practice of munching on precooked shredded, flaked, or granulated wheat, corn, oats, or bran was spreading over much of the civilized world.

Inasmuch as many of these new breakfast cereals sold for perhaps fifteen times the cost of their materials, their sudden popularity also quickly produced several memorable millionaires. One was W. K. Kellogg, a somber man whose immense philanthropies are believed to have arisen, in part, from a deep anxiety that his surviving relatives might get their hands on his fortune. Another was C. W. Post, remembered for—among other things—having once tried to produce rainfall by the simultaneous detonation of 150 sticks of dynamite, hoisted by twenty kites into the arid blue above his Texas ranch.

In the early nineties Charley Post was in poor health and poorer finances. He had been an inventor, and a salesman of farm implements, hardware, and real estate. The bankruptcy of a blanket company had left him with a stock of blankets that he traded for treatments—unsuccessful, he always maintained—at the Seventh-day Adventist sanitarium in Battle Creek, operated by an evangelical vegetarian named Dr. John Harvey Kellogg. Still sickly, Post stayed on in Battle Creek, making a precarious living as an inventor, mental healer, and proprietor of a small convalescent home called La Vita Inn. He also ran a mail-order business in patent suspenders made by his wife. Just a few years later, thanks to a magical touch at promoting his inventions, Postum and Grape-Nuts, he had become a high-spirited multimillionaire who, on a grand European tour, once paused to wonder how he might persuade the King of England to endorse Grape-Nuts.

Post's special and peculiar discovery was that foods could be effectively advertised as medicine —which in that time meant patent medicine. "Makes Sturdy Legs!" was headlined as a virtue

Wars

These are the friendly flakes that get a real hold on your appetite. Small moppets have been stowing them away and spilling a few in their bathrobe pockets for over 50 years. . . .
—Corn Flakes advertisement

of Grape-Nuts; "Makes Red Blood!" was the endlessly repeated virtue of Postum. Post also explored what has been called symptom-inducing advertising. "Lost Eyesight Through Coffee Drinking" was but one alarming headline used to scare customers over to Postum. Another advertisement showed coffee dripping slimily down the page, past the words: "Constant dripping wears away the stone. Perhaps a hole has been started in you. . . . Try leaving off coffee for ten days and use Postum Food Coffee. . . ." Rheumatism, heart disease, and general systemic poisoning were all laid at the door of the demon coffee; malaria, loose teeth, consumption, and appendicitis could be beaten back by the regular ingestion of Grape-Nuts. The Grape-Nuts box was small, true, but that was because the food was highly concentrated. This theme of compactness practically to the point of pemmican was underlined by ads showing explorers and prospectors setting forth with their pack animals heavily laden with boxes of Grape-Nuts. It was not made clear whether these were to be eaten by the men, the animals, or both.

In fact, the concept of Americans by the mil-

lions munching on horse-feed grains proved highly stimulating to humorists; and the makers of one cereal, H-O Oats, enhanced the image by also making and advertising special horse feed. But advertisers in general were not overly sensitive to such nuances in the early days; Ivory Soap once proudly announced that it was "most excellent for washing galled spots and scratches on horses."

Post did not limit himself to frightening his customers into hypochondria. As a practicing mental healer he knew the powers and uses of positive faith, particularly faith coupled with dietary eccentricity. Early purchasers of Grape-Nuts received with each box a tract Post had written first in his La Vita Inn days called "The Road to Wellville." He was also an instinctive copywriter, with a gift for compelling headlines and for bare and forceful language. His subtitle on an early version of the Wellville tract was "Worded for Plain People." Commenting on the headline "If Coffee Don't Agree—Use Postum," Gerald Carson, the contemporary historian of the breakfast-food business, has observed that Post could use a "powerful brand of farmer English." He was also capable of greater flourish, as when he plugged Grape-Nuts as an adjunct to female beauty: "There are no blotches on the face of Beauty when fed on Grape-Nuts. The true pink-and-white complexion is made on the *inside* of the body." Post spent hundreds of thousands of dollars dinning in the slogan "There's a Reason" as a catch phrase for both Grape-Nuts and Postum. This slogan, criticized and finally demolished by later and less imaginative advertising men (What reason? For what? Where's the name of The Product?), nevertheless captured exactly the faith-stained, hypochondriac mysticism that Post was striving for.

Sometimes advertising space was devoted less to selling The Product than to baring the teeth at the enemy.

The Kind with the Flavor—Made of the Best White Corn.

In much of his early advertising Post also made heavy use of testimonials, reworking letters of approval—under the guise of condensation—until they bore little resemblance to the pale and watery originals. To Charley Post, writing an ad seems to have been a form of self-expression, highly useful in argument and conflict. When in his later years he plunged into controversy with labor unions, he used advertisements as weapons, wielding them as dangerously as other men might brandish swords, guns, or lawyers.

Post's first verifiable exposure to the idea of a cereal coffee substitute appears to have been in 1892, when he was a patient at the Battle Creek sanitarium. Here Dr. John Kellogg provided various manufactured cereal foods, including a rather gritty one called Granola and a warm brown beverage, brewed from roasted grain products, called Caramel Cereal Coffee. Kellogg maintained a desultory sideline business in manufacturing his health foods, mainly for mail-order sale to ex-patients, but his numerous other activities, plus a wary caution about impairing his professional standing, kept the business small.

One story has it that Post proposed a joint commercial venture with the doctor and was turned down brusquely. Whether this was true or not, Post was no man to let a good thing slip. In 1894 he invested sixty-nine dollars in a second-hand stove, a peanut roaster, a coffee grinder, two bushels of wheat, 200 pounds of bran, and ten jugs of molasses. In a shed near La Vita Inn he set about inventing Postum.

The first year his coffee substitute was on sale, Post lost $800. But he was a tireless and effective salesman, and he had an unshakable faith in advertising. Many times he managed to persuade publishers to give him credit until cash came in from sales generated by the advertising they ran. He talked a Chicago advertising agency into placing his ads on a contingent basis. (Soon the agency held so many of Post's notes that it could easily have taken over the precarious little business, but it hardly seemed worth it.)

By its second year Postum began to make a little money, almost all of it poured back into

62

advertising and into renewing and expanding credit. Grape-Nuts, added early in 1898, displayed Post's highly developed pragmatism: not being a hot drink, it wasn't seasonal in sales, and it made a perfect companion product because some substances removed in its manufacture could be used up in Postum. The two products flourished. After the first lean years Post suddenly discovered that he had become a millionaire, and Battle Creek's first citizen. Soon this set off a wild boom there in the speculative manufacture of dozens of copycat cereals.

Post was also in a position of firmly established mutual hostility with Dr. John Kellogg. Kellogg felt Post was a plagiarist; Post, making oblique references to "vegetarian cranks," observed that he had known of coffee substitutes in his early Texas days, *years* before he first came to Battle Creek. Later, when the doctor's younger brother, W. K. Kellogg, broke free of the doctor's shadow and founded what would become the corn-flakes empire, the Post-Kellogg feud continued vigorously. The two large firms in Battle Creek regarded each other across their factory fences with unwinking, baleful eyes.

There were frequent forays, such as piracy-by-pay-raise of foremen believed to know manufacturing secrets. Once the Kellogg factory, being rebuilt after a disastrous fire, discovered that Post had alertly cornered the market in the special water-cooled steel rolls needed to make flaked cereals. Once the Post plant found itself short of coal and had the embarrassing innocence to ask if it could buy a carload from Kellogg's plentiful supply. And some years later, when the Kellogg Company was in a temporarily shaky financial position, and W. K. Kellogg was working desperately and successfully to set the firm back on its financial feet, he received several bland inquiries from across the way if he wanted to sell out at last—at distress prices.

A CHEERFUL dyspeptic named Henry D. Perky was the creator of another classic of the United States breakfast table. But as Perky ruefully admitted later, he had had no such intention

originally. For several struggling years, in fact, he clung faithfully to the belief that what he had *really* invented was a kind of wheat pudding.

Perky was variously and obscurely a storekeeper, schoolteacher, and lawyer in Nebraska and Colorado. (His legal training paid off later: his invention was so heavily studded with patents that pirates were successfully repelled until the twenties, when the patents expired.) He devoted his spare time to a favorite hobby—dosing a chronic state of indigestion. In his experiments, he came to the view that wheat, if steamed or boiled, was not only edible but indeed highly digestible—an almost perfect food. In Denver in

Fortifying the young for the rigors of winter play has long been a favorite gambit, as this 1909 ad suggests.

Warm it in a pan before serving

EGG-O-SEE 10¢

Cold Days Demand Energy
and Egg-O-See supplies it to old and young. It puts "snap" into business and home duties, into school and play, because there is real energy in it, power without over-taxing digestion, and deliciousness without injury.

Let the children eat all the EGG-O-SEE they wish—the more EGG-O-SEE the more health

Crisp it for a minute in the oven and eat with cream, and notice its flaky, appetizing nut-like flavor, and how much more perfectly it digests and how good you feel while it is digesting. Choice wheat, the true food, perfectly prepared by the original Egg-O-See process. Pure, palatable, perfect in satisfying and digestive power.

10 Liberal Breakfasts 10c.

In Canada and Pacific Coast territory the price of Egg-O-See is 15c, two packages for 25c. How to get well, keep well by natural means — bathing, exercise, food, etc.— and how to use Egg-O-See for every meal in the week is told in our expensively prepared booklet, "-back to nature," sent free. We are glad to send it. You will be glad to get it.

EGG-O-SEE CEREAL COMPANY
800 AMERICAN TRUST BLDG., CHICAGO, ILL.

-back to nature

63

the early nineties Perky devised a little machine to make his boiled wheat—a rather viscid mass—more manageable. It had a pair of steel rolls, one smooth and the other lightly grooved, that extruded the wheat into a comb of moist, stringy filaments. These could then be folded up into little mattresslike biscuits. Perky envisioned the possibility of commercial gain—in selling the extruding machines to bakers. He did manage to sell a few around Denver, but there was only a limited public taste for wheat puddings. Worse, the moist little mattresses showed an unappetizing tendency to turn moldy if not speedily eaten.

Then onto the scene came Dr. Kellogg of Battle Creek, stopping off in Denver on a Western trip to look into this new food idea. The two cereal enthusiasts had guarded but amiable conversations in which Kellogg put Perky on the road to riches. The doctor suggested that it would be more profitable to sell food than food machinery, and explained that moldiness could easily be licked by baking the biscuits dry after manufacture. He even offered to buy all rights to what was soon to become world-famous as Shredded Wheat. After almost concluding the deal, he finally broke off over a difference in price so small as to corrode his soul whenever he thought how close he had come to this well-patented gold mine. Perhaps he found a measure of solace when, back at the sanitarium, he tried some early Shredded Wheat on his patients. He received from one the observation that it was "about like eating a whisk broom."

But Kellogg's fiasco was Perky's triumph. He moved East and set about persuading the civilized world to eat Shredded Wheat. The first years were difficult: a tiny shop in Boston and another, in 1895, in Worcester, were his first "factories." He made largely unsuccessful efforts, via "tested menus" and traveling female demonstrators, to persuade people to buy what he still referred to as the "pudding proposition"—i.e., Shredded Wheat embedded in boiled vegetables and lubricated with gravy.

By 1900, however, there had accumulated enough experience and earnings to set the dys-peptic lawyer squarely on the road to success. He abandoned puddings for breakfast cereal. He built a show-place factory at Niagara Falls, described on every box as a "Palace of Food" and "Conservatory of Light." He systematically gave away samples by the hundreds of thousands —an excellent way of launching any strange new product. And, most important of all, he began to advertise heavily and skillfully.

Shredded Wheat advertising made great use of such potent concepts as naturalness, the excellence of wheat as a food (provided it wasn't debased by conversion to white flour), and (in the beginning at least) the perils of meat-eating. "Stomach Comfort in Every Shred" ran one early headline, with the copy beneath devoted to a pleasing little homily calculated to hook almost anyone who had lately had even a minor internal twinge. Perky also made shrewd use in his advertising of the appropriateness of Niagara Falls as a site for his Natural Food Company. Gradually the impression spread that the Falls not only powered the factory but also provided abundant supplies of cool, pure water which was somehow essential to the preparation of the product. Thanks to illustrations on the box, and frequent factory tours for visitors, Shredded Wheat soon became effectively associated both with one of America's foremost natural wonders and with the transports of a happy honeymoon. But during the great growing years of Shredded Wheat, Perky's ad-

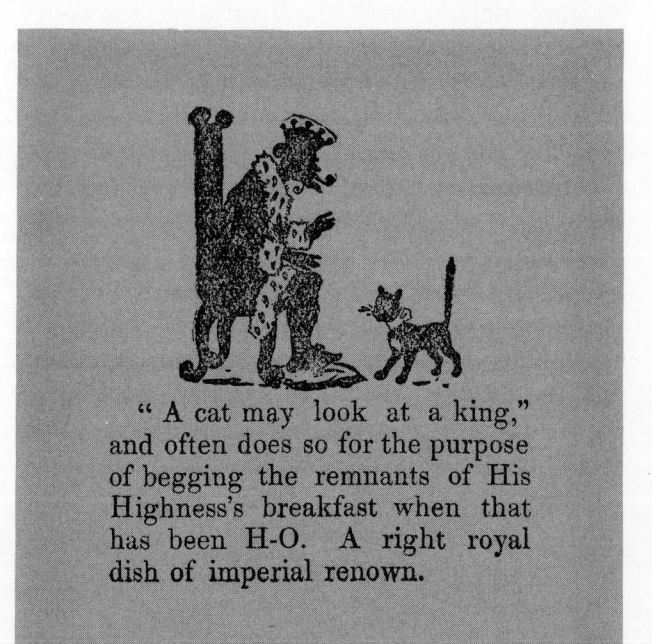

" A cat may look at a king," and often does so for the purpose of begging the remnants of His Highness's breakfast when that has been H-O. A right royal dish of imperial renown.

vertising concentrated most heavily on visceral themes. The ads usually aimed for that note of serene optimism that would comfort any man preoccupied with his gut: "These delicate shreds are retained and assimilated when the stomach rejects all other foods."

TRAILING for years in the shadow of Dr. John Kellogg was his dour younger brother, Will. He acted as business manager of the Battle Creek sanitarium and of the doctor's numerous other enterprises; he functioned as handyman-expediter in everything from investigating patients' credit to making (when necessary) funeral arrangements. He also collaborated in after-hours experiments in the kitchen, seeking new and nutritious ways to granulate and flake precooked grain. Anyone observing Will's glum demeanor and somewhat eclipsed personality in those days probably would never have predicted his golden future. For W. K. ("The Original Has This Signature") Kellogg was destined to become the corn-flakes king, and a man who personally supervised the expenditure of more than $100 million on advertising. He survived until 1951, the archetype of the crochety, wary, shy, and exceedingly human self-made multimillionaire. Illustrative of his personality was the occasion when, on a transcontinental trip, his Pullman flashed at dusk through a tiny Middle Western town. The train didn't stop, but W. K. managed to catch a glimpse of a Kellogg Company car parked on the street by the little hotel. He promptly wired the home office to check up on that salesman's expense account to be sure he didn't charge for a garage that night.

Relations between W. K. and his flamboyant elder brother, Dr. John, were always thorny. There were brief periods of guarded civility and long stretches of pungent acrimony, dotted with lawsuits. It was not until after 1906 that W. K. managed to cut free and found a cereal company of his own. At the helm, W. K. displayed a sure and unhesitant hand. Desultory mail-order sales to the sickly gave way to a concentration ·on retail sales to everyone, unhealthy or not. The moment

In two jiffies a flavory meal to satisfy the hungriest man —Kellogg's Crispy Corn Flakes.

1st It's a meal to make a hungry man beam with joy. With milk or cream, as satisfying as it is tasty.

2nd Good for every man who uses up a lot of body-fuel. Builds energy fast.

3rd It is ready to eat. No cooking. No waiting. Just pour in a bowl and serve.

Get the genuine Kellogg flavor by asking in full for Kellogg's Corn Flakes.

Kellogg's
CORN FLAKES

Oven-fresh always Inner-sealed waxtite wrapper keeps Kellogg's as fresh and crisp after opening as before—exclusive Kellogg feature.

A 1904 example of one of advertising's chronic problems: the idea
that sounds fine but comes out chaotic and dazed on paper.

he could afford it, W. K. lured away from Shredded Wheat an expert on retail food distribution, and in the very first months of his new company, before he had secured complete distribution for Corn Flakes, he blew $4,000 into a full-page ad in the *Ladies' Home Journal*. This single ad diminished the company's available cash reserves by about a third, but because it counseled housewives to badger their grocers into stocking Corn Flakes, it very successfully speeded up national distribution

W. K. rarely wrote advertising copy himself, though he felt himself an expert judge of it. He generally favored less lurid appeals than those used by his early competitors, and his techniques seem curiously modern for 1906. He showed a highly developed awareness of the value of repetition and continuity; he preferred mild claims repeated ceaselessly to showy but sporadic campaigns.

He even invented an early consumer-testing system for all advertising, promotion, and package designs: try them out first on Dayton, Ohio. Only if the Corn Flakes consumption of Dayton reflected a meaningful upward quiver would W. K. then splurge nationally with the new idea. He also had an obsession about the need for persistent sampling; crews of men were hired, trained, and turned loose on the land with orders to give away small trial boxes of Corn Flakes to every single housewife they could beat out of the bushes.

This once produced a minor panic in the town of Moberly, Missouri. The citizenry, suddenly discovering mysterious symbols chalked on front walks and gateposts, concluded—in a flash flood of rumor—that the town had been marked out for capture and rapine by a gang of criminals. Only after the rumors had produced considerable housewifely hysteria did it come out that the marks were left by a crew of Corn Flakes men to indicate which households had received their samples.

One of W. K.'s showiest triumphs took place in New York City, where he unfolded a brilliantly successful "teaser" campaign. For a week house-

Run

When You Hear 3 Rings

Hustle and open the door. For 3 rings means the man from Battle Creek—and he's got a big, FREE sample of Kellogg's delicious Toasted Corn Flakes for you.

It's "Kellogg's treat"—and it's too good to miss—so be ready to run when you hear the *3 rings*. It's a big sample—enough for breakfast—enough to let everybody taste the delicious and inimitable flavor that has made Kellogg's Toasted Corn Flakes the country's favorite food. *3 rings — remember!*

Look for This

W. K. Kellogg

67

wives there were exposed to a barrage of intriguing ads:

NEXT WEDNESDAY IS "WINK DAY" IN NEW YORK!
GIVE THE GROCER A WINK
AND SEE WHAT YOU GET!
—K-T-C

What they got—at the minimum—were free samples, since signature initials stood for Kellogg's Toasted Corn (Flakes). The wink campaign was an eye-opener in advertising circles: it received a lot of free publicity, and it shot Corn Flakes consumption in the city from less than two carloads a month to more than one carload a day.

Unlike Post and Perky, W. K. made little use of medical themes in his advertising (with the exception, of course, of bran cereals). Corn Flakes were endlessly described as fresh, pleasant, and nourishing in the extreme, but there was little effort to picture them as wonder drugs. This proved to be fairly farsighted; while the patent-medicine gambit was initially powerful, it became more and more ineffective as medical knowledge and public sophistication increased.

Millions of dollars were spent, however, in developing an "identity" of healthful deliciousness for Kellogg cereals, by using the endlessly repeated image of a eupeptic corn-fed maiden, surprised in the field while embracing a sheaf of the raw materials. The origin of this eidolon is disputed: one historian has it that she was originally a "type writer" employed in the Kellogg offices and pressed into service as a model. According to another and more circumstantial tale, a lithograph salesman turned up in 1907 with a drawing of a girl clutching a shock of wheat, made for a farm-implement company, but not satisfactory to them. W. K. was charmed by the picture, had corn substituted for wheat, and christened the girl "Sweetheart of the Corn." Company chroniclers do agree on one thing: it has been necessary to redraw and reengineer Sweetheart at least three times since 1907—for few things are more transient than the public concept of a toothsome maiden.

NOT all cereals were successes. The reports of the original gold strikes drew hordes of imitators to Battle Creek, most of whom failed dismally. There was a concoction of apple jelly and wheat flakes called Cero-Fruito; a grayish mixture of machined oats called Norka Oats; a celery-flavored substance called Tryabita. Breathing deeply, Bernarr Macfadden invented something he called Strengtho; it was a disastrous failure. There were other cereals named Orange Meat, Golden Manna, Hardy-food, and Vim. Harassed by gadfly competitors, Post himself put out an imitation of Postum christened Monk's Brew, cut the price on it steadily until his competitors collapsed or fled, and then took it off the market.

A few cereals, notably Apetizo and Egg-o-See, achieved moderate success. One, Malta-Vita, temporarily hit the jackpot. It earned several million dollars for its exhilarated backers—and then plunged into bankruptcy when its over-

The original, or 1907, model of the Sweetheart of the Corn. It has never been
clear what besides natural high spirits makes her wish to embrace the stalks.

SUNDAY Is Puffed Grain Day

Why So?

In a million homes Sunday seems to be the chief day for Puffed Wheat and Puffed Rice. So all of our evidence indicates.

Can you understand why that is so?

That is partly due to Sunday suppers—these bubble-like grains in milk. Then a great many people think of Puffed Grains as dainties, too good for every day.

That's a Great Mistake

Of course, Puffed Grains are dainties. They are light and airy, thin and flaky, with a fascinating taste. They are the food confections. But they are also more than that.

Puffed Wheat and Puffed Rice are whole-grain foods, with the grains puffed to eight times normal size.

They are scientific foods, invented by Prof. A. P. Anderson—a famous dietitian.

They are the only grain foods so prepared that every food cell is exploded. Digestion is made easy and complete, so that every atom feeds.

It's a great mistake to serve such foods infrequently. There are three kinds, so you get a variety. They make the ideal breakfast dish. Mixed with fruit, they form a delightful blend. In bowls of milk they are flavory, toasted bubbles, four times as porous as bread.

Salted or buttered, like peanuts or popcorn, they are perfect between-meal tidbits. In candy-making they are better than nut meats. They are flaky, toasted wafers for soups.

They are all-hour foods which never tax the stomach.

We seal the grains in huge guns; then roll them for an hour in 550 degrees of heat. That gives the nut-like flavor. All the inner moisture is changed to steam; then the guns are shot. A hundred million steam explosions occur in every kernel. Every food cell is exploded, so digestion can instantly act. That is why these Puffed Grains are such airy, flimsy bubbles. Keep all three kinds on hand.

Puffed Wheat   Puffed Rice
and Corn Puffs
Each 15c Except in Far West

The guns weren't shot off until the last paragraph of this 1918 Puffed Wheat and Puffed Rice ad, but the magic was at work. Note the Brisbane-like prose.

The Top Layer

The top layer in a barrel of apples is generally the best in the barrel. The "top layer" is always the best in everything—except in a

SHREDDED WHEAT BISCUIT

In 1907 Shredded Wheat was still recommending such delights as creamed oysters spooned over cereal, "a joy to those who love the savory bivalve."

worked factory began to deliver flakes that turned moldy in the box, a mischance that the public proved wholly unwilling to forgive.

Away from Battle Creek's Klondike atmosphere, a few breakfast foods managed to achieve independent success. The most notable, of course, was Shredded Wheat. Another was Force, a wheat flake made in Buffalo by a flashy entrepreneur named Edward Ellsworth, who lured his manufacturing staff from Battle Creek. His success, however, was largely due to some ingenious advertising jingles about a Force eater called Sunny Jim (see page 87). Other outside successes were two cold cereals marketed by the Quaker Oats Company, long the maker of a hot cereal that produced on its eaters, according to its ads, "The Smile That Won't Come Off." This pair, originally known as Puff Berries and Wheat Berries, did poorly at first. Their sales, in fact, were distinctly

peckish until diagnosed by A. D. Lasker and Claude Hopkins, then resident geniuses at the pioneering advertising agency of Lord & Thomas. Hopkins advised the company to discontinue ads that showed Orientals eating rice, on the theory that this art might encourage befuddled housewives to believe that eating Puff Berries could induce an Oriental cast of features. Further, he recommended, the cereals should be given a coupled set of names, such as Puffed Rice and Puffed Wheat. And they should be priced higher, in order to seem more valuable. Finally, heavy advertising campaigns should be built around the memorable image, "Shot from Guns," and its inventor, Professor A. P. Anderson. Once this advice was acted on, the peckish pair of cereals began to sell at so feverish a pace it became necessary to carry the money to the bank by truck.

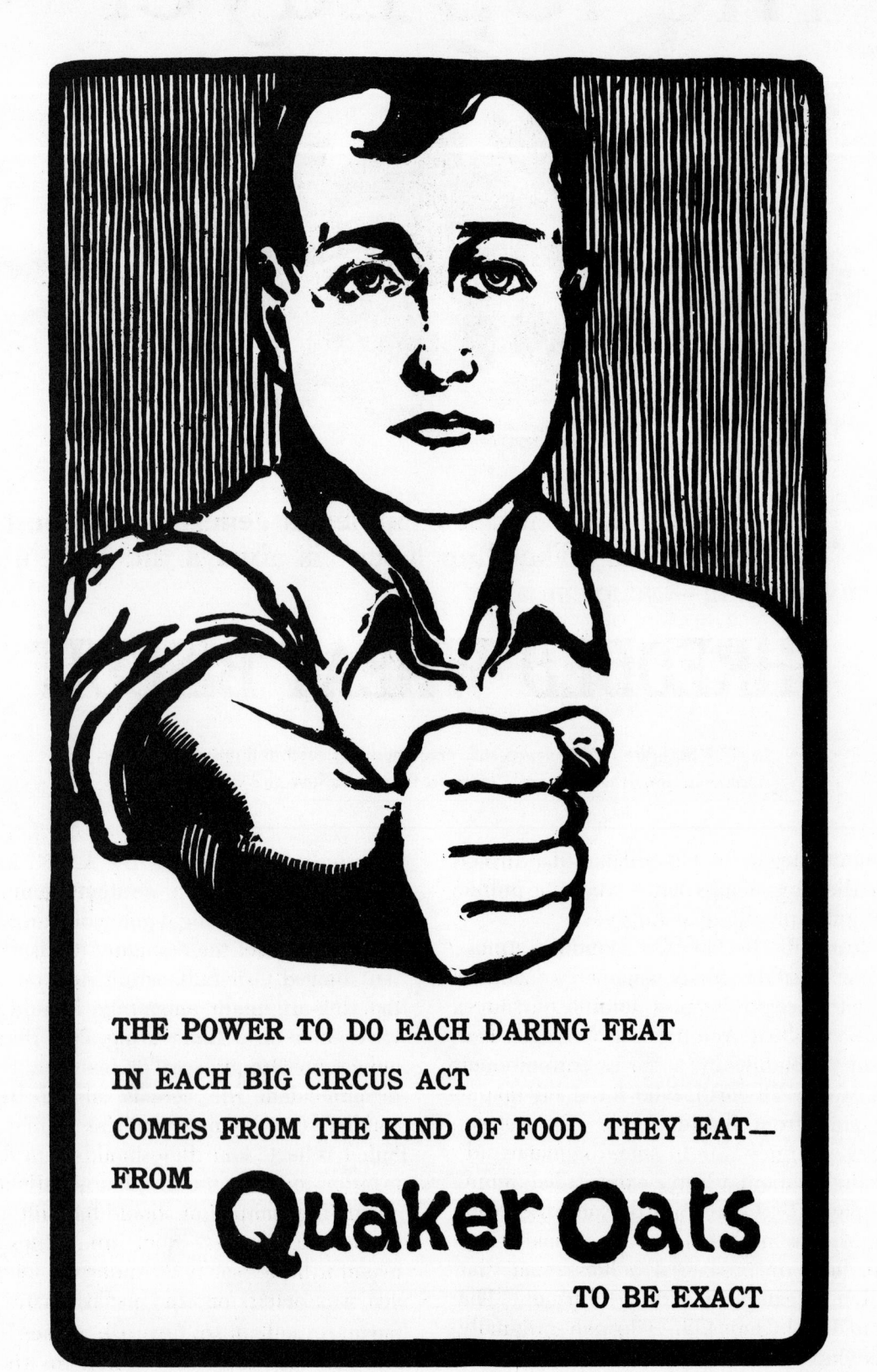

THE POWER TO DO EACH DARING FEAT
IN EACH BIG CIRCUS ACT
COMES FROM THE KIND OF FOOD THEY EAT—
FROM **Quaker Oats**
TO BE EXACT

Says Phoebe Snow
About to go
Upon a trip
To Buffalo:
"My gown stays white
Both day and night
Upon the Road of Anthracite."

And:

When nearly there
Her only care
Is but to smooth
Her auburn hair.
Her face is bright,
Her frock still white
Upon the Road of Anthracite.

Like the earlier sequences, this was spun out with patient ingenuity over scores of jingles. Phoebe grew to be a kind of early pin-up girl; the ads were illustrated by paintings of a good-looking model, her attractiveness not noticeably impaired by her compulsive cleanliness. There was also a rudimentary continuity to these jingles (again foreshadowing comic strips) in which Phoebe successively met each member of the train crew, discovering that "day or night/ They're all polite/ Upon the Road of Anthracite."

Nor was the railroad's scenery neglected:

The wondrous sight
Of mountain height
At Water Gap
Brings such delight,
She must alight
To walk a mite
Beside the Road of Anthracite.

In later jingle sequences a romance flowered between Phoebe and a hero, also dressed in white, that she met on the train. Ultimately they were married en route by a bishop (also white-clad) who happened to be going along to Buffalo too.

Like other successful jingles, Phoebe had an enormous currency. As Calkins himself wrote, forty years later, she "had her day and became a proverb, a symbol, a simile in her time, and had her tribute of burlesque, parody, cartooning, and allusion that was evidence of a world's familiarity, and is now gathered into the limbo of outmoded advertising techniques. . . . Advertising styles share with theatrical productions the fate of disappearing without a trace once their brief moment is over."

Phoebe's inventor may perhaps have been too quick to inter his creation, for her memory and influence go marching on. Along with Sunny Jim and the pleasing citizens of Spotless Town, she is the direct ancestor of the singing commercials of radio and television. Here tinkling rhythms are used for precisely the same purpose that applied sixty years ago: to act as mental cockleburs to hold in your head the all-important identity of The Product.

One jingle Calkins wrote never did see the light of commercial advertising, though it was almost certainly the most skillful verse to come from his pen. A privately written spoof of advertising's brand names, it aped Lewis Carroll:

JAPALACKY

'Twas crisco, and the talc jonteel
    Did mum and lysol in the lux;
All thermos were the sanitas,
    And the tiz keds canthrox.
"Beware the Japalac, my son!
    The jaws that bite, the claws that peel;
Beware the zuzu bird, and shun
    The tootsie hupmobile."
He took his luxite sword in hand;
    Long time the shuron foe he sought—
So rested he by the postum tree,
    And stood awhile in thought.
And, as in armco thought he stood
    The Japalac with eyes of flame,
Came neolin through the jaffee wood
    And kodaked as he came.
One, two! one, two! and through and through
    The luxite sword went pebeco;
He left it dead, and with its head
    He went odorono.
"And hast thou slain the Japalac?
    Come to my arms, my fabricoid!
O cedar-mop! cutex! calox!"
    Uneeda 'nameloid.
'Twas crisco, and the talc jonteel
    Did mum and lysol in the lux;
All thermos were the sanitas,
    And the tiz keds canthrox.

Chapter 7 | The Trademark

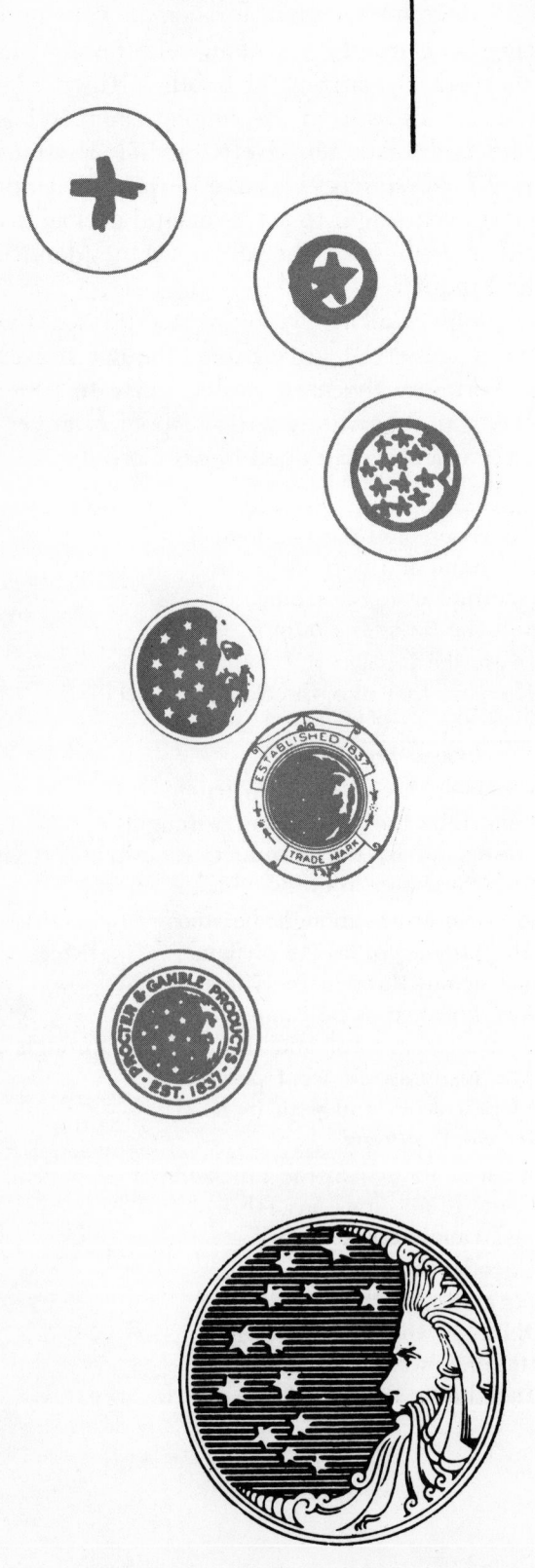

ADVERTISING has a crucial need to invest a product with special, pungent identity. For if The Product is one of several similar ones, and if its advertising fails to give it individual traits that penetrate to the supremely inattentive public mind, money spent plugging it will be almost wholly wasted. It can even be worse than wasted. The money may help to increase the sales of a *competitor's* product—about as corrosive an idea as a businessman's mind can entertain. Almost unimaginable labors have been devoted to furnishing everything from corn plasters to steamships with throbbingly individual personalities. It is only in this light that one really understands how a large and dignified corporation can come, for example, to christen one of its products "Oilzum."

This urgent desire for identity arises, in part, from the magic concept of brand, an idea as basic to the world we live in as, say, the internal combustion engine or the electron. The word "Brand" derives literally: a maker's name or symbol burned upon barrels, boxes, or wooden tool handles, like the ownership mark seared on a steer's hide. When tobacco, flour, and coffee came to the grocery store in bulk—and barrels of whisky and sugar were marked with Xs to aid unlettered clerks—makers' names didn't mean very much,

Menagerie

The great Art in writing advertisements is the finding out a proper Method to catch the Reader's eye; without which, a good Thing may pass unobserved. . . . Asterisks and Hands were formerly of great Use for this Purpose. Of late years the N.B. has been much in Fashion; as also little Cuts and Figures, the Invention of which we must ascribe to the Author of Spring Trusses. . . .

—Joseph Addison, in *The Tatler*, 1710

and advertising of them could accomplish little. But when commodities arrived in small sealed packages, endowed with identity in the form of well-advertised brands, the modern world arrived with a resounding crash and eerie electrical discharges. Consider a few of the implications: for the buyer, convenience, uniformity, and a new measure of protection from short weight or adulteration. For the storekeeper, reduced spoilage, potentially higher volume, and a higher markup. And for the manufacturer, intoxicating possibilities of staking out as his very own a huge—maybe even world-wide—slice of the market.

One early example was Log Cabin Syrup. In 1887 a Minnesota grocer, J. P. Towle, conceived the notion that it might be profitable to sell syrup in small, cheap tin cans—rather than filling from a common barrel the miscellaneous containers that his customers sometimes remembered to bring along. An enthusiastic admirer of Abraham Lincoln, Towle arranged for a trial supply of tin cans shaped like miniature log cabins, in honor of his hero's early years. He soon discovered that most customers would pay a trifle extra for syrup packaged this way, quite as much for novelty as for convenience.

The same conclusion was reached about a decade later with crackers. For generations crackers had arrived from the baker in barrels. The system was so familiar that a whole set of folkways had grown up around it: the open barrel placed not far from the stove (to keep the crackers from getting soggy in damp weather); the tendency for broken, dirty, or even weevily crackers to accumulate at the top, thanks to the picking-out process; the tradition of serving as a kind of miniature public utility, like the tin cup and roller towel by a pump; the cosy retreat for the cat.

Then, in 1899, amid brassy fanfares of advertising (blown by N. W. Ayer for the National Biscuit Company), the packaged soda cracker arrived. This was no casual appearance of a new product but the climactic raising of the curtain upon an elaborately planned venture. The cracker had its own box with an airtight inner liner; it had the name Uneeda to act as a fishhook to memory; and it had its trademarked symbol, a sprightly tad in oilskins, to denote imperviousness to wet weather. (The tad, by the way, is identifiable: he was Gordon Stiles, the nephew of an agency man, who was snatched from play, togged out in a bright yellow slicker, and hurriedly photographed as a guide for the artist.)

91

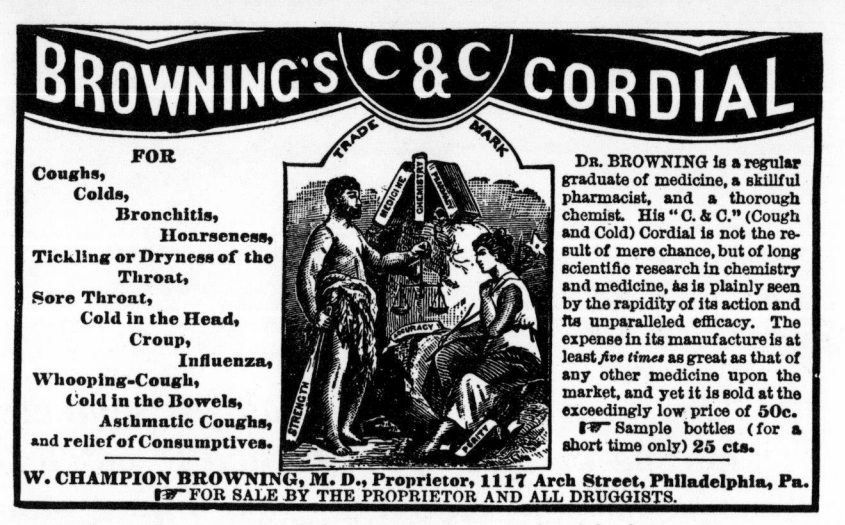

In the early days when a man sat down to invent a trademark, there was a pronounced tendency to come up with lots of symbolic figures and labels all over the scenery.

The new packaged soda cracker appealed strongly to housewives. It was hygienic and somehow virtuous—in contrast to those dirty old things that were pawed over by *ignorant loafers* that sat around the store *spitting*. Within months it became apparent that the Uneeda campaign was a brilliant triumph. N. W. Ayer & Son, flushed with pride over its share in the planning, became the first agency to start calling its customers "clients."

Identity was the key to successful brand advertising. The extent to which this was realized is reflected in the growth of trademarks registered in the United States Patent Office: 121 in 1871, more than 10,000 by 1906, some 650,000 today. (The first one registered, for the Averill Chemical Paint Company, was a seething mass of symbols: a defiant eagle standing on a rock labeled Chemistry, holding in its mouth a paintpot, a brush, and a banner inscribed with the words Economical, Durable, Beautiful, in front of a landscape containing a river, viaduct, steamboat, railroad train, "manufactories," and miscellaneous other things.)

Trademarks had a standing in common law long before the government began to register them. In the Middle Ages they were private symbols used by guilds to identify the group of craftsmen that had made a particular object. But under the pressure of advertising's critical need for identity, trademarks grew into a whole new pantheon of domestic deities. There were downy chicks, cuddlesome kittens, and nobly fierce lions and tigers. There were chubby cherubim, delectable angels, and fairies complete with wings, filmy nightgowns, and star-tipped wands. There were occult symbols that ranged from writhing monograms to monads, swastikas, triangles, keystones, and unbroken chains; bundles of grain, rocks, columns, and oak and pine trees; gartered legs, clasping hands, hammer-brandishing arms, and enucleated but all-seeing eyes that floated in space. People, too, were part of this new collection of folk symbols: plump and big-headed infants, winsome little girls, energetic housemaids, fatherly Quakers and Pilgrims, noble red men, several extremely Gallic chefs, bearded men and others surprised while shaving, and, in vast numbers, toothsome maidens.

THE ORIGINS of these distinguishing symbols are highly varied. Some of the animals actually lived. The prototype of the Camel cigarette camel was apparently an elderly dromedary named Old Joe, serving with the Barnum & Bailey circus when it put in at Winston-Salem in 1913. He caught the eye of an R. J. Reynolds employee who knew that the firm was preparing to launch a new cigarette tentatively named "Camel." There were difficulties, though, in taking photographs for the use of an artist. The circus management wasn't cooperative in parading Old Joe for his picture until representations were made to the head keeper that the company had, after all, let its people out that afternoon to go to the circus. Then Old Joe himself began to act up, perhaps made skittish by strangers thrashing about with black cloth and tripod off his port bow. He

The New Salesman Rebuked.

"Excuse him, Madam. He has not yet learned that our best class of customers all mean **PETER'S** when they ask for Eating Chocolates. They know from long experience that it deserves its great reputation for Purity, Wholesomeness, and Digestibility."

Lamont, Corliss & Co., Sole Agents, New York.

It took some pretty stern and strenuous selling to establish brand names among products which were previously sold anonymously in bulk.

kept turning and advancing strongly on the photographer. Finally his impatient keeper gave an extra-hard tug on the bridle and the dignified dromedary, deeply vexed, assumed that offish, hoisted-tail stance that has since been reproduced billions of times.

Old Joe's debut as a cigarette, incidentally, was in a historic four-stage teaser campaign. It ran in newspapers, and the first ad was simply a drawing of Old Joe, not on a package, with the single word "Camels." The second stage carried the line: "The Camels are coming"; the third conveyed the alarming intelligence that "Tomorrow there'll be more Camels in this town than in all Asia and Africa combined." The fourth ad in the series showed the package and bore the line: "Camel cigarettes are here." Unaware of all these shenanigans, Old Joe continued on in his morose and dignified career until, some years later in

Bridgeport, Connecticut, he was killed in a railroad wreck.

Another immortalized animal, the Victor talking-machine dog, also had a real-life existence. So many varying and conflicting details have gathered about him, however, that scholars suspect that he is being rapidly encrusted in folklore, a kind of accidentally cultured pearl. As far as can now be determined, he was an obese fox terrier responding to the name of Nipper. His original owner died in the nineties and a brother, a London artist named Francis Barraud, took Nipper in. One day he saw Nipper peering with cocked-head curiosity into the morning-glory trumpet of an early gramophone. Barraud promptly envisioned a sentimental, narrative painting of the sort then highly popular. It would be titled "His Master's Voice" and it would show an ever-faithful dog in the foreground by the gramophone—

Real people were the original models for some trademarks, including the demure Baker waitress, the beamish Cream of Wheat chef, and ever-loving old Aunt Jemima.

and his deceased master stretched out in an open coffin behind. At Barraud's request, the Gramophone Company lent him a shiny new brass instrument for the picture. On studying the completed work, the company was so pleased that it bought the painting and tactfully persuaded Barraud to paint out the mortuary details in the background.

In 1901 rights to United States use of Nipper were acquired by the Victor Talking Machine Company, and the picture made a much-discussed debut in a center-spread ad in *The Saturday Evening Post* for April 25, 1903. Soon Nipper grew to be one of the world's best-known trademarks. The managing director of the Gramophone Company gave strict orders to the company firemen that the *first* thing they were to do in case of fire would be to carry out the original painting from its place of honor on the wall of the directors' board room. In his later years Barraud was pensioned by the British firm as additional recompense for his services. But today Nipper's image (presently the property of RCA) faces a flawed future: whole generations are growing up who don't know what the strange machine is that the dog is inspecting so intently.

The trademark menagerie is a crowded one. It includes the Bull Durham bull, rampant since 1871; and the Cortecelli kittens, all tangled in silk for more than sixty years. (Chesapeake & Ohio's Chessie is a kitty-come-lately; this relative newcomer first appeared in 1933.) There are many others: Greyhound's greyhound; Knopf's borzoi; Bull Dog Suspenders' bull dog; Hartford's elk; and of course Borden's Elsie the Cow—derived in part from a real cow of great charm and high butterfat output named, impractically, "You'll Do Lobelia."

As might be predicted, a tendency toward coy whimsy has occasionally marred the use of animal emblems. One instance was the carefully nurtured uncertainty over whether the object protruding from Chessie's coverlet was a paw or a tail. Another example has been the recurrent appearance in Elsie the Cow advertisements of a pin-up on the wall of her boudoir; it shows the

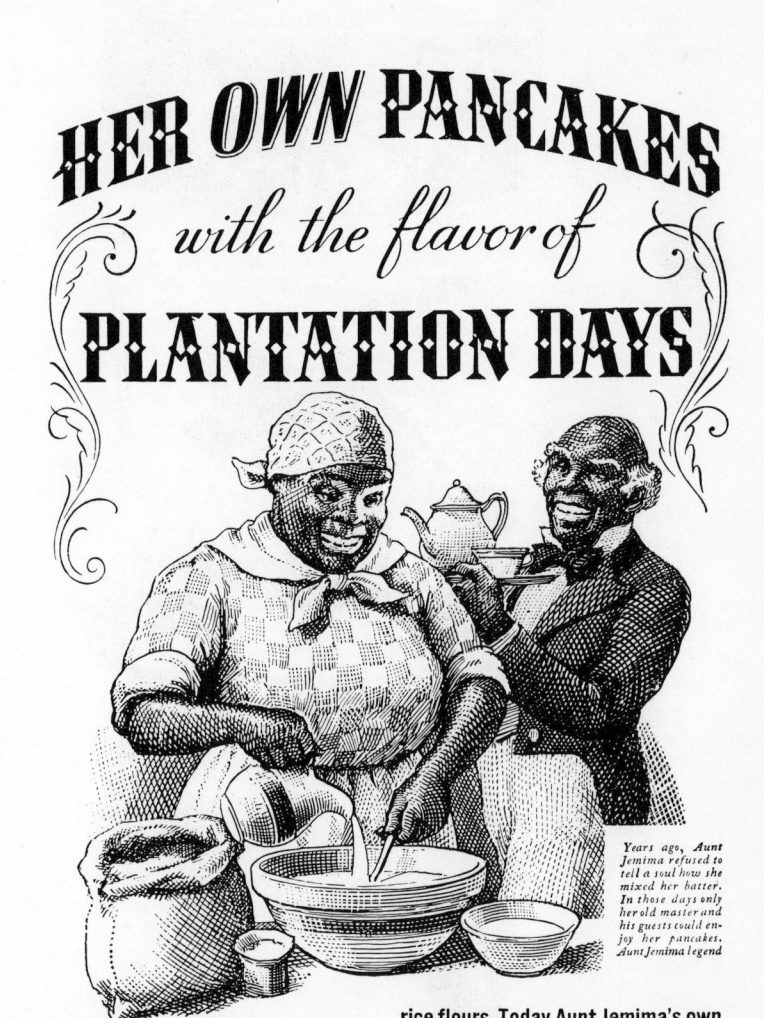

Years ago, *Aunt Jemima refused to tell a soul how she mixed her batter. In those days only her old master and his guests could enjoy her pancakes.* Aunt Jemima legend

SUCH light and tender pancakes! The real old-fashioned kind—with a matchless plantation flavor. For years Aunt Jemima's Pancakes were famous all over the South. The recipe was that old cook's secret...a knack of combining wheat, corn, rye and rice flours. Today Aunt Jemima's own ingredients come to you ready-mixed. Just add milk or water to Aunt Jemima Pancake Flour, bake and serve. It's that easy to have Aunt Jemima's real plantation pancakes—pancakes with the same wonderful taste as those she made herself. The Quaker Oats Company, Chicago.

quick-easy!

AUNT JEMIMA PANCAKE FLOUR

Aunt Jemima Pancake Flour in the red package; Aunt Jemima for Buckwheats in the yellow

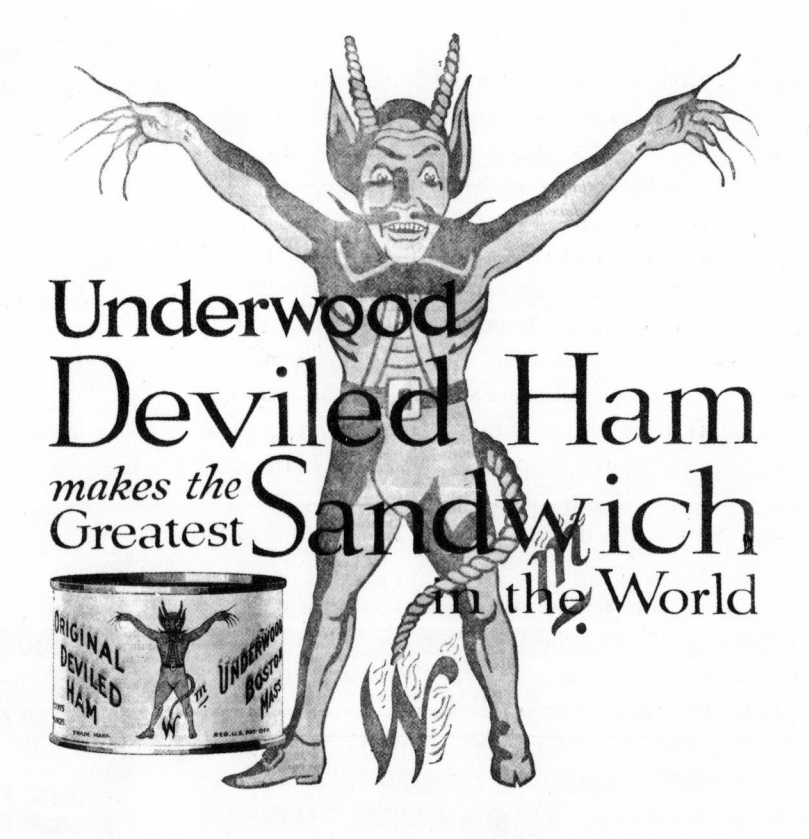

Familiar after years of heavy advertising, symbols like these came to have an almost independent existence. Then if one changed, as Old Dutch did, a part of the past was lost.

Bull Durham bull and is labeled "Her Hero."

One of the most widely known animal trademarks is M-G-M's Leo the Lion. It was devised about 1916 by Howard Dietz, and was reportedly chosen because Dietz had attended Columbia University, where lions are a local fetish.

Leo was not only real but repeatedly so. Every time one of the M-G-M executives happened on a new, freshly imported, and decorative lion, he tended to give orders to have him photographed and substituted for the older and inevitably mangier model. Pretty soon "official" Leos began to pile up. To end the confusion M-G-M decided to put out the warming tale that as a reward for his valued services to M-G-M, the "real" Leo was to be taken back to Africa and set free in the jungle. To the studio's dismay, this stirred up a storm of protest from animal lovers who contended that a lion reared in captivity would have a dreadful time in the harshly competitive jungle. Poor lovable old Leo, all soft from Hollywood, would either starve or be killed by his tougher cousins.

Press agents hastily revised the story to say that the "real" Leo would not be sent to Africa after all; he would be pensioned off to live out his days in a spacious and comfortable zoo. Actually, nobody at M-G-M was quite certain which lion of the number that had come and gone was the one all the fuss was about.

Some of the human characters used as trademarks were real too. Ever since 1825 Walter Baker & Company has identified its cocoa and chocolate with a painting of a capped and tray-bearing waitress apparently gliding to the right on invisible wheels. The story goes that she was actually Anna Baltauf, the buxom daughter of an impoverished knight, who in the early 1740s was compelled by harsh circumstance to work as a waitress in a Viennese chocolate café. One day, in the best fairy-tale tradition, a young Austrian nobleman, Prince Ditrichstein, spotted Anna as she came bearing cocoa. He was deeply smitten and kept coming back for more cocoa. In the course of time, awash with cocoa, the Prince married the girl, possibly so he wouldn't have to

drink more. But at any rate, he commissioned a Swiss artist, Jean Etienne Liotard, to paint Anna in the setting and costume she wore when first he saw her. Skeptics about this sweet-chocolate tale are referred to the Dresden Museum, where for more than two centuries Liotard's *"La Belle Chocolatière"* has hung in the royal collection.

Several other probably actual people—including the Cream of Wheat chef and Aunt Jemima—have been translated into the official hagiography of trademarks. It is necessary to say "probably" because both the fragrance of folklore and an occasional whiff of press-agentry float past the scholars who search for truth in this area. Few company advertising departments like to admit that they don't know how some treasured symbol came to be used, or that it was originally the invention of Chester Snodgrass in Shipping who happened to catch the old man in a receptive mood.

The Cream of Wheat chef is supposed to have been a man who, one day in 1896, caught the eye of Col. Emory Mapes, the head of the company. A smiling Negro restaurant chef, he made such a strong and pleasing impression on the Colonel that a photographer was immediately summoned to capture him for the artist. Aunt Jemima is equally shadowy. The legend runs that she was a cook who worked for Colonel Higbee, of the Mississippi Higbees, and who greatly enhanced the Colonel's reputation for hospitality with her celebrated hot cakes, made from a secret recipe. In 1886 she is supposed to have sold her formula to the R. T. Davis Mill Company, a firm that gratefully included her among its exhibits at the 1893 World's Fair. Though not registered as a trademark until 1903, Aunt Jay has beamed from advertisements ever since 1889.

Unquestionably real were the models for well-known trademarks built with frank pride on the hairy faces of company proprietors. There was the handle-barred W. L. Douglas, whose piercing gaze and unmistakable probity testified to the merit of his $3 Shoe for Gentlemen. And there was the luxuriantly mustached John H. Woodbury, for whose Facial Soap for the Skin, Scalp, and Complexion the claim was once made: "If beauty is only skin deep, we can make you beautiful." (This early appeal to the contrary, Woodbury's Facial Soap continued for decades to be presented as a dermatological aid, a way of beating back blackheads and eczema. It was not until the twenties that its agency, the J. Walter Thompson Company, came out with the tactile, not to say sexual, appeal: "The Skin You Love to Touch.")

Perhaps most famous of all are the perennial Smith Brothers, Trade and Mark, decorating each box of cough drops—which previously were sold out of glass jars on store counters and called James Smith & Son's Compound of Wild Cherry Cough Candy.

However, most trademarks (the term, by the way, has often been used loosely to describe, not a specifically registered design, but simply a characteristic feature of advertising) make no pretense at reality. They are simply invented symbols or characters. Such a one is the compulsive housekeeper who for decades brandished a stick in

Now obtainable everywhere at popular prices

Nipper the Curious Dog is probably the world's most cherished trademark. One reason, aside from the high esteem commonly given to man's best friend, is that any narrative picture is usually dear to the human heart.

behalf of Old Dutch Cleanser. She was originally a goosegirl in a painting at the home of a Cudahy Packing Company official. When the company was preparing to launch its cleaner, he took the painting to the office and pointed out that her briskly hostile posture (originally assumed to drive geese out of the garden) was ideally suited to the slogan "Chases Dirt." Advertising artists concealed her face in a large bonnet, matroned her figure, and produced a trademark that was soon known to millions. She quickly became familiar enough to supply Theodore Roosevelt's opponents with a weapon of derision when he enunciated his foreign policy of speaking softly and carrying a big stick. Only recently did the company discard the angry creature, replacing her with a stylized, vanilla-flavored blonde of the sort rarely encountered outside the imagination of advertising art directors.

Trademarks without known prototypes include the Campbell Soup twins, a brace of cherubim first drawn in 1904 by Grayce Gebbie Drayton. For more than five decades they have gamboled like Peter Pan in the sunlight of perpetual childhood, symbolizing the charms of healthy prepubescence and the nourishing qualities of soup. Another tyke prevented from enjoying normal growth is the Fisk Tire boy, the lad who although he is tottering so sleepily off to his wee trundle bed that with one hand he drips candle wax on the floor, is nonetheless capable of hefting an auto tire onto his shoulder with the other. Sleepyhead was, in a sense, born by accident. In 1907 Burr E. Griffin, a commercial artist who was trying to develop an advertisement for Fisk, was working fruitlessly until late at night on ideas that didn't pan out. He gave up, told himself that it was time to retire—and snapped his fingers as a happy revelation came upon him. The company was delighted with his "Time to Re-Tire" slogan and sketch, and has used it ever since, though with occasional tinkering. In 1928 Sleepyhead's yawn was replaced with a smile, and, in 1930, with a grin. Both the tire and the lad's nightclothes were modernized. Shortly thereafter the company lurched into receiver-

R. J. Reynolds Tobacco Co.

A wily circus dromedary, known to his Barnum & Bailey associates as Old Joe, was the original Camel cigarette model. His stagy stance was deftly captured by the artist.

99

Stop and listen, your eyes will glisten—
    This signal is meant for you.
There's joy and health, the best of wealth,
    In Campbell's Thirty-Two!

Conscious cuteness, a trait now somewhat out of style, was successful for years in selling Campbell's Soup, among other things. The ad below had this message: "I am Doctor Wisengood/ And here's my best advice./ You'll find this simple wholesome food/ Worth many times the price."

ship. Though no one claimed there was a causal relationship, when Fisk resumed operation, as a division of the U.S. Rubber Company, the lad was back yawning again.

A liberally advertised and memorable trademark can grow to be highly valuable; it becomes, in the eyes of accountants, the embodiment of a company's good will. It often has, in addition, a strangely impish capacity for making trouble. This was demonstrated once when rights to use Buster Brown, an early comic-strip character drawn by R. F. Outcault, were purchased by the Brown Shoe Company. Shortly after the first ads showing pumpkin-headed Buster began to appear, the company discovered to its distaste that it had inadvertently renamed itself. Nothing thereafter could prevent the massively imprecise public from calling it the "Buster Brown Shoe Company." A more serious mishap occurred when the Sherwin-Williams Paint Company, straining for a graphic image appropriate to paint, began using a trademark that included a chameleon. This sophisticated allusion didn't seem to help business a bit. Before long came the explanation: too many people thought that the chameleon was a snake. Once the repulsive creature was replaced with the messy but nonreptilian "Covers the Earth" symbol, sales took a turn for the better.

Trademarks have been found in diverse and sometimes *outré* places. When preparing to register its trademark abroad in 1922, Munsingwear decided that it could do with an extra touch of swank. It sent researchers into the library to rummage about in heraldry. They emerged beaming with a drawing of a shield, embellished with "cupped and fretted chevrons," and reported that a device such as this was borne in battle by a metal-clad valiant in the First Crusade—but they never explained quite why this was appropriate for an underwear manufacturer. Planters' Peanuts, on the other hand, had no truck with heraldry when it was on the hunt for a trademark. It simply held a trademark contest in 1916, open to the schoolchildren of Suffolk, Virginia, for a prize of five dollars. The winner was the familiar top-hatted peanut, though the

TIME TO RE-TIRE
"GET A FISK"

An illustrated pun, Old Sleepyhead at the left has been agape for more than fifty years. Changed tire design has necessitated frequent tinkering with the drawing. The Gold Dust pickaninnies appeared over the pleasing if doubtful advice to: "Let the Gold Dust Twins Do Your Work."

company did employ a commercial artist to add such touches as the monocle and the crooked-leg stance.

Many advertisers have attempted to harness the potentialities of pretty girls in their trademarks, generally with mediocre results. For a variety of technical reasons, pretty girls have proved to be slippery creatures that don't harness easily. One difficulty is in style of clothes, which may have to be modified every year or two to keep the poor creature from turning into a frump. An even greater difficulty arises from the inconstancy of public tastes in the ideal female.

The ideal woman is continuously fighting and losing the battle of obsolescence. Every few years she needs to be rebuilt, not only with new hair arrangements, but also with a new figure and carriage, a new expression, new mouth and eyebrows, and, preferably, a reshaped skull. W. K. Kellogg, as already noted, had to have his Sweetheart of the Corn sent back to the shop for overhaul a number of times, and as a plain country lass, she has undoubtedly been better shielded against obsolescence than a smart city girl would be.

The perils of pretty-girl trademarks were graphically shown by a dentrifice, Sozodont, which was the first big advertiser to try to establish a female-character trademark. The Sozodont Girl appeared in the eighties as a woodcut and in the nineties as a halftone—a close-up portrait, pronouncedly dental, of what started out as a handsome woman and ended up, years later, as something with which to threaten unruly children.

Numerous attempts have been made over the years to circumvent this tendency toward rapid aging by female trademarks. One ingenious approach has been to pin hopes on the durability of historic or fictional characters: Diana or Pallas Athena, Pocahontas or a Pilgrim lass, a classical shepherdess or milkmaid, a busty and bunting-draped Columbia. This device does have the effect of preserving her against changes in clothes styles; in the case of some, like the Venus Pencil Venus, there are practically no clothes to fret about anyhow.

Unquestionably the most perfectly embalmed of all the trademark maidens is Psyche, the White Rock Girl. She has survived more than six decades

101

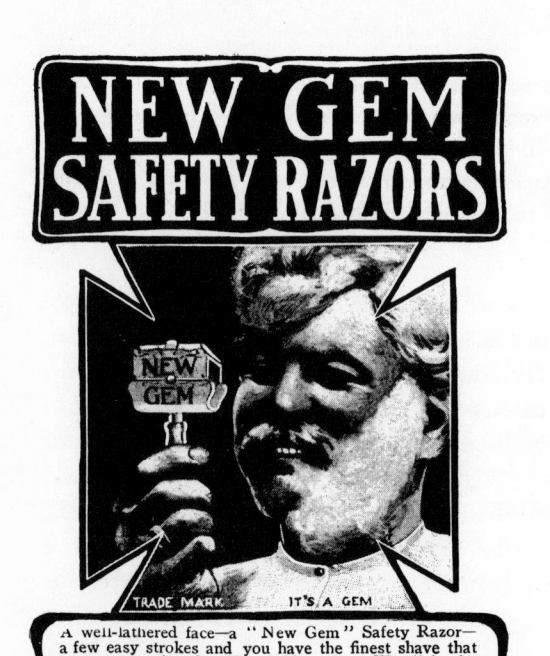

SMITH BROTHERS

TRADE   MARK

with only one major and a few minor overhauls.

In the nineties the owners of the White Rock Mineral Springs Company were an enterprising crew; they bottled something called Ozonate Lithia Water that issued from the ground near Waukesha, Wisconsin, and was then described as suitable for home water cures and general medicinal purposes. At the 1893 World's Fair in Chicago the proprietors discovered a painting by Paul Thurmann, a German artist, that delighted them. It was titled "Psyche at Nature's Mirror" and showed a solid Teuton maiden, minimally garbed and just sprouting the wings that denoted her transition from girl to goddess. She was kneeling on a stone and peering at her reflection in a pool, presumably to see what deification was doing for her.

The White Rock people immediately bought rights to use the painting in advertising. First they inscribed "White Rock" on the stone on which Psyche knelt. Then they set about energetic promotion of their find, starting off with a white wedding-cake pavilion at the Fair, built around a hastily manufactured statue. (The company was one that rarely missed any tricks at promotion. A few years later it vigorously spread the word that its bottles had been glimpsed on the banquet table at the coronation of Edward VII, and who had more celebratedly royal tastes in drink than that monarch?)

For thirty-one years Psyche survived almost untouched, save for a darkening of the sunny

102

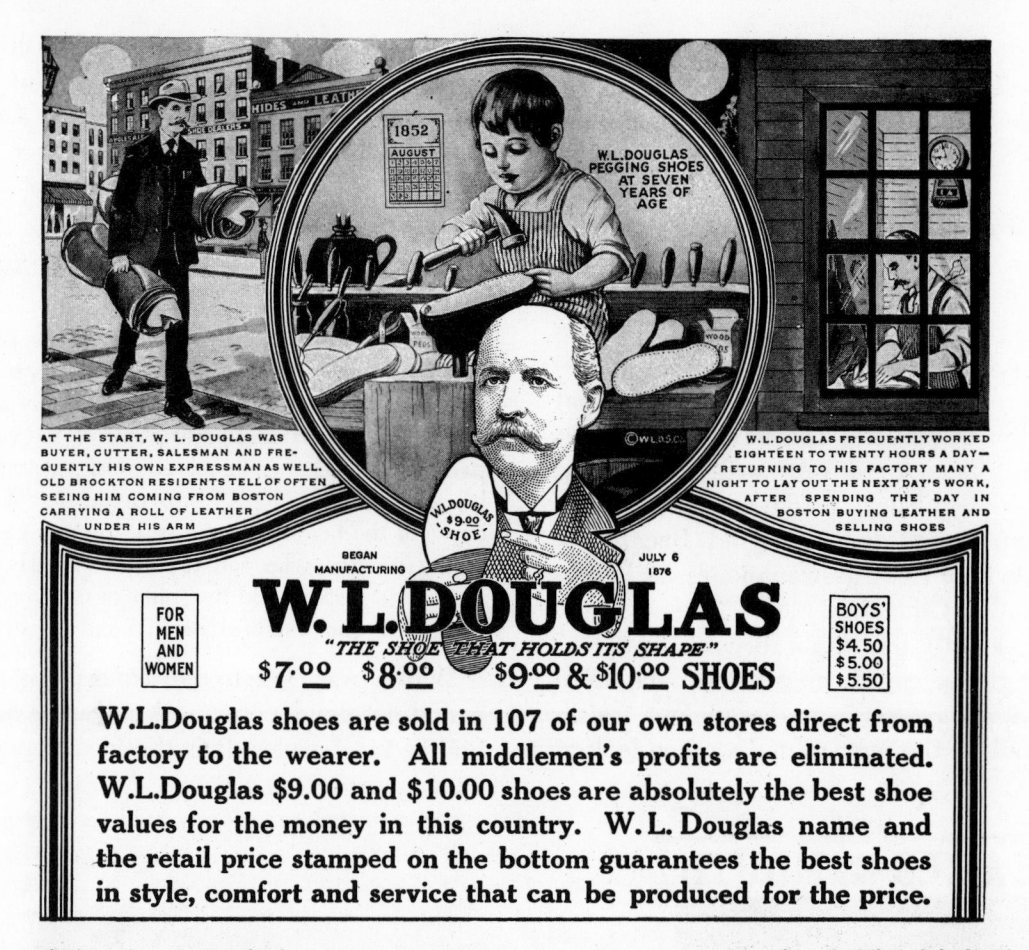

At the start, W. L. Douglas was buyer, cutter, salesman and frequently his own expressman as well. Old Brockton residents tell of often seeing him coming from Boston carrying a roll of leather under his arm

W.L. Douglas pegging shoes at seven years of age

W. L. Douglas frequently worked eighteen to twenty hours a day—returning to his factory many a night to lay out the next day's work, after spending the day in Boston buying leather and selling shoes

1852 AUGUST

BEGAN MANUFACTURING

JULY 6 1876

FOR MEN AND WOMEN

W. L. DOUGLAS
"THE SHOE THAT HOLDS ITS SHAPE"
$7.⁰⁰ $8.⁰⁰ $9.⁰⁰ & $10.⁰⁰ SHOES

BOYS' SHOES $4.50 $5.00 $5.50

W.L. Douglas shoes are sold in 107 of our own stores direct from factory to the wearer. All middlemen's profits are eliminated. W.L.Douglas $9.00 and $10.00 shoes are absolutely the best shoe values for the money in this country. W. L. Douglas name and the retail price stamped on the bottom guarantees the best shoes in style, comfort and service that can be produced for the price.

Whiskered or mustached company proprietors turn up in many an early ad. (The delighted shaver at left wasn't Mr. Gem.) W. L. Douglas, whose early trials are graphically described in the ad above, ended making 17,000 pairs of shoes daily. He was also Governor of Massachusetts.

glade in the background. The fact that her only garment was a filmy skirt undoubtedly helped a good deal. The only persistent difficulty the company ran into was the pronunciation of her name. It was often rendered as "Pishie." Company sales manuals kept pointing out that she was called SIGH-key, but admitted that she could be referred to, in a pinch, as "The White Rock Girl." By 1924, it was felt that some modification could not be postponed any longer. Her hair, caught up in a Psyche Knot—a coil in the style of the nineties—was thought to be giving her an unfortunately maternal look. Accordingly it was replaced with a chic marcel, reminiscent of Mary Pickford in her middle period.

Two more decades then passed with only trivial tinkering. Finally, in 1944, under the impetus of a new company management, Psyche was wholly rebuilt. One objective was to modernize her figure, an embodiment of 1893 Teutonic ideals, but rather chunky by later standards. It was also necessary to do something about her hair, the marcel having proved a ghastly mistake. Other objectives (not stated by the company) may have been to do something about her knees-apart posture, more pantherlike than ladylike. After long labors, the revised model of the goddess was unveiled, essentially the same Psyche around today. Compared to Thurmann's maiden, she is proportioned to be three inches taller, twenty-eight pounds lighter, and measures 35-25-35 instead of 37-27-38. She also has her knees demurely together, an updated hairdo, and a fine new coat of whitewash on the rock.

Many advertisers have preferred to avoid the risk of impairing anything so valuable as a trademark with a perishably pretty girl. But to capitalize on the excellent attention-getting value of a pretty girl who *hasn't* perished, they often use her as an advertising "character"—a distinctive person or type used in illustration, but not frozen in a trademark. This have-it-both-ways approach has been tried very widely in recent years (notably by Lucky Strike and other cigarette companies, and by Rheingold Beer), but here as elsewhere the way was pioneered by the Eastman Kodak Company.

As early as 1901 the public became aware of the Kodak girl, a conspicuously nice and even sisterly type. In response to the ancient truism that men look at the woman and women look at the dress, she was also presented with great attention to style and taste—just a *little* ahead of thoroughly established fashion. The Kodak girl, like many an advertising model since, actually influenced dress styles, popularizing a striped skirt in particular.

In 1902, the editor of *Cosmopolitan*, John Brisben Walker, observed:

> What is the psychology of using a pretty face [in advertising]? The humblest that travels and reads will tell you that he is mysteriously inclined to regard the mechanical adjustment of the covered apparatus which hangs at the charming young woman's hip as being of a highly superior order of merit because of the beauty of face and raiment. Certainly no young woman who can dress so cleverly and with such good taste would be guilty of carrying a camera not of the most skillful mechanical construction.

Walker was close to a discovery of a truth that would not dawn upon most magazine advertisers for several decades. It is the idea that you don't

The problem of preserving a pretty girl is almost insoluble. Sozodont tried and failed; Eastman Kodak avoided the issue; and Psyche has required two major overhauls to date.

1893   1924

necessarily *have* to sell The Product itself in an ad; instead, you can create an aura of prestige and glamour around it that will sell The Product for you. In the years since the Kodak girl smiled wholesomely at magazine readers, such advertising by association has grown into a powerful giant. Now whole campaigns are devoted not merely to establishing the individual identity of The Product, but to making that identity overwhelmingly attractive through carefully selected associations. The tattooed men who tout filter-tip cigarettes as a he-man's smoke, the resolutely convivial family groups who argue the innocence of beer, the weary but never vague adventurers who toil into the wilderness burdened by cases of whisky—these make the Kodak girl, and the simpler world of brands and trademarks from which she came, seem old-fashioned indeed by · comparison.

105

1944

Chapter 8 | My Luve Is Like a

I THINK SHE CAME FROM A LAND OF FIRE
On a summer day undreamed of by the fabled sea
a wonderful girl and a wonderful man and a Playbo
making three but not a crowd—lilting airs from
the cool sea floor—the scent of sea-blown blossoms
from the land.

Just loiter and let the world go by. You will kno
the meaning of sunset—you will talk the langua
of the stars. That is joy.

—magazine ad of the twent

What do you imagine this collection of words was
supposed to sell? A sea? Or a beach? Or the stars?
None of these—this farrago of sounds was intend
to make you dash out and demand a certain make
automobile.

—Helen Woodward, *Through Many Windo*

FEW INVENTIONS have had so many fathers as the automobile. In the nineties fully a dozen Americans—including Duryea, Apperson, Haynes, Maxwell, King, Maxim, Ford, Olds, and Winton—were under the impression, as they straightened up and wiped their hands on a piece of waste, that they had just built the first practical automobile. But similar vehicles had already been built by mechanically minded Frenchmen and Germans. It also turned out that an American, George B. Selden, had applied in 1879 for a patent on what was, at least on paper, a plausible gasoline-driven vehicle. Most historians award

106

Red, Red Convertible

honors to Daimler and Benz in Europe in the late eighties, and, in this country, to Charles and Frank Duryea, in 1892. Certainly by the latter date a number of men had managed to create man-carrying vehicles that, with luck, could wobble along in a fusillade of explosions for a few miles before something shattered.

Though slow a-borning, the automobile quickly grew to be a respectable piece of machinery. By the turn of the century, it had become a fairly capable mechanism, and would have been able to prove it if there had been adequate tires and suitable roads to run on. Much of the auto's early get-a-horse reputation arose from inconceivably bad roads and tires that went flat with dismaying frequency. Nevertheless, Alexander Winton was able to startle the country in 1899 by driving from Cleveland to New York in less than two days, and in that same year the Stanley brothers navigated a steam car to the top of Mount Washington in New Hampshire. By 1900 some 8,000 motor vehicles were loose in the land. Many of these were imported, of course, but dozens of United States manufacturers also invaded the field. (Bicycle makers, blacksmiths, machine-shop proprietors, and wagon manufacturers were particularly attracted by this marvelous piece of machinery.) These domestic builders turned out 4,192 American-born cars in 1900. The number included 20 or 25 shipped by a Detroit firm that, before it slid into bankruptcy, was guided by an ambitious and stubborn engineer for Detroit Edison named Henry Ford.

The question of whose were the first commercial auto advertisements is almost as shadowy as whose were the first autos. Evidently the Duryeas ran the first trade-journal and newspaper ads in 1896, and Alexander Winton the first magazine ads the following year. The Duryea ad, a simple and verbless announcement of the availability of "motor wagons, motors, and automotive vehicles of all kinds," showed a pair of bundled-up females sitting warily in a tiller-steered horseless carriage. The Winton ad, unillustrated and only one inch high, whispered hesitantly, "Gasoline Buggies For Sale."

Thanks to the bicycle craze, advertising was equipped to do better than this. Bicycle ads had long outgrown trade-journal approaches. The fashion was elegant ads, illustrated by romantic artists like Maxfield Parrish and the imitators of Aubrey Beardsley, with copy that strummed delicately on such themes as the joys of the open road and the opportunities for wind-blown companionship with the opposite sex. The latter approach was not particularly suited to early-model automobiles; although cars were later to have far-reaching effects on American mating habits, the earliest ones were so clamorous and spastic as to be wholly inappropriate for such purposes. It would be rather like advertising today the romantic potential of a guided missile.

The bicycle makers had learned much that could be used by the auto manufacturers. Some advertising men who worked on bike accounts were already looking ahead: if they could adver-

At a time when potential buyers were often skeptical of the reliability of cars, shrewd advertisers asserted that The Product was as reliable as clockwork. This 1904 Olds was obviously safe enough to carry ladies after dark.

tise $100 bicycles so effectively that one person in seventy owned one, and if that person was typically a young man to whom $100 was a large sum, there were enticing prospects in titillating the latent desires of older, more prosperous citizens for $800 or $900 cars. Plainly, the greater the amount spent for each unit, the greater the amount available for advertising it, and if by chance advertising and fashion should turn the item into a success, advertising appropriations could go up and the actual cost of advertising be lowered. A good case in point was that of Monarch bicycle, a proud wheel which bore the slogan "Faultless." In 1893 Monarch's advertising cost $5,000, and 1,200 bikes were sold; in 1896 the figures were $125,000 and 50,000 bicycles. With an increase in sales volume of almost fiftyfold, the cost of advertising actually dropped from $4.17 to $2.50 per bike. Most of this, it might be added, was devoted to magazine advertising, although $10,000 was set aside to support a factory racing team, and another $10,000 for balloon ascensions.

IN THE early years of the century, auto advertising grew only slowly in volume. Most makers had little cash to spare—income from autos shipped out was usually depended on to pay for materials and labor on autos being built—and plenty of low-cost promotion was available for the picking. It was a time of stunts, tours, endurance runs, and racing. Henry Ford's second car company was preoccupied with 999, a vicious monster that raced against time at Daytona and on the ice of Lake St. Clair; the Stanley brothers were setting amazing speed records with their whistling tea kettles; and Glidden Tours and Vanderbilt Cup races were filling newspapers.

The car ads that did appear in the first decade of the century for some reason did not profit by the example of the bicycle makers. Instead, they made use of a dry, innocent, cataloguelike approach. Even ads in general magazines and newspapers seem to have been designed for the pages of trade journals like *The Horseless Age* or *Motor*. The Product was often shown silhouetted, unoccupied, floating in space. Copy themes were baldly technical: horsepower, number of cylinders, kind of transmission, all couched in complex mechanical jargon.

Considerable effort was devoted to persuading readers that, though earlier and inferior cars may have indeed been unreliable, mechanical perfection had now been attained. Oldsmobile chanted, "The Oldsmobile Goes." Packard's theme was that "The Packard Gets You There And Back." In a Winton, the ads explained, "so long as your foot is on the button, you can go one mile or a hundred."

By 1910, a year when the young industry cranked out almost 200,000 vehicles, catalogue silhouettes were less common and the approach became less technical. Horsepower, weight, mechanical features, and performance claims were still mentioned, but in less loving detail. The main copy themes and the art were designed to put people in the scene. Often a touring car would be pictured rounding a bend at a spot of rustic beauty or parked at some grassy picnic glen. And artists quickly learned to heed that first

An advertised feature of the 1910 Reo was that it had lefthand drive: "This is the new and right way—convenient for dismounting to the sidewalk." The windshield and top were extras.

The headline for this Willys-Knight ad was a whimsical if irrational pun: "Memorable Days in a Knight." Mother, patient by the wheel, has been shrunken slightly by the artist to suggest roominess.

commandment of automotive art: don't put people on the near side—they'll obscure The Product. Instead, tuck them inside (shrinking them slightly, so it looks roomier in there), or else spot them on the wings of the scene, in postures of rapt admiration.

In the years before the first world war the auto began to develop at an accelerating and astonishing rate. Ford's Model T, on sale since the fall of 1908, proved to be just what the country needed: simple, sturdy, capable of bouncing through the roughest going with fenders a-flap, virtually unbreakable. (When after abuse and neglect, something *did* bust, you simply sent off for a spare part, screwed it on yourself, and cranked up.) Model Ts were sold in numbers that were a wonder of the age: 82,400 in 1912, 199,100 in 1913, and 308,213 in the twelve months ending on August 1, 1915. Though perfectly willing to advertise on occasion, Ford had begun to reveal his special talent at getting advertising space for nothing. His announcement of a minimum $5-a-day wage in 1914 brought more national attention than a lavish paid publicity campaign would have. His announcement the following year of a "profit-sharing" refund of $40 to $60 apiece to all purchasers of Model Ts in the previous twelve months was another inspiration.

Other auto makers, less adept at the manufacture of newsworthy publicity, were swarming into the advertising pages of newspapers and

magazines. Makers of tires, skid chains, batteries, spark plugs, and gasoline joined in the hunt for the public's dollars, until by 1915 autos and accessories together constituted a seventh of all national magazine advertising. It was a time when Lord & Thomas was weaving its artful magic, in advertising work for Chalmers, Willys, and Reo, and when an ex-newspaperman named Mac-Manus began to endow a number of makes with special personalities they were to bear for years.

Theodore Francis MacManus, born in Buffalo, gave up a city editor's job in Toledo to try his hand at writing advertising copy for Detroit's new industry. He turned out to be so expert at the glorification of automobiles that his name has been revered for forty years in Detroit. (It is also

Hard sell in the small type for this 1909 whizzer: "If it were a large car, we could not afford to make it so good."

Hupmobile $750

4 cylinders
20 H.P.
Sliding gears
Bosch magneto

Champs-Elysées · Paris

[Lincoln four passenger, two window Berline,
first shown at the recent New York Salon]

A haughty text block below this 1927 picture conveyed to the abashed reader the idea that a car so obviously at home on the Champs Elysées was good enough for him.

preserved in the title of a big advertising agency, MacManus, John & Adams, Inc.) Mac-Manus, who all his life remained quietly pleased with the fact that he had never learned to drive a car, wrote copy at one time or another for a host of makes, including Cadillac, Hupmobile, Dodge, Packard, Apperson, and Stearns-Knight. His particular specialty was the earnest, solid, dignified, reputation-building ad. Of these the most famous by far was a gem for Cadillac called "The Penalty of Leadership." It first appeared in *The Saturday Evening Post* for January 2, 1915, and its dignified, blandly snobbish message—that Cadillac had managed to overcome the personality problems resulting from its incomparable superiority to all

other motor cars—struck so responsive a chord in the public that Cadillac and its agency have been filling requests for reprints ever since. Apparently people admired, and "identified with," a pride so overweening that MacManus did not deign even to mention The Product in the copy.

MacManus, whose ads made him a millionaire and who seems to have derived unusual pleasure from nonparticipation, once had a private golf course built on his estate, but never learned to play the game. He did occasionally stomp around the course to get a little exercise and, in the words of James Playsted Wood, "to dispel his dislike of advertising . . . too much of [which], he had concluded, was cheap, blatant, and tricky."

111

This ad, which ran in *The Saturday Evening Post* on October 3, 1908, was the first public appearance of the Model T Ford. Few would have guessed that more than 15,000,000 of them would follow, nor that this homely but willing car would change the face of the nation.

ABOUT 1915 auto advertising took a decisively different turn. Up to this point the chief themes were mechanical excellence and the joys of the open road. But now a powerful new one was added: an automobile should be valued for its smart and elegant looks. This was an idea of revolutionary importance, later to spread from autos into advertising in general, until in the twenties it was used for the advertising of everything from power boats to rotary can openers. It marked the beginning of the era of the stylist, the dawn of the time when kitchen stoves and toasters had to have rocket-ship lines, and when virtually every metal object designed for public sale had to be tricked out with brightwork, spears, arrows, fins, skirts, and gleaming chromium slash marks.

At the beginning, before the appeal of styling became detached from reality, it served two useful purposes. First, it helped pave the way for the closed car, a development that, with the self-starter, changed autos from seasonal vehicles operated by hardy, duster-swathed adventurers to full-time conveyances for the whole family. The second advantage accrued to advertising, since styling greatly widened the potential of the art. Only mechanically sophisticated persons were capable of pulsing to the charms of, say, Packard's aluminum-pistoned Twin Six engine. But everybody with at least one working eye could be led to feel qualified to appraise the car's swanky lines and details, down to the elegant red hexagons enameled on the hubcaps.

Under the influence of eye appeal—which made every man in America his own auto connoisseur —subtle changes began to develop in the owner-auto relationship. Previously a man had bought a car as a machine for transportation and, perhaps, for suggesting to neighbors and associates that he was a mildly prosperous and forward-looking fellow. But now, and increasingly with every passing year, he bought a particular car because it enhanced his self-esteem and fitted his image of himself as, say, a man of judicious moderation (Chalmers, Peerless, Chandler), a man of quiet elegance (Locomobile, Cunningham, Pierce-

Arrow), or a man of sporting tastes (Templar, Stutz, Wills St. Clair).

The latter car, incidentally, was the work of the unforgettably named Childe Harold Wills, a highly individualistic engineer who also worked, in the early days, for Ford. One of his contributions was the vanadium steel alloy that added to the sturdiness of the Tin Lizzie. Another was the familiar cursive lettering of "Ford" that graced so many million flivvers. Childe Harold Wills had set up the lettering from type that came with a toy printing press he had been given as a youngster and had kept in the attic ever since.

While the job of creating a car's personality was partly the task of its designers, it was also very much the responsibility of advertising men. The illustrations in the ads were especially crucial. The limousine was classically shown on a bluestone drive, just emerging from wrought-iron gates in the charge of a haughty chauffeur, and bearing within its satiny cave persons of unearthly refinement. A roadster, on the other hand, would be occupied by a gay young couple, and its details would be dashing—three spares racked at the rear, and a great spotlight on its running-board pedestal. And one of those interesting new closed sedans might be shown rolling through the city park, carrying a pretty mother, a fragile grandmother, immaculate and mannerly

Undiluted snobbery was the ad theme for this stately 1920 Locomobile. There was only one chaste and arresting line: "America's Finest and Most Expensive Motor Car."

113

Templar
The Superfine Small Car

New makes proliferated in the twenties. But even newcomers to auto advertising knew instinctively that people in the illustrations should be smart, clever, and not placed in front of The Product.

children, and one red rose in the cut-glass vase affixed to the window post.

The notorious love affair between Americans and autos was certainly intensified by this glory-of-it-all advertising approach. As in all infatuations, it was necessary to look at the love-object with a misty, imaginative eye, somewhat imperceptive of literal reality, seeing it as a symbol of ecstatic fulfillment. Such affectionate and uncritical vision was something that advertising worked hard to develop. Just a few years after the car was first presented as a thing of beauty and a joy until next year, the national love affair was in full fever. In 1919 the country had six million cars—a number that impressed the world. But in just ten more years Americans had scrapped practically all of these and had bought 23 million new ones.

As the affair continued, the auto was discovered to be a mistress with a delightful variety of enticements. The auto offered something for everyone: it provided mobility, escape,

and an intoxicating sense of power; it bore promise of happy vacations, mild explorations, and convenient romance; it made everyone an expert car critic; gave its driver a chance to display virtuosity and daring; served as a portable billboard of social and economic status; allowed a confirmed tinkerer to get his hands joyously dirty; and tolerated being rubbed down every week with loving chamois and affectionate wax.

In the twenties an engagingly batty salesman-poet named Ned Jordan turned up with a car ideally attuned to this enraptured relationship. Jordan, an ex-newspaperman, had served his sales apprenticeship at National Cash Register, where the celebrated John H. Patterson was a tough but instructive tyrant. Then Jordan went to work for the makers of the Rambler and Jeffrey cars, serving variously as advertising, sales, and general manager. (Years later he described himself then as "a bright boy of 28, wearing white spats, telling other people what to do.")

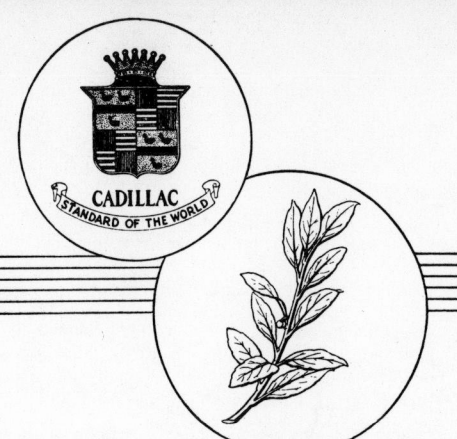

The Penalty of Leadership

IN EVERY field of human endeavor, he that is first must perpetually live in the white light of publicity.

Whether the leadership be vested in a man or in a manufactured product, emulation and envy are ever at work.

In art, in literature, in music, in industry, the reward and the punishment are always the same.

The reward is widespread recognition; the punishment, fierce denial and detraction.

When a man's work becomes a standard for the whole world, it also becomes a target for the shafts of the envious few.

If his work be merely mediocre, he will be left severely alone—if he achieves a masterpiece, it will set a million tongues a-wagging.

Jealousy does not protrude its forked tongue at the artist who produces a commonplace painting.

Whatsoever you write, or paint, or play, or sing, or build, no one will strive to surpass or to slander you unless your work be stamped with the seal of genius.

Long, long after a great work or a good work has been done, those who are disappointed or envious, continue to cry out that it cannot be done.

Spiteful little voices in the domain of art were raised against our own Whistler as a mountebank, long after the big world had acclaimed him its greatest artistic genius.

Multitudes flocked to Bayreuth to worship at the musical shrine of Wagner, while the little group of those whom he had dethroned and displaced argued angrily that he was no musician at all.

The little world continued to protest that Fulton could never build a steamboat, while the big world flocked to the river banks to see his boat steam by.

The leader is assailed because he is a leader, and the effort to equal him is merely added proof of that leadership.

Failing to equal or to excel, the follower seeks to depreciate and to destroy—but only confirms once more the superiority of that which he strives to supplant.

There is nothing new in this.

It is as old as the world and as old as the human passions—envy, fear, greed, ambition, and the desire to surpass.

And it all avails nothing.

If the leader truly leads, he remains—the leader.

Master-poet, master-painter, master-workman, each in his turn is assailed, and each holds his laurels through the ages.

That which is good or great makes itself known, no matter how loud the clamor of denial.

That which deserves to live—lives.

Somewhere West of Laramie

SOMEWHERE west of Laramie there's a broncho-busting, steer-roping girl who knows what I'm talking about.

She can tell what a sassy pony, that's a cross between greased lightning and the place where it hits, can do with eleven hundred pounds of steel and action when he's going high, wide and handsome.

The truth is—the Playboy was built for her.

Built for the lass whose face is brown with the sun when the day is done of revel and romp and race.

She loves the cross of the wild and the tame.

There's a savor of links about that car—of laughter and lilt and light—a hint of old loves—and saddle and quirt. It's a brawny thing—yet a graceful thing for the sweep o' the Avenue.

Step into the Playboy when the hour grows dull with things gone dead and stale.

Then start for the land of real living with the spirit of the lass who rides, lean and rangy, into the red horizon of a Wyoming twilight.

JORDAN MOTOR CAR COMPANY, Inc., Cleveland, Ohio

In 1916, after a short trick as a copywriter for Lord & Thomas, Ned Jordan determined to become an auto manufacturer. He wrote later:

"You see, I'd been selling Ramblers and Jeffreys for ten years according to the engineers' ideas of promotion—offset crankshafts, straight-line drives, and ejector manifolds. Then Kettering perfected the starting system. Now any woman could crank a car without breaking her arm. A brand-new market had been created. So we got together $300,000 and started for town and made a car with everything that women want in a car."

Collecting the $300,000 was a neat little triumph in itself. Jordan called in a group of friends and showed them sketches based on a glimpse he had had of a sporty and lavish roadster Flo Ziegfeld was having custom-built for Billie Burke. After an hour's intensive salesmanship, Jordan persuaded his friends to cough up $200,-000. (They were destined to get back 1,900 per cent on their investment.) Then he sped to Cleveland and sold bankers there on investing another $100,000. He called in parts manufacturers and persuaded them to lend him some engineers. His plan was to make a high-priced "assembled" car in Cleveland, put together from parts made by suppliers. One model, to be called the Playboy (with a bow to playwright Synge), was to be a rakish roadster with an aluminum body, soft leather upholstery, and a fitted vanity case on the dash.

Ned Jordan rattled out an advertisement to run in *The Saturday Evening Post*, the magazine that had grown to be a kind of national show window for auto ads:

We might as well tell it . . . the secret will soon be out . . . It's a wonderful companion for a wonderful girl and a wonderful boy. How did we happen to think of it? Why . . . a girl who loves to swim and paddle and shoot described it to a boy who loves the roar of a cutout. So we built one just for the love of doing it . . . and stepped on it . . . AND . . . the chickens ran and the dogs barked. It's a shame to call this Playboy a roadster . . . so full is this brawny thing of the vigor of boyhood and morning.

Nobody had ever written automobile ads like this before—wildly inexplicit, composed in an eccentric free-verse manner, rich in easy imagery and commercially desirable associations (there are no less than three "loves" and three "wonderfuls" in that brief ad). During its first year on the market, priced to yield a profit of $500 per car, 2,000 Playboys were sold to people who responded to Ned's unusual prose. And that first million dollars was only the beginning.

In several other good years, sales climbed up near 5,000 units, and the little company could shave its unit profit down to $150 and still net $750,000. As Jordan reminisced later, "We *did* make a lot of money *awfully* fast." His low-volume, high-price approach was eyed askance by the big Detroit manufacturers dedicated to contrary views. Most of the time, though, the

A few auto executives clung tenaciously to the belief that engine features made glorious ads. Admire our ingenious sleeve valves, the ads argued, and then hasten out to buy.

Jordan Motor Car Company was a trivial gadfly that Detroit did not take seriously—especially when it recalled that Henry Ford frequently built more than twice as many cars in a single day as Jordan did in an entire calendar year.

But the demonstrated power of the giddy little Cleveland company's advertising was taken seriously indeed. In *The Saturday Evening Post* for June 23, 1923, Ned's most famous and influential ad appeared, a 173-word lyric headlined "Somewhere West of Laramie." It had a remarkable public impact; people talked about it, quoted it, tore it out and saved it as if it were a moving little poem. To analytical advertising men it indicated that the day of unadorned nuts-and-bolts copy was fading fast. "Laramie" was a little obscure in its reference, and was initially faulted for this by conventional advertising men. (It has long been an article of faith that all copy should be instantly comprehensible by near morons.)

Perhaps it wasn't immediately clear whether Jordan was vending a horse, a girl, a car, or Wyoming real estate. What *was* clear, however, was that an incalculably large number of people had noted, read, and remembered the ad; that it conveyed to many of them the concept that the Playboy was almost achingly desirable; and that it achieved this commercially useful result with neither a mechanical or performance claim nor an informative illustration.

"Somewhere West of Laramie" and "The Penalty of Success" are usually hailed as the greatest auto ads ever run. Of the pair, Jordan's was the more influential. It fathered a kind of copywriting that has spread far beyond autos, and has become a valuable tool for the sale of fashionable clothes, resorts, liquor, furs, jewelry, and perfumes. One term for such copy is "word magic"—a phrase not necessarily opprobrious, though it commonly has derisive overtones. The allusive, ecstatic, faintly fey approach, its pearls often strung on a fragile garland of triple periods, has grown to be one of advertising's standard gambits. Clear traces of the ancestral lass, lean and rangy, who rode into the red horizon of the Wyoming twilight can be detected in such latter-day classics as DeBeers's shimmery apothegms about how a diamond is forever, or in Tabu's shaggy violinist who has been maddened, utterly maddened, by the smell of his accompanist.

Jordan cars and ads continued through the turbulent twenties. Some of Ned's efforts (notably the one quoted at the head of this chapter) missed the mark, and none of them equaled "Laramie" in currency. High-priced and vulnerable to the depression, the Jordan car expired in 1931. Jordan himself confessed later he had started liquidation in 1928, when "we could see

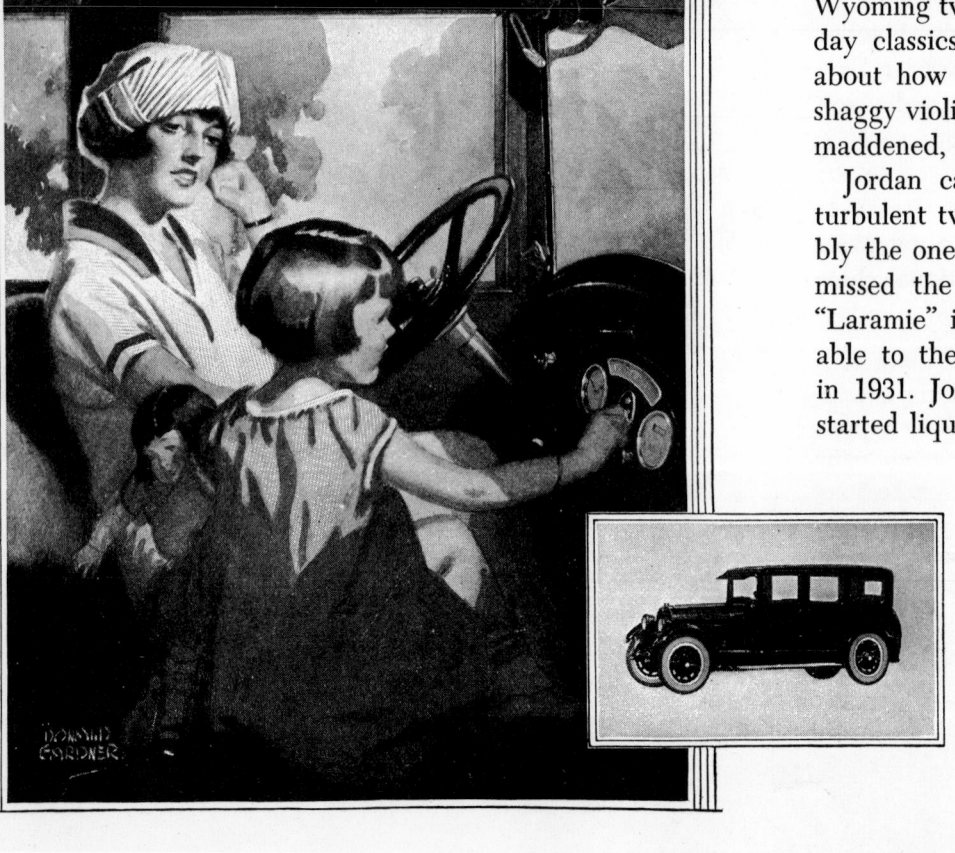

Often a leader in deft merchandising, Cadillac began this 1925 ad: "One quality which women deeply admire in the Cadillac is its unrivalled capacity for *remaining young.*"

CADILLAC

the depression looming up over the horizon. Thank the Lord we quit just in time. Our families have since been enjoying the trust funds which the Playboy earned."

Ned Jordan died in 1958 at the age of seventy-six, his later years having been spent in sardonic observation of the Detroit scene. Not long before his death he observed that the auto industry needed much more gazoompah—a Jordanism defined as "a quality possessed by certain old-fashioned Americans . . . cold efficiency, tempered with technique, experience, and judgment: GA—from the Babylonian for guts; ZOOM—denoting speed; PAH—diminutive for 'that's that.' "

FASCINATING paradoxes turn up in the history of the automobile. One is the fact that, though developed in Western Europe, a land of moderate distances and, in 1890, good roads, it grew most luxuriantly in America, where its initial usefulness was restricted by long distances and primitive roads. This paradox is a favorite parade ground of Detroit historians, who see it as testimony for the American Way, free enterprise, and the dogma of "we'd-never-have-done-it-if-Reuther-had-been-around." Scholars not working for the Automobile Manufacturers Association are willing to acknowledge the importance of the laissez-faire climate of the early days, but they also tick off such general factors as prosperity, an expanding population, less debilitation through war and military expenditure than in Europe, and the fact that the auto's most effective missionary, the Model T Ford, didn't give a hoot if it traveled primitive roads.

Another anomaly, less often mentioned by industry historians, is the speed with which the auto managed to demolish a deep-seated Ameri-

Chrysler "70" Royal Sedan
$1795, f. o. b. Detroit

Chrysler's characteristic early appeal was to performance. Of this Model 70 shown shooting up a hill in 1926, it was said: "Chrysler Model Numbers Mean Miles Per Hour."

can prejudice against installment buying. It is not easy today to realize the extent to which, in the nineteenth and early twentieth centuries, debt was equated with depravity. Thrift was then a preeminent virtue. To covet, let alone buy, something that couldn't be paid for in cash was held to indicate weak moral fiber. One general exception was a mortgage for the purchase of a home; and there was grudging sanction for the installment purchase of such lifetime possessions as sewing machines and pianos. As late as 1909, nevertheless, Edward Bok printed in the *Ladies' Home Journal* a resounding blast titled "A Trap For The Unwary," warning against the corrupting perils of installment buying, a human frailty virtually at one with alcoholism, wife beating, and taking dope.

Bok's article was one of the last boosts that

The tiny, not to say subnormal, humans peeping out of this 1922 Chandler show advertising craftiness: Make the people midgets so The Product will then seem massive.

119

If- I had only put on- WEED TIRE CHAINS

The selling leverage of anxiety, lightly dusted with guilt, was fully explored in the twenties. In this scene of anguish, carefully plotted to sell The Product, note such Belasco touches as the broken umbrella, the shocked passers-by, and the pointing finger of the surviving child.

old-fashioned thrift was to get. The automobile, its gleaming enticements spread far and wide by advertising, soon made debt socially acceptable. It accomplished this feat, in fact, with a speed that casts doubt on the familiar assumption that man's ethical attitudes are hard and slow to change. Autos could be bought on credit from a few enterprising dealers as early as 1912. The idea spread across the country in two or three years. In 1916 the Maxwell car came out with an advertising campaign based on the slogan, "Pay As You Ride!" This frank credit system seemed shocking in Detroit at first, and other companies (including Buick, Reo, and Cadillac) protested to Maxwell over what was termed its unsound marketing measure. Actually, Maxwell's terms would seem excessively conservative today, since they stipulated a minimum down payment of 50 per cent.

In just a few years, under the stimulus of climbing sales, heavy advertising, invigorating competition, and a contagious feeling that the

country had achieved a plateau of permanent prosperity, the auto industry forgot its prissy reluctance about credit. For one thing, it was observed that "handling auto paper" was itself a highly nourishing business. Besides, credit boosted sales immensely, and that settled the matter. Soon the vendors of home appliances, oil burners, power boats, fur coats, and a host of other desirable possessions—including cemetery lots—jumped into the act. As early as 1927, according to *Printers' Ink,* the American consumer was $4 billion in debt, although too busy enjoying what he hadn't paid for to worry visibly about it. An erstwhile oddity became a commonplace: a man could take delivery of a new car, drive it for thousands of miles, and then trade it in—all without ever paying completely for it.

In the boom years auto accessory advertising also grew greatly in volume, if not in quality. Many battery makers, for instance, could think of nothing better for their ads than to show The Product looming large and clean on the page,

"Forty miles before we hit even a service station! We'll be in a nice fix if we have a blowout, with no spare!"

"I'm not worrying about blowouts; we've got Kelly-Springfields on all around. It's the gas I'm thinking about."

The he—she cartoon, familiar from *Judge*, *Life*, and *College Humor*, made readers feel at home in these ads.

or else cut away to show that its interior arrangements and juices were demonstrably nicer than anyone else's. Tires were peculiarly subject to this sort of unimaginative giantism in advertising art; they were all too often shown rolling hugely but irrelevantly across the countryside. One exception to this sterile approach was a series of ads run from 1918 to 1931 for Kelly-Springfield tires. They used large line or wash drawings by Laurence Fellowes, and showed smart people and a sporty car togged out in Kelly-Springfield tires. A short caption would be arranged beneath in the manner of a he-she joke from the pages of *Judge* or the old *Life*. The series' high readability and deceptively soft sell disposed of a lot of tires.

When accessory manufacturers tried to vary the monotony of their ads, the results were often unfortunate. There was frank dalliance in the twenties with the scare-'em-silly theory of advertising. Fire extinguishers for cars were pushed as a means of avoiding not only the unfortunate combustion of your car, but also of your loved ones. In battery ads a car full of doomed and desperate mortals, presumably equipped with the defective product of a competitor, would be shown stalled on the tracks in front of a looming locomotive. To encourage the sale of skid chains an anguished driver might be shown at the roadside attending the last conscious moments of a golden-haired girl, struck down one icy day because of parsimony or neglect.

At the end of the decade, when advertising fashion was swinging in favor of photographic art, one brisk young agency man on an insurance account won a great reputation for his marvelously compelling pictures. His technique, he revealed later, was to wait in a Manhattan hotel suite with a crew of photographers and professional models. He had a line to the police communications network, and whenever a particularly violent auto accident was reported, he would speed with his cohorts to the scene. As soon as the genuine victims were carried off to the hospital or morgue, the brisk young account executive would arrange his models about the shattered metal in commercially effective poses of anguish and pain.

QUICK ACTION BRAKES
EXTRA LARGE AND EXTRA SAFE

In the construction of Dodge Brothers Motor Car, every consideration has been given to the owner's safety.

This is particularly evident in the brakes, which, with their 14-inch drums and 2¼ inch lining, are appreciably larger than the average. The extra surface thus provided develops greater friction when the brake bands contract over the drums— and it is this friction which stops the car.

Connecting levers are designed to transmit the maximum of power with the minimum of effort. The slightest pressure on the brake pedal has an immediate effect. This pressure is distributed evenly between the two rear wheels by a highly efficient equalizer, which prevents skidding because it retards both wheels simultaneously.

And the brake bands grip evenly all around the drums. This protects the lining against irregular wear and enables the driver to stop quickly, quietly and safely.

DODGE BROTHERS

The price of the Touring Car is $880 f. o. b. Detroit

© D. B.

Distinctive typography and a plain, old-shoe copy appeal characterized many Dodge ads. The earnest, dogged text nicely mirrored the car's frumpy, run-forever personality.

If The Product didn't lend itself to the blatant use of terror—as gasoline, motor oil, and spark plugs did not—it was always possible to draw on the rich heritage of patent medicine. After all, these commodities worked deep in the insides of a car; and everyone knew that owners identified so closely with their cars that they gave them pet names and almost wept at trade-in time. So the character of the copy written to sell such products often bore a detectable kinship to that for Lydia E. Pinkham's Vegetable Compound. Buy our gasoline and motor oil, and your engine will eliminate its harmful internal deposits and feel young again. Buy our competitors' products, and your engine will become fatally freighted with sludge, carbon, varnish, acids, and gummy deposits.

Such an approach was especially useful for the advertising of proprietary gasoline additives, special carburetors, and imaginative gadgets supposed to save gasoline, "fatten the spark," and deliver almost frightening increases in power. Since many of these devices were akin to the electric belts of the medicine men, it was no cause for surprise that the advertising of them was only marginally honest. What is surprising, perhaps, is that plenty of large and reputable oil firms did nearly the same. They began to skate on the thin ice of half truth with the development, in the late twenties, of premium-grade gasoline. Under the stress of competition, gaso-

line ads soon began to claim that for maximum power, greatest fuel mileage, easiest starting, and longest engine life, premium grades were the best that money could buy. Such claims, though hallowed by years of usage, still exasperate auto engineers who know, as the public in general does not, that the *sole* difference between premium and regular grades lies in antiknock characteristics. Other virtues, if any, exist chiefly in the mind of the innocent buyer.

THE ROLE that Henry Ford played in auto advertising was a starring one, and one that nobody else in the industry has been able to assume. He was much in the news columns, usually in a favorable light. Derisive but affectionate jokes about the flivver could be heard from every vaudeville stage in the land. The ten-millionth Model T, in 1924, and the fifteen-millionth, in 1927, were built at the Rouge plant among staged rites that won nationwide publicity, and that somehow made all Americans feel pleased and a little proud. Ford's pronouncements on everything under the sun were immediately put out on news wires; his luxurious camping trips with Edison and John Burroughs were followed vicariously by millions. Publishing circles whispered the story, possibly true, about a big magazine that couldn't seem to get any Ford advertising. "I can't understand it," the publisher is supposed to have said. "We're certainly important to any manufacturer, and the Lord knows we've given Ford enough editorial attention." Whereupon the publisher had a sudden inspiration; his editor was ordered not to mention Ford's name again, and in six months a fat advertising contract arrived at the business office.

The announcement of the Model A Ford on December 2, 1927, as the long-awaited replacement to the Tin Lizzie, was Ford's masterwork of showmanship. Although he spent almost $1,-500,000 on newspaper and magazine ads during the week of announcement, the ads were just the cherry atop the most successful publicity sundae in business history, the climax of eight months of carefully timed leaks and deftly managed mystery. More than 100,000 people filed through Ford's Detroit showrooms that December 2. In Cleveland mounted police were barely able to save the plate-glass windows. In Chicago the waiting queue was encircling the block before noon. In many cities the public schools were closed so that the little ones might have an early chance to see The Product.

During the lean years of the thirties auto advertising reflected the depression in a number of ways. One was an increasing prominence given to price in ads. (It is sometimes forgotten today that right up to Pearl Harbor prices were an important part of most auto ads; only since 1945 have the amounts become so swollen that most ads discreetly omit them.) Another depression development was much heavier use of photographic illustration, as agency art directors decided that photos had more "conviction of truth" than paintings.

Anyone who has ever observed advertising photographers at work is apt to wonder about this conclusion, since agency photos of automobiles are about as spontaneous and casual as a high-church wedding. There are committee meetings, test shots, and memoranda galore before even the setting is determined—whether on the driveway before the gracious house, at the yacht or country club, under the ambassador's porte-cochere, by the marquee of the distinguished hotel, or even, democratically, at the curb near the smart market. Then exact camera location and lenses must be chosen to produce maximum elongation of The Product, in harmony with the fundamental advertising premise that bigger equals better. Then once the car is maneuvered onto the set and jockeyed into exact position, the hubcaps on each visible wheel must be pried off and replaced so that the insigne on them is right side up. Hundreds of pounds of lead blocks or sandbags are stowed inside so that the car hunkers down on its springs to look lower and longer. The lighting is adjusted for hours or even days until the brightwork glistens, in Paul Kearney's phrase, like a mouthful of gold teeth.

Fully as much care goes into the selection and placement of models. If a girl is to be photographed within the car, she should be small, so that The Product will appear to be exceptionally roomy; but if she's to be stationed outside, she should be a lady basketball player, to make the car look lower. All models used, whether the doorman at the hotel, the ambassador at the porte-cochere, or the ambient millionaires at the yacht club, must be able to assume on command that special admiring and bright-eyed appearance believed most likely to sell The Product.

Copywriting in the thirties also reflected the times. General Motors, after making a study that indicated that buyers valued reliability, came out with scores of ads suggesting that its cars were *intensely* reliable. During hard times it is difficult for advertising to stick to the bland assumption that the competition doesn't exist, and a great

Only Hudson and Essex Have the Coach

It Gives All Closed Car Comforts and at Open Car Cost

So Why Buy an Open Car?

Students of automotive art often find that the car is much clearer than its gray, fogbound setting. A 1920 Chandler.

many sidelong glances were evident. Chevrolet bore down on the theme that it was the only car in its field to have Knee Action; Plymouth dinned in the message that it was the only car in its field to have Floating Power; Ford missed few chances to point out that it was the only car in its field to use a V-8 engine.

During this period, it was discovered that competition could work *for* you as well as against you. In the winter of 1931–32 Ford was tooling up for its new engine, and had already started a powerful publicity build-up for its announcement in the spring. This left Plymouth, then only a few years old and without a strong following, out in left field. It was a difficult marketing problem for Plymouth, but provided a shining opportunity for a singular young man named J. Stirling Getchell.

Getchell had started his own little advertising agency in the year of the crash. Bursting with enterprise, he produced (on speculation, for he didn't have the Plymouth account) a memorable ad headlined "Look at All Three." It won notice by its unconventional admonition to the reader to look at competitive products. More important, it gave Plymouth a free ride on Ford's immense publicity build-up, which came to a climax the same week that Getchell's ad came out. It is now sometimes said that the ad marked a turning point in Plymouth's sales history. It shortly brought Getchell, who was then thirty-one, both fame and the Plymouth account.

Throughout the thirties Getchell continued to move swiftly. His agency was built up rapidly to multimillion-dollar size. He showed a fondness for screaming tabloid headlines, for layouts of rectilinear orderliness, and for strips of photos used to hammer home simple selling points. He was one of the first to employ Ernest Dichter, later a celebrated soothsayer-psychiatrist in advertising, setting him to work on the symbolism of the auto. (Dichter reported back his famous discovery that a convertible is like a mistress, a sedan like a wife.) Getchell was a pioneer in the shotgun approach to photography, dispatching crews of photographers to expose hundreds of

negatives when only one picture could be used. He worked day and night, fired people on whim, lived in a state of almost continuous excitement, and was tough, profane, nakedly direct, and, though demonic and haggard-looking, seemingly inexhaustible. Quite unable to relax, Getchell occasionally would try tennis, but would end up galloping heavily about the court in a fierce desire to win. Banished on doctor's orders to a sanitarium bed for rest every weekend, he took along copies of everything the agency had produced the previous week, and spent each weekend tearing it to pieces and reworking it. In 1940 he died very suddenly, forty-one years old, a legendary meteor of advertising prematurely burnt out.

By the time that the first Japanese bombs shut off all civilian auto manufacture, it was clear that the American car had changed the face of the land far more than had the steamboat and the locomotive. It had reshaped cities, created suburbs, abolished rural isolation. It caused far-reaching changes in medical care, schools, vacation habits, retail distribution, and nearly every form of business. Directly and indirectly it supported about seven million workers. And on the automobile was spent almost a tenth of the total national income; government figures showed that even families in straitened circumstances spent almost as much on their cars as on their clothing, and approximately a third of what they spent for such necessities as food and drink. The automobile had proliferated until it was by far the most important manufactured product in America. It was advertising's proudest triumph.

Deaf Persons Can Now Hear

Wonderful Invention Has Delivered Thousands from the Handicap of Deafness.

Don't think you have to worry along if you can't hear well. Every deaf person is at a hopeless disadvantage, deprived of social pleasure, barred from active business. Any dullness of hearing is a constant mortification.

But now this misery is unnecessary. Every deaf person can hear as well as ever before by simply wearing a pair of

WILSON'S EAR DRUMS

A wonderful little device that fits into the ears without the slightest discomfort. Invisible when inserted—so tiny, so perfect, that you forget you are wearing them. And the effect is magical.

This marvelous invention was perfected by Mr. Geo. H. Wilson, after years of suffering from hopeless deafness. They enabled him to hear perfectly. And this miracle has been repeated for 200,000 persons.

Send today for a book written by Mr. Wilson that tells the whole story—gives hundreds of letters from grateful users. This priceless book is FREE for your name on a postal. Just ask for Mr. Wilson's book. It will come by return mail. Address **Wilson Ear Drum Co.,** 430 Todd Bldg., Louisville, Ky. (2)

This was one account on which young Albert Lasker first "practiced the craft." But a Gene Katz was the actual copywriter.

Great Man

I am sure I would fail if I tried to advertise the Rolls-Royce, Tiffany & Company, or Steinway pianos. I do not know the reactions of the rich. But I do know the common people. I love to talk to laboring men, to study housewives who must count their pennies, to gain the confidence and learn the ambitions of poor boys and girls. Give me something which they want and I will strike the responsive chord. My words will be simple, my sentences short. Scholars may ridicule my style. The rich and vain may laugh at the factors which I feature. But in millions of humble homes the common people will read and buy.

—Claude C. Hopkins

The task of a copywriter is that of administering shock effects, tropismatic reactions, animal orientations, forced movements, fixation of ideas, verbal intoxication . . . a trading on the range of human infirmities which blossom in devout observances, and bear fruit in the psychopathic wards.

—Thorstein Veblen

A REVOLUTION in advertising comparable in significance to the harnessing of electric power took place in the first decade of this century. It was the discovery that *nothing* could sell The Product faster than the skillful use of emotional appeals. The possibilities that opened up were as wide as the range of human feelings. On the surface were low-voltage, socially acceptable emotions like patriotism, nostalgia, and benign attitudes toward children, mothers, and dogs. Beneath this level were categories of higher voltage and greater amperage as well. There were, for example, the emotions associated with inadequacy and guilt; and the powerful feelings of shame, anxiety, alarm, and fear. Above all was the huge category of self-interest, which included ambition and envy, pleasure and indulgence, vanity and pride, acquisition and preservation, and the many-colored, tingling delights of sex.

Advertising men were entranced by the possibilities of special emotional combinations designed for a particular product. As techniques developed, there appeared such recipes as anxiety mixed with inadequacy for the sale of fire insurance, revolvers, and antiskid chains; fear, vanity, and sex for the sale of lotions, tooth paste, and deodorants; and pride blended with remorse and guilt for the sale of tombstones and guaranteed-waterproof coffins.

It would be inexact to suggest that the pioneers of emotional advertising suddenly appeared with a highly developed new approach. The rationale —the realization that the essential ingredient was emotional appeal—came later. It was the initial impression of these pathfinders that they were introducing the idea of sales argument, in contrast to simple brand identification. Actually, they were incomparable salesmen, much better at disposing of The Product by the carload than at analyzing how they did it. They were also strange men—original, intense, theatrical, egotistic, fonder of intuition than research. They laid out the patterns for what is now called the hard sell; they invented a number of advertising's most obnoxious traits. Historically, they gave immense new importance to advertising agencies, and they established the copywriter as the crucial agency magician.

For all these services they were richly rewarded. One of them averred that he never did manage to find out how much money he had made. This was Albert D. Lasker, and the uncertainty amounted to plus or minus $10 million. He was sure he'd earned more than $40 million—but probably less, he guessed, than $60 million. When he retired in 1942, Lasker took the name of his agency into retirement with him. His associates were allowed to buy Lord & Thomas but not the name; it was reborn as Foote, Cone & Belding. As many noted at the time, it was a gesture with Viking overtones: a proud and ceremonial killing of the faithful war horse that had borne the famous warrior.

THE MOST influential copywriter of all was Claude C. Hopkins (see pages 58 and 71). He was born in 1866 into an impoverished Michigan home. Sickly but energetic, young Claude was at ten the part-time janitor of two schools and one church, and, in his spare time, a newspaper boy and distributor of handbills. Characteristically, he charged a premium over other kids for the handbills he gave out, on the grounds that he *really* distributed them, as could be verified by a comparison of results. He also sold from house to house a silver polish that his mother made; he made the vital discovery of successful door-to-door selling—that he could sell only one housewife in ten when he was unable to get beyond the door, and almost nine women in ten when he managed to win his way to the pantry and demonstrate it.

Claude's father, a minister, died when the youngster was ten. His mother was so acutely devout that he was permitted no activity on Sundays beyond reading the Bible, except when listening to five obligatory sermons and attending to his churchly janitoring. The intensive Bible reading was helpful later; all his life Claude, who had only fragmentary schooling, wrote in prose of great simplicity and force, with rolling King Jamesian tones. Aimed toward the ministry, he

became a lay preacher at seventeen, and at eighteen, after he had preached against Fundamentalist views, he had a violent break with his mother. He was, she told him, "no longer her son," and he left home, rarely to see her again.

After a brief term in a Grand Rapids business school (of such mediocrity, to hear him tell it later, that it might have been invented by Charles Dickens in an exaggerating mood), Hopkins got a job with the Bissell Carpet Sweeper Company. In months, thanks to extreme industriousness, he became head bookkeeper. He was fretting over the fact that weeks had gone by without further promotion when he happened on a pamphlet written by the great John E. Powers, then at the height of his fame. Hopkins heard that this man was able to earn a glittering $12,000 a year just by composing his deceptively simple ads. At once bookkeeping permanently lost its charm, and the youngster set out on the advertising career that was to make him a multimillionaire.

He wangled a chance to write some sales pamphlets sent out to carpet-sweeper dealers. They were unlike any that Bissell had tried before. Earlier ones had described the excellence of the mechanism, with its wonderful spinning brush and its husky capability for gathering dirt. Hopkins convinced himself that most carpet sweepers were bought by women and that women didn't understand machinery. They didn't even want to hear about it, he felt. So he wrote pamphlets that were packed with what seemed to be irrelevant reasons for buying carpet sweepers. He stressed that they could be obtained in special woods—handsome birch or opulent walnut, golden maple or rich mahogany. Bissell executives explained, in case this strange and intense young man hadn't got it straight, that the kind of wood didn't make the slightest difference in a sweeper's ability to pick up dirt. But after his first efforts produced a phenomenally high percentage of orders, rebuke vanished. His pamphlets, tested and revised and then sent out in large batches, brought in floods of orders—more than those turned in by the firm's fourteen road salesmen.

Elated, Hopkins pressed on with variations.

My Book Is Free

My treatment too—if that fails.

But if it helps—if it succeeds,
If health is yours again,
I ask you to pay—$5.50.

The book tells all.
I send it to you free
If you but write.

And further, I will send the name of a druggist near
you who will let you take six bottles of my remedy,

Dr. Shoop's Restorative

On a month's trial.   If it succeeds, the cost to you is
$5.50.   If it fails, the druggist will bill the cost to me.

Don't Wait Until You Are Worse.

Taken in time, the suffering of this little one
would have been prevented:—

"Two years ago my little girl was sick continuously for
six months. We tried many doctors, but they failed, yet
it took only two bottles of your remedy to cure her, and
she has remained cured. You can tell others of this cure if
you so desire."   Mrs. C. H. Avery, Rockdale, N. Y.

The wife of Omer Andrus, of Bayou Chicat,
La., had been sick for 20 years. For 8 years
could do practically no work. He writes:

"When she first started taking the Restorative she
barely weighed 90 pounds; now she weighs 135, and is easily able to do all her housework."

J. G. Billingsley, of Thomasville, Ga. He
writes:

"I spent $250.00 for other medicines, and the $3.00 I
have spent with you have done me more good than all the
rest."

Both money and suffering might have been
saved.

And these are only three from over 65,000
similar cases. Such letters—many of them—
come every day to me.

How much serious illness the Restorative has
prevented I have no means of knowing, for the
slightly ill and the indisposed simply get a
bottle or two of their druggist, are cured, and I
never hear from them.

But of 600,000 sick ones—seriously sick,
mind you—who asked for my guarantee, 39
out of 40 have paid.

If I can succeed in cases like these—fail but
one time in 40 in diseases deep-seated and chronic, isn't it certain I can cure the slightly ill?

All You Need Do.

Simply write me—that is all. Tell me the
book you need. The offer I make may sound
extravagant. But it isn't. It would mean
bankruptcy to me, though, were it not for my
discovery. That discovery—the treatment of
the inside nerves—taught me a way to cure.
I do not doctor the mere organs. I doctor the
nerves that operate them—that give them
strength and power.

And failures are seldom—so seldom that I
make this offer gladly, freely—so that those
who might doubt may learn without risk.

Tell of it, please, to some sick friend. Or
send me his name. That's but a trifle—a
minute's time—a postal. He is your friend.
You can help him. My way may be his only
way to get well.

If I, a stranger, will do this for him, you
should at least write.

Drop me a postal to-day,

Simply state which
book you want and
address Dr. Shoop.
Box 3397, Racine, Wis.

Book 1 on Dyspepsia
Book 2 on the Heart
Book 3 on the Kidneys
Book 4 for Women
Book 5 for Men
Book 6 on Rheumatism

Mild cases, not chronic, are often cured with
one or two bottles. At druggists'.

**Here was salesmanship in print, 1903 style. The ad was written by John E. Kennedy
when he was a highly paid copywriter for Dr. Shoop. From *Advertising Age*.**

Your first shave

will prove, beyond all doubt, the claims men make for this unique shaving cream

Let us send you a 10-shave tube to try

WE'VE built Palmolive Shaving Cream to a national business success by making few claims for it. We let it prove its case by sending a 10-day test tube free to all who ask. In that way, we've gained leadership in a highly competitive field in only a few years.

130 formulas tried

Before offering Palmolive Shaving Cream, we asked 1000 men their supreme desires in a shaving cream. Then met them exactly.

We tried and discarded 130 formulas before finding the right one. We put our 60 years of soap experience behind this creation. The result is a shaving cream unlike any you have ever tried.

Five advantages

1. Multiplies itself in lather 250 times.
2. Softens the beard in one minute.
3. Maintains its creamy fullness for 10 minutes on the face.
4. Strong bubbles hold the hairs erect for cutting.
5. Fine after-effects due to palm and olive oil content.

Just send coupon

Your present method may suit you well. But still there may be a better one. This test may mean much to you in comfort. Send the coupon before you forget.

THE PALMOLIVE COMPANY (Del. Corp.), CHICAGO, ILL.

He seems to have been the first person to promote the household appliance as a Christmas gift. He thus planted an idea that would reach flower decades later with ads showing the entire family on the stairs Christmas morning, cataleptic with delight over a ribboned refrigerator tagged, "For Mom, With Love."

One memorable Bissell pamphlet told, in reverent language, how some few carpet sweepers were to be made up in a rare wood called vermilion. A strange and beautiful wood, it was imported at great expense from India, where vermilion trees were felled by chained convict gangs working deep in the jungle, and where elephants (he didn't call them "lumbering") carried the logs out to the storied banks of the Ganges. After this piece of imagery hit the mails, Bissell earned more money in six weeks than in any previous year. And young Claude developed a conviction that he could sell almost anything to almost anybody.

Long before success made him famous, Hopkins showed startling self-assurance. Swift & Company advertised for an ad manager. After scouting the firm and finding it acceptable, he showed up at the offices and announced that he had come to take the job. He was told that there were 105 other applicants. "I was astounded," he noted. "One hundred and six men considered themselves fitted for that high position. What effrontery!" But capturing the job was child's play. For three weeks he wrote a newspaper column on advertising for nothing, sending each issue to Swift, and he also had the firm deluged with laudatory letters about him, written by every conceivable acquaintance that he could mobilize in a short, sharp campaign.

At Swift the problem child was a shortening called Cotosuet, and Hopkins was unable to find any way in which it differed from its competitors. So he simply sold it—in record amounts—by the use of circus methods, mainly pitchmen-demonstrators in stores. To draw crowds he had Cotosuet used in the baking of giant cakes, put on display as the Biggest Cake in the World. Publicity that P. T. Barnum would have applauded marked the promotion in each city. Local papers were carefully primed with tales about the record crowds elsewhere ("so big that women fainted and police reserves had to be called out") and newsboys were bribed to cry, "All About the Big Cake!" But Swift proved to be an uncongenial home for Hopkins; he felt that they "didn't understand the basic principles of advertising" when they refused to let him use a coupon offering free samples. He moved rapidly on to writing ads for a patent medicine—Dr. Shoop's Restorative—and for Schlitz beer.

At Schlitz there were glimpses of Hopkins's developing technique. Previous beer ads had generally apostrophized The Product as "pure." He snorted at this: "Platitudes and generalities roll off the human understanding. The claim made no impression. The bigger the type used, the bigger the folly." Hopkins went through the brewery, searching for "reasons-why." His ads came out with torrents of them. There was the wonderful "mother yeast cell" that had been selected after 1,018 different experiments to obtain that matchless flavor; there were the special wells driven 4,000 feet into the ground; the snowy filters through which every drop of beer was passed; and, as evidence of unceasing concern for the best, the fact that empty bottles were sterilized with live steam. The most powerful ad in the campaign was headlined: "Washed With Live Steam!"

Like the Bissell people before them, Schlitz executives had a feeling that Hopkins must have been woolgathering on the plant tour. Did he not realize that *all* breweries cleaned their empties with steam? Hopkins huffed that he hadn't claimed Schlitz was the only brewery to do it, and besides, competitors would now be reluctant to make what would seem like copycat claims. Just be the first to make a claim, he pontificated, and you preempt it as your own. He was pleased but not surprised when sales of Schlitz beer shot from fifth place to a tie for first.

Another kind of jaunty realism appeared in his work for Dr. Shoop. Here it was not enough to make claims; patent-medicine ads seethed with claims. Some new selling lever was needed. He devised a two-pronged scheme: the customer was offered six bottles for the price of five, and if after taking as directed and still feeling his health unimproved, the customer could apply to the druggist for a warrant that would get him his money back. This approach turned out to be very successful, with low redemption costs on the money-back offer. Dr. Shoop's Restorative was never healthier. Hopkins theorized that it worked on the psychological principle underlying all patent-medicine successes: the ads appealed to suggestible people who, in general, *did* feel better after gulping down the stuff.

The theory was sound enough as far as it went, but this seems to have been one of the few times where, in the light of later findings, Hopkins may have missed a bet. In the 1930s and 1940s another self-assured advertising man named Duane Jones explored further the shadowy recesses of the money-back offer. (Jones, by the way, is still remembered with awe as the fellow who once imported ten tons of rock from an Irish quarry not far from Blarney Castle. His ads pulled a flabbergasting 408,000 orders for Blarney Stone Charm Bracelets, offered for twenty-five cents plus a label from The Product. The stunt alarmed the Irish government into a hasty regulation prohibiting the exportation to America of Blarney-type stone, lest it impair the tourist trade.)

Jones discovered that if you entice a housewife into buying several bars of soap or a few cans of food by means of a money-back offer, and if you require her to make just a little effort to obtain the money (return the labels with a letter explaining why the product was not satisfactory), the natural laws of human inertia hold redemption costs down to low levels. This handy finding was one that Hopkins almost, but didn't quite, discover.

With the country guided toward marked increases in consumption of Cotosuet and carpet sweepers, Schlitz and Dr. Shoop's Restorative, Hopkins's career was fairly on its way. The elements that were to make him one of advertising's most golden practitioners by the twenties were already evident by 1907. He was abnormally hard-working; he loathed golf; during one ten-year period he worked every night until midnight and almost every weekend. He believed fervently that to sell in mass he had to speak to people in the mass, with utmost simplicity and force. He had to give them scores of reasons why they should want The Product—simple, selfish, self-advantaging reasons. Hopkins had a disenchanted view of people as buyers: "People are like sheep. They cannot judge values; neither can you and I. We judge things largely by others' impressions, by popular favor. We go with the crowd. The most effective thing I have ever found in advertising is the trend of the crowd."

After his whirl with Dr. Shoop, Hopkins came upon Liquozone. It was an ailing and moribund germicide, and he received a part interest for promoting it. He plunged with furious energy into this promotion, and drove it up to a net of $1.8 million in his first year. After five years Liquozone was a world-wide success, and Hopkins had driven himself into a nervous breakdown. He spent three months in resting furiously and drinking milk.

Meanwhile a chance encounter between two men then strangers to him switched his career onto a new track. Albert Lasker, leading light of the booming Chicago agency of Lord & Thomas, chanced to meet Cyrus H. K. Curtis in the diner of a train. Curtis, an abstemious man whose thriving magazines carried no liquor ads, announced that he was going to order a bottle of beer for the first time in his life. He had just read a remarkable ad for Schlitz beer. Why didn't Lasker find out, he went on, knocking the ash from his cigar, who had written the kind of ad that could do that?

"SO FAR as I know," Hopkins once observed, "no ordinary human being has ever resisted Albert Lasker." He was explaining why he came to work at Lord & Thomas at a time when he didn't want the job, and the explanation was almost adequate. Lasker *was* one of the most persuasive men in the history of American business.

Lasker had been born in 1880 in Galveston. A genial and energetic lad, he had at twelve written, sold ads for, and published the standard juvenile newspaper. (A sense of dramatic timing was already evident: his ten-year-old brother was appointed collector of advertising revenue, and "as I walked out of the place he would skip in to collect the money.")

In his teens Lasker worked as a stringer for a New Orleans newspaper, and years later he admitted to a classic cub-reporter embarrassment. Assigned to cover a play in the Galveston Opera House, he filed a judicious but purely imaginary review and then went off to see a girl —only to discover the next day that the Opera House had burned down. It is not recorded if this is what ended his newspaper career; but in any event he shortly presented himself, a bright and shining lad of eighteen, at the offices of Lord & Thomas in Chicago. He was hired as a clerk at ten dollars a week. What followed outdid Horatio Alger. In six years, at twenty-four, he was a partner in the firm, taking home $52,000 a year.

One element in this extraordinary rise can be discerned during his earliest apprenticeship. He went to A. L. Thomas, one of the agency's founders, and asked if he could "practice the craft" on one or two old, small accounts. The first one on which he "practiced" was the sleepy little account of the Wilson Ear Drum Company; and such was his persuasiveness that the firm was startled to find that it had suddenly begun to sell unprecedented numbers of Ear Drums. Speaking years later, Lasker admitted that "I hadn't known what advertising was. I was like the fellow who uses electricity but who doesn't know what force it is. Sometimes he doesn't get the right results; sometimes he does."

His failings, if any, as a knowing copywriter were unimportant. Lasker quickly developed into a superb salesman, and his specialty was selling Lord & Thomas. He was a prototype of what has come to be a crucial agency partner: the quick-witted, hard-driving, slightly piratical person who

Magic

Lies in pretty teeth—Remove that film

Why will any woman in these days have dingy film on teeth?

There is now a way to end it. Millions of people employ it. You can see the results in glistening teeth everywhere you look.

This is to offer a ten-day test, to show *you* how to beautify the teeth.

Film is cloudy

Film is that viscous coat you feel. It clings to the teeth, enters crevices and stays. When left it forms the basis of tartar. Teeth look discolored more or less.

But film does more. It causes most tooth troubles.

It holds food substances which ferment and form acid. It holds the acid in contact with the teeth to cause decay.

Germs breed by millions in it. They, with tartar, are the chief cause of pyorrhea.

Avoid Harmful Grit

Pepsodent curdles the film and removes it without harmful scouring. Its polishing agent is far softer than enamel. Never use a film combatant which contains harsh grit.

You leave it

Old ways of brushing leave much of that film intact. It dims the teeth and, night and day, threatens serious damage. That's why so many well-brushed teeth discolor and decay. Tooth troubles have been constantly increasing. So dental science has been seeking ways to fight that film.

A new-type tooth paste has been perfected, correcting some old mistakes. These two film combatants are embodied in it. The name is Pepsodent, and by its use millions now combat that film.

Two other foes

It also fights two other foes of teeth. It multiplies the starch digestant in the saliva. To digest starch deposits on teeth which may otherwise cling and form acids.

It multiplies the alkalinity of the saliva. To neutralize mouth acids which cause tooth decay.

Lives altered

Whole lives may be altered by this better tooth protection. Dentists now advise that children use Pepsodent from the time the first tooth appears. It will mean a new dental era.

The way to know this is to send the coupon for a 10-Day Tube. Note how clean the teeth feel after using. Mark the absence of the viscous film. See how teeth whiten as the film-coats disappear.

See and feel the new effects, then read the reasons in the book we send.

Cut out the coupon now.

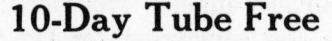
133

goes out and drags in the business. The new account sometimes must be pried away from some other agency; this has of course been most common in recent decades. But in Lasker's early great days there was a high proportion of "missionary work." This consisted of finding firms that didn't advertise—or not enough, or not in the right way—and grasping them by the corporate lapels and explaining, charming, and persuading them into employing Lord & Thomas.

In seeking new accounts Lasker discovered that his agency, like others, was weak in the special services it could offer. In 1898, the year he was hired, Lord & Thomas had one staff copywriter, paid forty dollars a week, and one staff artist, paid thirty-five. This was not skill of sufficient order, particularly for the kind of agency salesmanship Lasker was good at. Further, it contrasted unfavorably with the situation at some businesses that already advertised heavily, notably the patent-medicine makers. Here individual firms often had better copywriters than the agencies, and paid them more. Aware of this weakness, Lasker buttressed his solicitations by describing, in glowing terms, all the gifted newspapermen that he would put on the job.

This was changed dramatically a few months after he became a partner. Lasker was chatting with Thomas one afternoon when a card was sent up from the barroom downstairs. It bore the name of John E. Kennedy, and scribbled on it was the question: "Do you know what advertising really is?" Neither Lasker nor Thomas had ever heard of Kennedy, but Lasker, with a flicker of curiosity, invited the stranger up. He proved to be a lanky and handsome eccentric, an ex-member of the Royal Canadian Mounted Police. He was now the star copywriter for Dr. Shoop

in Racine. "Advertising," this oracle pronounced with maximum portentousness, his handle-bar mustaches quivering like antennae, "is Salesmanship in Print!"

Lasker hired Kennedy away from Dr. Shoop (unwittingly creating the opening through which Claude Hopkins got his patent-medicine training). He paid Kennedy a then-unprecedented $28,000 a year plus expenses—and promptly set about publicizing it. Lord & Thomas had captured for its clients the most gifted and costly copywriter in the world, fresh from patent-medicine triumphs. Salesmanship in Print became the agency's war cry—the magic ingredient that distinguished Lord & Thomas from lesser agencies that were able to offer only futile "sloganizing." A hint of the impresario introducing the unique artist marked Lasker's management of Kennedy. He let it be known that he himself sat at Kennedy's feet, to learn all he could of Salesmanship in Print. Kennedy's dogma—that advertising should be plausible, persuasive, and emotion-oriented—was also imparted to a group of bright young ex-newspapermen.

It was far from being *all* theatrics. Lasker and Kennedy deliberately set out to make a third of Lord & Thomas's volume mail-order accounts. This form of advertising was demanding but also highly instructive. The comparative mail response to different appeals provided a sensitive meter of success; mail order was the best way to measure how powerful an approach actually was. Then, after a few years of learning while earning, Lasker gradually dropped most of the mail-order accounts, for they were potentially less profitable. As Lasker put it: "They were the great laboratory in which to learn, but after you have learned it, it is like having learned to be an actor in the hard school of stock company in a small town. The reward is on Broadway."

Lord & Thomas boomed under this mixture of hoopla and shrewdness. Billings doubled and quadrupled; and Lasker predicted, correctly as it turned out, that this was only the beginning. Kennedy resigned in 1907, to the accompaniment of such jets of praise from Lasker as to lead

Hired away from Dr. Shoop, John E. Kennedy was billed as Lord & Thomas's great find, the best and most highly paid copywriter in the world. This photo is from *Advertising Age*.

to the speculation that his departure did not occasion real grief: "It was our good fortune that he came to us as the instrument through which to make known his principles to the world. But we also are . . . entitled to be given the credit, just as they have to give the credit to Queen Isabella and King Ferdinand for sending Columbus on his trip." The agency then had more copywriters than any other, but Lasker felt the need to describe a new resident genius when soliciting new accounts.

So when Cyrus Curtis ordered his bottle of Schlitz, Lasker sought out Hopkins, then convalescent from his breakdown. It seems to have taken little effort for Lasker to persuade him to give up free-lancing and Liquozone—though Hopkins did keep his hand in on the latter, rather as a hobby, like blooded cattle, until the Federal food and drug laws took the fun out of it. Lasker's persuasion was made up of a shrewd combination: a judicious reminder that the days of Liquozone were numbered; the seductions of profit sharing; a fat advertising contract from Van Camp Packing Company that had been the despair of lesser copywriters—all presented with lavish applications of Lasker charm. For a moment Hopkins hesitated; he wasn't really well yet. So Lasker set the hook: if Hopkins would just dash off three Van Camp ads, Mrs. Hopkins could buy herself the most luxurious auto she could find in the city of Chicago, and charge it to Lord & Thomas. That did it, and Hopkins joined the firm at $1,000 a week (a sum soon doubled and tripled by commissions). Lasker himself delivered the ultimate accolade: "I soon found that Mr. Hopkins was even a stage further advanced than Mr. Kennedy had been."

FOR SEVENTEEN YEARS, until Hopkins left Lord & Thomas in 1924, he and Lasker were *enfants terribles* of American advertising. Each was restless, fast-moving, enormously energetic, and compulsively driven to salesmanship. They alternated in having nervous breakdowns—later described as taking a few months off for reasons of health. (Lasker's first, in 1912, came shortly after he became the sole proprietor of Lord & Thomas at thirty-two; and it was peculiarly incapacitating for so fluent a salesman: he could not talk for more than five minutes without crying.) The two men worked together well as a team, considering that few such intensely egotistic people had walked the earth since Napoleon I.

Their teamwork showed off at its best in a rite known behind the scenes at Lord & Thomas as "staging." This consisted of building up, to a prospective client, the Lord & Thomas official that he was about to meet for the first time. As a rule Lasker would not approach a prospect until underlings had paved the way, explaining that by great good fortune the prospect was about to meet the brilliant and farsighted young proprietor of Lord & Thomas. Then Lasker would appear, charming, disarming, impressively informed about the client's affairs. With fine dramatic artistry Lasker would tell the fellow that, by good fortune, he was to have a chance to meet the greatest copywriter in the world, the selling genius, the incomparable. When Claude Hopkins then strode in on cue, an employee once noted, the prospect was moistly prepared to shake hands with deity. More important, the situation had changed by imperceptible steps from that of a potential client to that of a supplicant.

Such charades would have meant little except for the fact that Hopkins *was* an incomparable copywriter and a marketing man of great acumen. His diagnosis of Puffed Wheat and Puffed Rice (page 70) was so profitable that the company remained a client until 1938, six years after Hopkins's death, when Lasker resigned the account in a moment of exasperation. Hopkins's early auto advertising set patterns that the industry followed for years.

His work for Van Camp's pork and beans was followed with admiration throughout the food industry. Van Camp's beans had posed a problem. As Hopkins noted later: fine beans but in no way different from competitors' beans. So with an instinct for the illogic that appears to motivate the mass housewife, he argued that since husbands often chose them for lunch in restaurants,

A $100,000 Dish

New-Type Baked Beans Which College-Trained Scientific Cooks Have Spent Years in Perfecting

It has cost us at least $100,000 to perfect Van Camp's Pork and Beans.

Modern culinary experts—men with college training—have devoted some years to this dish. Able scientists and famous chefs have co-operated with them.

This Was Wrong

Old-style baked beans were very hard to digest. They were always under-baked. Yet the baking crisped them and broke them—made some hard and some mushy.

In the Van Camp kitchens each lot of beans is analyzed before we start to cook. They are boiled in water freed from minerals, because hard water makes them tough.

They are baked in steam ovens by live steam under pressure at 245 degrees. They are thus baked for hours—baked as beans should be—without bursting or crisping a bean.

856 Sauces

The zestful sauce which we bake with Van Camp's would itself give the dish distinction.

But these scientific cooks made 856 sauces before they attained this perfection. This ideal tang and savor came only through months of development.

A far greater accomplishment was to fit baked beans for easy digestion, while leaving them mealy and whole.

This Is Perfect

The result is a new-type dish which will change your whole idea of baked beans. It will multiply their popularity. Above all, it will not tax digestion.

And it costs you less—all ready-baked—than do home-baked beans. Please order a trial meal.

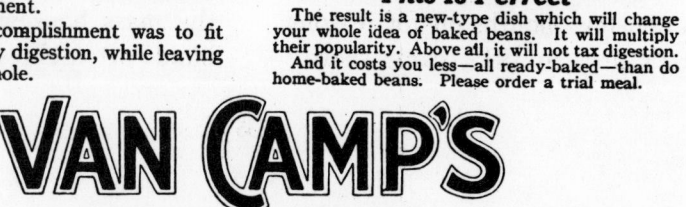

VAN CAMP'S

Pork and Beans

Baked With the Van Camp Sauce — Also Baked Without the Sauce

they should get the same beans at home. He scattered out coupons for free samples like Johnny Appleseed (get them to *ask* for a sample and they value it more highly than an unsolicited gift; besides, they've already read the ad, which means they're prepared to find the characteristics described; and finally, relative coupon returns let you compare the strength of different appeals). When a survey suggested that as much as 94 per cent of all housewives were in the habit of baking their own beans, Hopkins speedily mounted a campaign that inveighed against this pernicious practice:

I told of the sixteen hours required to bake beans at home. I told why home baking could never make beans digestible. I pictured home-baked beans, with the crisped beans on top, the mushy beans below. I told how we selected our beans, of the soft water we used, of our steam ovens where we baked beans for hours at 245 degrees. Then I offered a free sample for comparison. The result was an enormous success.

Lasker, meantime, in part to show his faith in Lord & Thomas advertising, invested money in Van Camp until he owned a quarter of the firm. (Both men tended, in the heat of selling enthusiasms, to buy pieces of client companies. At least, it helped hold the client.) It was through Van Camp that in 1918 Lasker met Will H. Hays, himself a highly persuasive type, who pointed out that the Republican Party was then in sorry shape. "The thing they needed most was propaganda," Lasker commented, and they wanted someone who'd had experience with "sick businesses and had made them well." This was the start of Lasker's public-relations labors for the Republican Party—an immeasurably important factor in the election of Warren G. Harding—and of Lasker's later service as chairman of Harding's Shipping Board.

As though to prove that his virtuosity was not limited to low-priced products, Hopkins took enthusiastically to auto and auto-accessory advertising. In the early days of auto advertising the problem was not so much to pack in selling reasons-why, but to make potential buyers believe that cars had really become practical.

Hopkins's formula was to dramatize the "man behind the car"—the company owner or the chief engineer—on the theory that if the public could be led to have confidence in the man, it would then have confidence in his product.

This worked well, and once too well. After Hopkins got through plugging Howard E. Coffin, chief engineer for the Chalmers car, the government stepped in and plucked him out to head the aircraft board in World War I. John Willys—a small auto dealer who had picked up his auto company more or less inadvertently by paying its $450 payroll in time of crisis—was advanced $200,000 worth of advertising by the agency, and then rapidly turned into a national figure. But perhaps the ultimate in this man-behind-the-car approach occurred when Reo applied for the privilege of some Lord & Thomas magic. R. E. Olds was told that his company would be acceptable to the agency on a number of conditions. One was that he would have to sign the ads with his name. "Then I stipulated," Hopkins said later, "that he call it 'My Farewell Car.' That to signify a degree of finality, and his satisfaction with it. 'But,' he replied, 'I don't intend to retire.' I said that was unnecessary. Sarah Bernhardt made seven farewell tours. He could have two or three. Every farewell is subject to reconsideration."

During the great growing years no one could predict when, under the warming light of a new appeal, an insignificant account would spurt up into a dazzling multimillion-dollar one. One bright morning two Milwaukee businessmen arrived at Lord & Thomas to talk about advertising their Galvanic Soap, a laundry soap. After some palaver it was regretfully decided to avoid entering so competitive a field. Did they have anything else? Well, there *was* a toilet soap made from olive and palm oils, but it had almost no distribution. "Sensing the germ of an advertising opportunity," Lasker and Hopkins persuaded the soapmakers to blow $700 on a test campaign in Benton Harbor, Michigan. It would stress the "beauty appeal" and it would end with a coupon offering a cake of Palmolive soap at any drugstore. (This

Hopkins touch is unmistakable in the ad at left: the
less numerical details; the jabbing sentences; and
t medicine's Not-This-But-Instead-This argument.

was a developing way of "forcing" distribution: the retailer would stock the product so that he could get the redemption money from the manufacturer.)

The little Benton Harbor trial was very promising; similar tests in different cities confirmed the results; a national magazine campaign was hastily mounted. It proved to be even more successful than the local trials. "We had only dimly recognized the strength of the beauty appeal," Hopkins explained, busily preparing ads that indicated that Cleopatra, as well as the most stunning Roman beauties, habitually used soaps remarkably like Palmolive.

One of the agency's greatest triumphs was the Goodyear tire account. It had been fairly small at first, about $40,000 a year; but with the growth of the industry and Hopkins's intensive plugging, Goodyear developed into one of the country's biggest tire makers, spending from $1,500,000 to $2,000,000 a year on advertising. Accordingly, it was an abrupt shock when Goodyear suddenly took the account away. Lasker put the loss at his own door; the client had wanted more and better art, he said, but he had not given it to them. Hopkins, somewhat tartly, put the loss down to himself: "There developed a desire for institutional advertising which I could never approve. It is natural. Great success brings to most men a desire to boast a little. Boasting is the last thing people want to hear. It isn't salesmanship."

But a third explanation arose from something that has brought nightmares to many an agency proprietor since: loss by defection. Several young Lord & Thomas executives resigned and formed a new firm (it later became Erwin Wasey & Company), and when the dust settled, it could be seen that the Goodyear account was its nucleus. Later, with fitting irony, several young executives resigned from Erwin Wasey to form what became the Kudner Agency, and the Goodyear account was *its* nucleus. Even when they didn't take accounts with them, young men trained in the ways of Lord & Thomas were constantly disappearing, either pirated away at higher salaries elsewhere, or else plunging into the enticing gamble of self-employment. An astonishing number of advertising-agency men in the twenties and thirties received their original training at Lord & Thomas.

To virtually everyone in the business Hopkins remained the First and Greatest of the copywriters. As such, he allowed himself the luxury of a few eccentricities. One was an attitude of guarded suspicion toward the art department. It was *words* that sold The Product, he maintained, and not space-wasting pictures. (This position has made Hopkins a kind of patron saint for all subsequent copywriters, because a classic cobra-mongoose relationship prevails in most agencies between copywriters and art directors. The latter complain that copywriters are dim-eyed barbarians who come around with ghastly scrawls they call "roughs." Copywriters hold that most art directors are semiliterate charlatans more concerned with superficial looks than with content.)

Another Hopkins quirk was opposition to any effort to inject playfulness or humor into advertisements. "Money comes slowly and by sacrifice," he wrote, battering his point home by sledge-hammer sentences. "Few people have enough. The average person is constantly choosing between one way to spend and another. Appeal for money in a lightsome way and you will never get it. People do not buy from clowns."

The same instinct for the jugular showed up in his contempt for soft, gentle, or fuzzy ads:

The people that you address are selfish, as we all are. They care nothing about your interest or your profit. They seek service for themselves. Ignoring this fact is a common mistake and a costly mistake in advertising. Ads say in effect, "Buy my brand. Give me the trade you give to others. Let me have the money." That is not a popular appeal. Whatever people do they do to please themselves.

The great man's attitude toward research was, to use a word he would have scorned, ambivalent. He had no objection to what he called "data" —information about the product. As his time grew inconveniently valuable, he would send others on the plant tour, to write memoranda on

Palmolive

The successor to ordinary toilet soaps in Particular Homes. Made of Pure Imported Olive and Palm Oils skillfully blended and combined with Cocoa Butter. **Palmolive** is not merely a cleanser, it combines all the virtues of the wonderful ingredients from which it is made. It allays irritation and inflammation and supplies the necessary oils for harsh skins and dry scalps.

Palmolive exercises the skin in that it stimulates the action of the many tiny pores and glands. The removal of all obstacles allows free circulation of the blood, and the delicate nourishment embodied in **Palmolive** supplies just the necessary impetus to restore the skin to its proper condition after cleansing it. Continued use will produce a beautiful, healthy, rosy complexion. There is no complexion that **Palmolive** cannot improve. If your dealer cannot supply you, send us his name and 15 cents and we will forward, prepaid, a full size cake.

Send four cents in stamps, to cover cost of mailing, and the *names of your grocer and druggist*, and we will send one of our beautiful oriental photogravures without advertising upon it, suitable for framing, size 10 x 16 inches. Address,

B. J. JOHNSON SOAP CO., 318 Fowler St., Milwaukee, Wis.

One of the early successes of Lord and Thomas was the promotion of Palmolive Soap. Here a noble Egyptian—Cleopatra, possibly, or Pharaoh's daughter—sports anachronistically with the Product. Attendants stand by with the ingredients.

Claude C. Hopkins in the 1920s. A *Printer's Ink* photo.

how The Product was made. But he was often thorny about research that purported to tell him about the public. He claimed that knowing the public was *his* job; he spent days and weeks, even at a time when his earnings were $300,000 a year, in poring over coupon returns, and in going out and talking to people. His forays to chat with the public were far more useful, he once said acidly, than "impressions gained from golf-club associates."

He did concede that market research might tell you what people thought they wanted of a product, thus permitting you to tell them that the product did indeed have just these traits. This technique once gave him a showy success, after Palmolive put a shaving cream on the market for the first time. Hopkins had hundreds of men interviewed to find out what they most desired in a shaving cream. Then he took the results to Palmolive's chief chemist and asked for specific, numerical values for claims in these areas—that

the cream multiplied itself in lather 250 times, that in less than one minute the beard absorbed 15 per cent of the water in the lather, and so on. (He was a great one for specific, numerical claims: "General statements count for little; a definite statement is usually accepted.") Again he was pleased but not surprised when sales of Palmolive's shaving cream shot upward.

Probably Hopkins acquired some of his skepticism about research from Lasker, who bragged that he would discard any research, however elaborate, if it didn't coincide with his own intuition. Hopkins resembled Edison in being scornful of scholarly disciplines, as compared to his own endless tinkering and testing. One of his most celebrated triumphs was with a tooth paste, Pepsodent, and here he used a coupon and free trial offer as a mechanism to test every detail in the ads. (It was a profitable account, even apart from commissions. He bought a $13,000 share in the tooth paste; it paid him $200,000 in dividends,

140

Albert D. Lasker as a young man. From *Advertising Age*.

and then he sold the stock for $500,000.) By the time Hopkins had his Pepsodent ads polished up, they read like the distilled essence of selling copy. Even now, more than thirty years later, his short, jabbing sentences pound at a reader with an echo of the force that propelled Hopkins into advertising immortality. In a typical one there is a small, cheap drawing of a woman having teeth of unearthly whiteness. Reeling groggily behind her is an enraptured male ("women desire beauty largely because of men—always show them using their beauty, as women do use it, to gain maximum effect"). There are stacked up three tested and proven headlines:

THOSE PEARLY SMILES

Do what they do——millions of them
Fight the dingy film on teeth

There is a way to whiter teeth, to greater beauty, sweeter smiles. You know that if you look about.

Millions are using a new way of teeth cleaning. They combat the film, which other millions leave.

Go now to your dealer and ask for a free test of this new-day method.

Most teeth are unclean

Most teeth are coated more or less by film. You feel it now—that viscous coat. Leave it and it soon discolors, forming dingy coats. That is how teeth lose luster.

No ordinary toothpaste effectively combats it. So well-brushed teeth may suffer.

Film causes most tooth troubles. It holds food substance which ferments and forms acid. It holds the acid in contact with the teeth to cause decay. Germs breed by the millions in it. They, with tartar, are the chief cause of pyorrhea.

A serious matter

Film is a serious matter. So dental science has long sought ways to fight it. Two have been found. One disintegrates the film at all stages of formation. One removes it without harmful scouring.

Many careful tests have proved these methods effective. A new-type toothpaste has been created to apply them daily. The name is Pepsodent.

[and so on for several hundred more words]

141

Chapter 10 | Send No Money

He Never Amounted to Much in School— *But Look at Him Today!*

OFTEN advertising seems to produce absolutely no results. An agency may capture a promising new client, devote its best skills to generating an advertising campaign, test and polish its ads until they shine with a high commercial gloss, and confidently launch the campaign—only to have it disappear into silence. Sales of The Product may continue to inch downward, upward, or sideways in precisely the same way as before the campaign. The large sums spent may, for all that can be measured in sales, have just as well been donated to the Society for the Propagation of Polynesian Missionaries, or used to light the client's cigars.

This absence of visible results is too commonplace to be surprising. But if a difficult client does hoist an eyebrow, there are dozens of ways, also tested, by which to account for it. Survey reports are usually available to show that the ads had remarkable readership, and the figures can be interpreted to show something called "steadily increasing penetration of the product

142

Just Pay Postman

One of the greatest advertising men I have ever known once said, 'If you can place an advertisement in a publication and get a traceable response from 1/10 of 1% of the readers of that publication, you have an outstandingly successful advertisement.'
—Aesop Glim, in *Printers' Ink*

image." If more figures seem to be called for, there are always such meaningful barometric indices as deseasonalized department-store sales, new Federal figures about the incidence of three-children families in one-family dwellings, and the recent abnormal rainfall in the Mississippi Basin. Doubts can be delicately planted about pricing, packaging, or a hidden dry rot that has begun to assail the dealers. It is possible to discourse with great persuasiveness about repetition, continuity, saturation, the need to fill consumption pipelines, and the fact that Rome was not built in a single campaign. The ads can be interpreted as a commercial as well as an artistic triumph: "Just think of how terrible sales would have been if you *hadn't* had the foresight to authorize that campaign!"

It must be remembered, moreover, that ads are run for other reasons than selling The Product. They may be intended to make the dealers feel deeply loved, or to encourage salesmen in the faith that the home office is back of them every inch of the way. Not a little advertising— including many automobile and insurance ads— is aimed at *current* owners of The Product. The intent is to confirm the wisdom of the purchase, to give clues to The Product's virtues,. and to cultivate loyalty against the day of replacement.

Occasionally ads are slanted toward the firm's stockholders who, like product owners, are known to read "their" ads with great assiduity. Still other ads are planned to wage psychological warfare against competitors or regulatory agencies, to impress the firm's president's social acquaintances, or to cosset the board chairman's wife, an inaccessible and often dangerous critic.

A great deal of national advertising is thus obscure not only in result but in intent—a kind of costly faith offering, spent in part to avert the misfortunes that traditionally await firms that let their advertising slide, and in part to achieve a variety of other results. Nothing could be farther from the truth, however, in one special subdivision of advertising. This subdivision is mail order, and it is a world where almost everything, rather than nothing, is known. In mail order results can often be tabulated to the penny—an exact casting-up of costs in comparison with earnings. Misty faith is replaced in mail order with an exactness approaching that of the physical sciences.

Mail-order advertising is generally, but not necessarily, identifiable by the presence of a coupon in the ad. (It shouldn't be confused with direct-mail advertising, where the ad itself arrives in the mail, masquerading as a letter.

"Here's an Extra $50, Grace
—I'm making <u>real</u> money now!"

"Yes, I've been keeping it a secret until pay day came. I've been promoted with an increase of $50 a month. And the first extra money is yours. Just a little reward for urging me to study at home. The boss says my spare time training has made me a valuable man to the firm and there's more money coming soon. We're starting up easy street, Grace, thanks to you and the I. C. S.!"

The appeals of extra money, ecstatic female admiration, and a lordly gesture set thousands to filling out the coupon. This correspondence-school ad first appeared in 1919.

Correspondence schools, phonograph records, marriage manuals, and such oddments as genuine horse-shoe dinner gongs are typical products advertised by mail order. Appeals in the mail for magazine subscriptions, or soft-shell pecans, or a new dormitory for your university are direct mail.) Mail-order advertising is worth examination because it is an island of rocky truths in the sea of general advertising, and because its tough teachings are at the core of all earnest efforts to persuade in print.

MAIL-ORDER advertising reached ripe maturity in the twenties, but it was in existence long before that. Seventy-five years ago magazines carried ads inviting their readers to buy by mail. In the eighties some advertisers had already invented "keys"—inconspicuous variations in the firm's address, or special box numbers, drawers, or departments. These were important because they permitted comparing the effectiveness of different ads, or different magazines and papers. The feasibility of selling, delivering, and collecting by mail was demonstrated early by the success of Richard W. Sears, whose little catalogues for watches grew rapidly into the mammoth Sears, Roebuck and Company.

The idea of a coupon in the corner of an ad—a device to stimulate a person to immediate action, to remind him to give his name and address, and to identify the ad and magazine that brought him to this desirable state of activity—was invented shortly before the turn of the century by Ralph Tilton. A picturesque early ad man, son of the Mrs. Tilton in the celebrated Tilton–Henry Ward Beecher scandal in Brooklyn in the 1870s, Tilton contributed an original and often bizarre note to everything he touched. He was always attended on calls about New York City by an elegant expense-account hansom cab. Once he chartered a special train from New York to Chicago in an effort to win an account, loading it with associates, friends, chorus girls, cigarettes specially monogrammed for the occasion, and a favorite French chef installed in the diner. The stunt did help him win the account although the expense, to Tilton's vexed surprise, was higher than the commissions it brought in.

He once solved a troublesome advertising problem by an expedient much whispered about in the trade. He was at the time ad manager of a large women's magazine and was about to lose an important corset account. The difficulty was that all photographs of models displaying The Product were unsatisfactory to the client—the best photographers in the city couldn't keep The Product from looking bunchy and wrinkled. So Tilton had the models photographed in the nude, and then had The Product air-brushed onto the pictures, sleek, unwrinkled, and a delight to the client.

One early success for mail-order advertising was in the sale of books. At first, near the turn of the century, this was a low-volume, high-markup business in which impressively bound sets of classics were sold to middle-class housewives, a group then becoming increasingly sensitive to status. Pope, Dickens, and Carlyle were favorites; a singularly unreadable set of tomes called Ridpath's *History of the World* was a big seller. At first it was rarely possible to complete the transaction by mail; most coupon returners hesitated to spend fifty or seventy-five dollars for even the

"See Here, Tockstein, We Need You in Our Business"

How a Patriotic Letter Carrier Came to be Deluged with Fine Business Offers

In Fresno, California, there is a wide-awake young man named Tockstein. Until recently, he wore the blue-gray uniform of the Post Office and delivered letters for Uncle Sam. He was ambitious, and he knew that to get on he must not look for aid outside himself but within.

He had very little time and he was always very tired when he was through with his day's work. But he found a way—and that way is open to you too. The first result of his new way was that he sold 37,744 thrift stamps in one day—breaking all records—simply because he had learned a new way to do the work of three people in one short day without getting tired.

And the next result was that because of his record-breaking feat, he has had offer after offer from responsible business houses at a big increase in salary. He hasn't decided yet which to take—they are all so good.

Now what he did was simple. He sent a coupon like the one at the bottom of this page for

An arresting headline, and an anecdote to set prospects dreaming, led here to a mail course in "personal efficiency."

145

"He Deposits $500 a Month!"

"See that man at the Receiving Teller's window? That's Billy King, Manager for Browning Company. Every month he comes in and deposits $500. I've been watching Billy for a long time—take almost as much interest in him as I do in my own boy.

"Three years ago he started at Browning's at $15 a week. Married, had one child, couldn't save a cent. One day he came in here desperate—wanted to borrow a hundred dollars—wife was sick.

"I said, 'Billy, I'm going to give you something worth more than a loan—some good advice—and if you'll follow it I'll let you have the hundred, too. You don't want to work for $15 a week all your life, do you?' Of course he didn't. 'Well,' I said, 'there's a way to climb out of your job to something better. Take up a course with the International Correspondence Schools in the work you want to advance in, and put in some of your evenings getting special training. The Schools will do wonders for you—I know, we've got several I. C. S. boys right here in the bank.'

"That very night Billy wrote to Scranton and a few days later he had started studying at home. Why, in a few months he had doubled his salary! Next thing I knew he was put in charge of his department, and two months ago they made him Manager. And he's making real money. Owns his own home, has quite a little property beside, and he's a regular at that window every month. It just shows what a man can do in a little spare time."

Employers are begging for men with ambition, men who really want to get ahead in the world and are willing to prove it by training themselves in spare time to do some one thing well.

Prove that *you* are that kind of a man! The International Correspondence Schools are ready and anxious to help you prepare for something better if you'll simply give them the chance. More than two million men and women in the last 28 years have taken the I. C. S. route to more money. Over 100,000 others are getting ready in the same way right now.

Is there any reason why *you* should let others climb over you when you have the same chance they have? Surely the least you can do is to find out just what there is in this proposition for *you*. Here is all we ask: Without cost, without obligating yourself in any way, simply mark and mail this coupon.

The mail-order ad in its full flower. Note the enticing picture and headline, the anecdotal lead, the progressively smaller type, and the coupon.

Once mail-order testing techniques brought an ad close to perfection, it was sometimes run for years without change.

most decorative and culturally redolent volumes. (It was discovered, though, that a fair number of near-miss sales could be recaptured by the mailed offer of a discount of 10 or 15 per cent for "a very slightly imperfect set just found in our warehouse." Many thousands of Ridpath sets, all invisibly imperfect, were sold in this way.) But most sales had to be consummated by a silver-tongued salesman, calling in person. Akin to the lightning-rod artists of an earlier day, these men at their most brilliant were able to earn up to $35,000 a year in commissions. To use such experts in "cold" house-to-house calls was plainly inefficient, so that advertising that provided a supply of coupon leads was necessary.

Gradually mail-order book advertising moved in the direction of complete sales by mail, though on expensive sets salesmen were kept ready—as they still are—to close in on faltering customers. One spectacular early success was *The Photographic History of the Civil War*, published by the *Review of Reviews* in 1910 and advertised for several years to the tune of $350,000 a year. To the surprise of many ad men, the copy was written by a woman, Helen Woodward, one of the first female copywriters of record. She proved to be an expert practitioner of the mail-order arts, for several hundred thousand sets of *The Photographic History* were disposed of before the newer horrors of World War I cut into the business.

Mrs. Woodward later had triumphs in the mail-order sale of O. Henry and Mark Twain, but, as she noted later, she also had her failures:

Richard Harding Davis went well but Stevenson only after we had cheapened him. This was a disappointment. We had prepared such glamorous advertising of Stevenson with dashing pirates by Howard Pyle and gory captions like "One More Step and I'll Blow Your Brains Out." But the public didn't want Stevenson's pirates. With some disgust we finally succeeded in forcing Stevenson down the throat of the public by the use of such headlines as "He Wanted the Woman I Love" and "Husband or Lover—Which Did She Save?"

Mail-order book ads launched other careers. Bruce Barton—later to become not only a resident deity of Batten, Barton, Durstine & Osborn, but also author of *The Man Nobody Knows*, a book about Jesus Christ that compared His principles with those of advertising—began as a copywriter for books. He was working for P. F. Collier & Son in 1912 when he wrote his first ad for Dr. Eliot's Five Foot Shelf of books. Barton found a repossessed set kicking around the office, tore out a picture and had a cut made, and wrote the headline:

THIS IS MARIE ANTOINETTE
RIDING TO HER DEATH

He appended nine paragraphs of emphatic and persuasive copy (". . . the fascinating story of how Dr. Eliot of Harvard has picked out the few *really worth while* books out of the thousands of useless ones . . ."), and was himself immediately riding to a distinguished career—because Marie

The owner of this company once turned down a bid from a big-time copywriter. Everything about our ad, he said, was tested and perfected; we wouldn't change even a word.

pulled more than eight times as many coupons as the best that Collier's had been able to do before.

Bruce Barton turned out to be a specialist in warm, moist, inspirational copy. He pioneered in the use of something that grew to be an advertising fad in the twenties—the narrative ad, often in the form of an allegory or parable. Another specialty of his, according to partner Roy Durstine, was sincerity. ("If a man is sincere you can forgive him almost anything," Durstine once wrote. "There ought to be something about an advertisement as contagious as the measles. Without sincerity an advertisement is no more contagious than a sprained ankle.")

Barton found a chance to display practically all of these attributes in a celebrated series of coupon ads for a correspondence school, the Alexander Hamilton Institute. One particularly effective one, a kind of reverse Rake's Progress, was illustrated with a drawing showing a man standing at the foot of a large hill. He had a child perched on one shoulder, and standing beside him were a wife and second tot. Up the hill, curving slightly but leading to the gloriously sunlit hilltop, was a road. The ad began:

THE GLORY OF THE UPWARD PATH
As told in the letters of men who are traveling it

Two paths begin at the bottom of the hill of life.

One of them winds about the base, thru years of routine and drudgery. Now and then it rises over a knoll representing a little higher plane of living made possible by hard earned progress; but its route is slow and difficult and bordered with monotony.

The other mounts slowly at first, but rapidly afterwards, into positions where every problem is new and stirring, and where the rewards are comfort, and travel and freedom from all fear.

Let us glance for a moment at the letters men write who are treading this fortunate path. Such letters come to the Alexander Hamilton Institute in every mail; they are the most thrilling feature of the Institute's business day.

Exultant letters they are, full of hope and happiness; the bulletins of progress on the upward path.

My income has increased
750 per cent

Here is one from an official in the largest enterprise of its kind in the world. "In the past eight years my income has increased 750%. The Course has been the foundation in my business training."

Another from an officer in a successful manufacturing company: "Last Friday was a happy day for me: I was elected a member of the Board of Directors of this company. The day when I enrolled with

Mail order was a fine way of selling book sets, though the actual volumes were often less readable than the ads. And they gave tone to a bookshelf.

See How Easily You Can Learn to Dance This New Way

If you can do the step illustrated in the chart in lower corner, there is no reason why you cannot easily and quickly master all the latest steps through Arthur Murray's method of teaching dancing right in your own home.

the Alexander Hamilton Institute was the turning point of my career."

The glory of the upward path was spelled out for another eight paragraphs before it came to the crucial coupon.

International Correspondence Schools, an exceedingly successful mail-order advertiser, preferred to avoid the risk of confusing the reader with parables, however explicit. ICS kept close to the same themes that Barton used—a hunger to be admired, to get ahead, to have money, power, and security—but it preferred to outline them directly. In 1919 it unveiled an ad that turned out to have phenomenal pulling power. The illustration showed a man thrusting some money toward a woman. She was so ecstatic that her hands were pressed together in a gesture of delighted adoration. The headline that captioned this arresting scene:

"HERE'S AN EXTRA $50, GRACE
—I'M MAKING REAL MONEY NOW!"

A happy-reverie element was strong in a great many correspondence-school ads. Readers by the million were invited to dream of trudging powerfully up Mount Parable to the exhilarating plateaus where directorships could be plucked like edelweiss. Even those whose past careers were wholly lacking in signs of distinction weren't excluded:

FIRST PART
Forward Waltz Step

1. Begin with left foot and step directly forward weight on left foot.
2. Step diagonally forward to right placing weight on right foot (see illustration).
3. Draw left foot up to right foot weight on left.
   That's all. Simply follow the numbers in the foot-prints. Master this part before going further.

A mail-order campaign of 1923, selling a 16-lesson course in learning to dance at home, just naturally wanted to be illustrated with a still from Rudolph Valentino's "The Four Horsemen." Prospects skeptical of their ability to tango like Valentino were given a diagram of the waltz.

The Man with the "Grasshopper Mind"

"I guess I'll take up $elling"

"Ought to put over that Money-making Idea"

"Think I'll try to make my Evenings worth Something"

"Believe I'll do some Good Reading"

"Some Day I'm going to Start Out for Myself"

"Think I'll change my Job"

THE PELMAN INSTITUTE OF AMERICA

Suite 873, 71 West 45th Street, New York City

The Pelman Institute of America
Suite 873, 71 West 45th Street
New York City

Please send me without obligation your free booklet,
"Scientific Mind Training." This does not place me
under any obligation and no salesman is to call on me.

Name..

Address...

City........................State..............

HE NEVER AMOUNTED

TO MUCH IN SCHOOL—

But Look at Him Today!

Sort of a nobody in school, he was. Not stupid—just a drifter. He seemed born to be merely a cog in the world's machinery. No one would have given him a second thought if suddenly he hadn't begun to rise in his job, and to go up and up . . .

And for those whose reveries ran in different directions, there were many promising other fields such as body-building and the manly art of jujitsu. (As the lead paragraph in an ad for one set of booklets pointed out: "You are more than able to take care of yourself if you know Jujitsu. In any emergency you become a panther-like fighting machine that is best left alone.")

Narrative mail-order ads, chatty and anecdotal, were highly popular in the early twenties. It was only when a reader had made his way deep in

the ad that he discovered what was being sold him, and the discovery was usually good-humored. A few ads grew to become national jokes but the humor was affectionate as well as derisive. For obscure reasons—perhaps the rhythm of his name, or a fleeting suggestion of inexpressible fatuity—Addison Sims of Seattle became a kind of American comic hero. It was especially surprising in view of the small part that Mr. Sims played in the famous 1921 memory-course ad:

HOW I IMPROVED MY MEMORY
IN ONE EVENING
The Amazing Experience of Victor Jones

"*Of course* I place you! Mr. Addison Sims of Seattle.

"If I remember correctly—and I *do* remember correctly—Mr. Burroughs, the lumberman, introduced me to you at the luncheon of the Seattle Rotary Club, three years ago in May. This is a pleasure indeed. I haven't laid eyes on you since that day. How is the grain business? And how did that amalgamation work out?"

The assurance of this speaker—in the crowded corridor of the Hotel McAlpin—compelled me to turn and look at him, though I must say, it is not my usual habit to "listen in" even in a hotel lobby.

"He is David M. Roth, the most famous memory expert in the United States," said my friend Kennedy, answering my question before I could get it out. "He will show you a lot more wonderful things than that, before the evening is over."

And he did.

Unquestionably the most beloved of all the mail-order ads, and a magnificent piece of Walter-Mittyism, was the memorable "They Laughed When I Sat Down at the Piano But When I Started to Play!—" (Buried deep in that wordy headline is the powerful patent-medicine appeal: before-and-after-taking.) This classic advertisement was written in 1925 by John Caples, then a cub copywriter at Ruthrauff & Ryan and recent graduate from the Naval Academy. Caples is still busy in advertising, incidentally, a vice-president at Batten, Barton, Durstine & Osborn and a specialist in using mail-order techniques to measure the effectiveness of general ads. Though

"Laughed" was long—more than a thousand words—it was one of the most effective pieces of happy-reverie copy ever written:

As the last notes of the Moonlight Sonata died away, the room resounded with a sudden roar of applause. I found myself surrounded by excited faces. How my friends carried on! Men shook my hand—wildly congratulated me—pounded me on the back in their enthusiasm! Everybody was exclaiming with delight—plying me with rapid questions . . . "Jack! Why didn't you tell us you could play like that?" . . . "Where *did* you learn?"—"How long have you studied?"—"Who *was* your teacher?"

Not all mail-order ads were warmly happy, of course. Some were precisely the opposite, and set themselves to gnawing away erosively at the pillars of the reader's confidence. They unfolded the very real possibility that he was ignorant, lonely, ineptly gauche, and puny—and all needlessly so since he could perfectly well fill out that coupon *today*. In scores of magazines Lionel Strongfort, his triceps and deltoids a-bulge contemptuously, jeered at his prospective customers:

OH, YOU SKINNY!

Why stay as thin as a rail? You don't have to! And you don't have to go through life with a chest that the tailor gives you; with legs you can hardly stand on. And what about that stomach that flinches every time you try a square meal? Are you a pill feeder?

Do you expect Health and Strength in tablet form —through pills, potions and other exploited piffle?

A marked truculence, as though they could barely keep their temper when faced with these hollow-chested prospects, was evident in some of the copy from the muscle builders. Earle E. Liederman, under a glowering portrait, headlined:

DEAD FROM THE
NECK DOWN

"He thought he was alive because he worked with his brain—but his body was fit for the undertaker."

Can you imagine such a fellow calling himself a man? And still there are thousands like him narrow chested, round shouldered, weak-kneed specimens of humanity. They would rather take a box of pills than do five minutes exercise.

After several hard-sell paragraphs, Liederman finished with a notable burst of sweat-shirt prose:

If there is a spark of manhood left in you, I will give you a body to be proud of. I guarantee to put one full inch on your arms in the first 30 days. And from then on, just watch 'em grow. I will build out your chest, broaden your shoulders and put real pep in your old backbone. You will have the flash to your eye and the spring to your step of a real athlete. Your whole body (inside and out) will function as it should, sending life-giving blood to your brain and every part of your system. I don't just promise these things. I guarantee them. Come on now and make me prove it. That's what I like.

Thanks to precisely aimed advertising, a comparative late-comer named Angelo Siciliano, rechristened Charles Atlas, became in the thirties the titan of the muscles-by-mail industry. A measure of promotional instinct had been evident early in his career, and Bernarr Macfadden

Make Your Mind a File—Not a Pile
Stop Forgetting
By Prof. Henry Dickson

*The Average mind resembles a
scrap pile*

*The Dickson Trained mined is
as well ordered as a cross-
index file*

Lurking behind Professor Dickson's very graphic images was a potent principle: the patent-medicine ad device of Before and After. A suggestion of inadequacy helped, too.

"Of Course I Place You! Mr Addison Sims of Seattle"

had titled him "America's Most Perfectly Developed Man" in ceremonial rites at Madison Square Garden. Atlas possessed also a fine feeling for publicity, as when he would tow a railroad car for the edification of feature writers and photographers. But success came largely from his advertising. His strongest headline, run in conjunction with a photo showing the Atlas muscles rampant, was "I was a 97-Pound Weakling!" The copy explained that transition from a flimsy teen-ager, too feeble to climb stairs, to rippling muscularity had been achieved by "dynamic tension." This was a technique for pitting muscles against each other to obtain beneficial exercise; no equipment was needed; fill out the coupon today.

Atlas's advertising won plenty of snickers. But it was exactly on target for the biggest market for mail-order muscles: young men of sixteen to twenty-one with a pervading sense of personal inadequacy. The ads outlining Atlas's remarkable physical redemption caused young men to sign up by the hundreds of thousands.

A later modification of the campaign was quite as powerful. A puny lad, losing his girl and pride to the depredations of a beach bully, signed up for the course and promptly grew formidable muscles. Then he returned to the scene of his humiliation, poleaxed the bully with one blow, and thus won back either the original girl or a reasonable facsimile. This was essentially a saga of the heroic kind that has engrossed mankind since the beginning of history, and, when pre-

sented in comic-strip form, one that proved singularly effective in selling muscle courses. Charles Atlas, whose business still thrives and who at sixty-six has muscles that still bulge theatrically, estimates that he has by now almost a million alumni.

Of the mail-order ads that railed at their readers, one of the most widely used was for the Sherwin Cody School of English. Under the headline "Do You Make These Mistakes in English?" the bearded Mr. Cody glared hypnotically at the reader, impelling him to flee guiltily into the jaws of a powerful lead paragraph:

Many persons use such expressions as "Leave them lay there" and "Mary was invited as well as myself." Still others say "between you and I" instead of "between you and me." It is astonishing how often "who" is used for "whom" and how frequently we hear such glaring mispronunciations as "for MID able," "ave NOO," and "KEW pon." Few know whether to spell certain words with one or two "c's" or "m's" or "r's" or with "ie" or "ei," and when to use commas in order to make their meaning absolutely clear.

It was obviously desirable, when peddling something as academic as an English course, to handle the prospect gingerly, and in particular to avoid touching any sensitive scars that might have been incurred during passage through the school system. He had to be made to feel that he wasn't to blame for being a prospect; the fault was, instead, the system's:

Here is our mother-tongue, a language that has built up our civilization, and without which we should all still be muttering savages! Yet our schools, by wrong methods, have made it a study to be avoided—the hardest of tasks instead of the most fascinating of games! For years it has been a crying disgrace.

The Sherwin Cody ad was written in 1918 by Maxwell Sackheim, an enterprising ad man who has specialized in mail order since 1908. (He was one of the founders of that triumph of mail order,

152

John Caples was only twenty-five, and barely able to get through "Chopsticks," when he wrote "They Laughed" but its fame has followed him in advertising ever since. A minor contributing factor to its endurance has been such parodies as "They Laughed When I Sat Down at the Piano—Somebody Had Taken Away the Stool!" Caples had a second big success almost immediately afterward, an ad for a language course headlined "They Grinned when the Waiter Spoke to Me in French—But Their Laughter Changed to Amazement at My Reply."

"Can he really play?" a girl whispered. "Heavens, no!" Arthur exclaimed. "He never played a note in his life."

They Laughed When I Sat Down At the Piano But When I Started to Play!~

ARTHUR had just played "The Rosary." The room rang with applause. I decided that this would be a dramatic moment for me to make my debut. To the amazement of all my friends I strode confidently over to the piano and sat down.

"Jack is up to his old tricks," somebody chuckled. The crowd laughed. They were all certain that I couldn't play a single note.

"Can he really play?" I heard a girl whisper to Arthur. "Heavens, no!" Arthur exclaimed. "He never played a note in all his life...But just you watch him. This is going to be good."

I decided to make the most of the situation. With mock dignity I drew out a silk handkerchief and lightly dusted off the keys. Then I rose and gave the revolving piano stool a quarter of a turn, just as I had seen an imitator of Paderewski do in a vaudeville sketch.

"What do you think of his execution?" called a voice from the rear.

"We're in favor of it!" came back the answer, and the crowd rocked with laughter.

Then I Started to Play

Instantly a tense silence fell on the guests. The laughter died on their lips as if by magic. I played through the first bars of Liszt's immortal Liebestraume. I heard gasps of amazement. My friends sat breathless—spellbound.

I played on and as I played I forgot the people around me. I forgot the hour, the place, the breathless listeners. The little world I lived in seemed to fade—seemed to grow dim—unreal. Only the music was real. Only the music and the visions it brought me. Visions as beautiful and as changing as the wind-blown clouds and drifting moonlight, that long ago inspired the master composer. It seemed as if the master musician himself were speaking to me—speaking through the medium of music—not in words but in chords. Not in sentences but in exquisite melodies.

A Complete Triumph!

As the last notes of the Liebestraume died away, the room resounded with a sudden roar of applause. I found myself surrounded by excited faces. How my friends carried on! Men shook my hand—wildly congratulated me—pounded me on the back in their enthusiasm! Everybody was exclaiming with delight—plying me with rapid questions.... "Jack! Why didn't you tell us you could play like that?" ..."Where *did* you learn?"—"How long have you studied?"—"Who *was* your teacher?"

"I have never even *seen* my teacher," I replied. "And just a short while ago I couldn't play a note."

"Quit your kidding," laughed Arthur, himself an accomplished pianist. "You've been studying for years. I can tell."

"I have been studying only a short while," I insisted. "I decided to keep it a secret so that I could surprise all you folks."

Then I told them the whole story.

"Have you ever heard of the U. S. School of Music?" I asked. A few of my friends nodded. "That's a correspondence school, isn't it?" they exclaimed.

"Exactly," I replied. "They have a new simplified method that can teach you to play any instrument *by note* in just a few months."

How I Learned to Play Without a Teacher

And then I explained how for years I had longed to play the piano.

"It seems just a short while ago," I continued, "that I saw an interesting ad of the U. S. School of Music mentioning a new method of learning to play which only cost a few cents a day! The ad told how a woman had mastered the piano in her spare time at home—and *without a teacher!* Best of all, the wonderful new method she used required no laborious scales—no heartless exercises—no tiresome practising. It sounded so convincing that I filled out the coupon requesting the Free Demonstration Lesson.

"The free book arrived promptly and I started in that very night to study the Demonstration Lesson. I was amazed to see how easy it was to play this new way. Then I sent for the course.

"When the course arrived I found it was just as the ad said—as easy as A. B. C.! And as the lessons continued they got easier and easier. Before I knew it I was playing all the pieces I liked best. Nothing stopped me. I could play ballads or classical numbers or jazz, all with equal ease. And I never did have any special talent for music."

* * * *

Play Any Instrument

You, too, can now *teach yourself* to be an accomplished musician—right at home—in half the usual time. You can't go wrong with this simple new method which has already shown almost half a million people how to play their favorite instruments *by note.* Forget that old-fashioned idea that you need special "talent." Just read the list of instruments in the panel, decide which one you want to play and the U. S. School will do the rest. And bear in mind no matter which instrument you choose, the cost in each case will be the same—just a few cents a day. No matter whether you are a mere beginner or already a good performer, you will be interested in learning about this new and wonderful method.

Send for Our Free Booklet and Demonstration Lesson

Thousands of successful students never dreamed they possessed musical ability until it was revealed to them by a remarkable "Musical Ability Test" which we send entirely without cost with our interesting free booklet.

If you are in earnest about wanting to play your favorite instrument—if you really want to gain happiness and increase your popularity—send at once for the free booklet and Demonstration Lesson. No cost—no obligation. Sign and send the convenient coupon now. Instruments supplied when needed, cash or credit. **U. S. School of Music, 812 Brunswick Bldg., New York City.**

Pick Your Instrument

Piano	Harmony and
Organ	Composition
Violin	Sight Singing
Drums and	Ukulele
Traps	Guitar
Mandolin	Hawaiian
Clarinet	Steel Guitar
Flute	Harp
Saxophone	Cornet
'Cello	Piccolo
	Trombone
Voice and	Speech Culture
Automatic Finger	Control
Piano Accordion	
Banjo (5-String, Plectrum or Tenor)	

Both Are Embarrassed—Yet Both Could Be at Ease

And now, at the table, both are embarrassed. Indeed, can there be any discomfort greater than that of not knowing what to do at the right time—of not being sure of one's manners? It is so easy for people to misjudge us.

THEY started out happily enough at the beginning of the evening. He was sure he had found ideal companionship at last. She was sure that she was going to impress him with her charm, her cultured personality.

But everything seemed to go wrong when they entered the restaurant after the performance at the theatre. Instead of allowing her to follow the head waiter to their places, he preceded—and when he realized his mistake he tried to make up for it by being extremely polite. But he made another humiliating blunder that made even the dignified waiter conceal a smile!

And now, at the table, both are embarrassed. He is wondering whether he is expected to order for both, or allow her to order for herself. She is wondering which fork is for the salad, which for the meat. Both are trying to create conversation, but somehow everything they say seems dull, uninteresting.

They will no doubt be uncomfortable and ill at ease throughout the evening, for it is only *absolute knowledge of what is right and what is wrong* that gives calm dignity and poise. And they do not know. She finds herself wondering vaguely what she will say to him when they leave each other at her door—whether she should invite him to call again or whether he should make the suggestion; whether she should invite him into the house or not; whether she should thank him or he should thank her for a pleasant evening. And similar questions, all very embarrassing, are bothering him.

The evening that could have been extremely happy, that could have been the beginning of a delightful friendship, is spoiled. He will probably breathe a sigh of relief when he leaves, and she will probably cry herself to sleep.

How Etiquette Gives Ease

Are you always at ease among strangers, are you always calm, dignified, well-poised no matter what happens, no matter where you chance to be? You can be—if you want to. And you *should* want to, for it will give you a new charm, a new power. You will be welcomed in every social circle, you will "mix" well at every gathering, you will develop a delightful personality.

By enabling you to know exactly what to do at the right time, what to say, write and wear under all circumstances, etiquette removes all element of doubt or uncertainty. You know what is right, and you do it. There is no hesitancy, no embarrassment, no humiliating blunders. People recognize in you a person of charm and polish, a person following correct forms and polite manners.

Every day in our contact with men and women little problems of conduct arise which the well-bred person knows how to solve. In the restaurant, at the hotel, on the train, at a dance—everywhere, every hour, little problems present themselves. Shall olives be taken with a fork or the

Shall she invite him into the house? Shall she ask him to call again? Shall she thank him for a pleasant evening? In rapid confusion these questions fly through her mind. How humiliating not to know exactly what to do and say at all times!

fingers, what shall the porter be tipped, how shall the woman register at the hotel, how shall a gentleman ask for a dance—countless questions of good conduct that reveal good manners.

Do *you* know everything regarding dinner etiquette, dance etiquette, etiquette at the wedding, the tea, the theatre, the garden party? Do you know how to word an invitation, how to acknowledge a gift, how to write a letter to a titled person? Do you know what to wear to the opera, to the formal dinner, to the masquerade ball, to the luncheon?

The Book of Etiquette
Complete in Two Volumes

In the famous two-volume set of the Book of Etiquette the subject of correct form for every occasion is covered completely, authoritatively. It is recognized as the most thorough and reliable book on the subject available today. It is encyclopedic in scope, answering every problem of etiquette that may be puzzling you in a clear, definite, interesting way. Nothing has been forgotten. Even the ancient origin of customs has been traced, and you are told exactly why rice is thrown after the bride, why black is the color of mourning, why a tea-cup is usually given to the engaged girl.

With the Book of Etiquette to refer to,

you need never make embarrassing blunders. You can know exactly what to do, say, write and wear at all times. You will be able to astonish your friends with your knowledge of *what is right* under all circumstances.

A great deal of your happiness depends upon your ability to make people like you. Someone once said, "Good manners make good company," and this is very true. Etiquette will help you become a "good mixer"—will aid you in acquiring a charming personality that will attract people to you. Because you will rarely be embarrassed, people who associate with you will not feel embarrassed—your gentle poise and dignity will find in them an answering reflection and you should be admired and respected no matter where you are or in whose company you happen to be.

Sent Free for 5 Days' Examination

The Book of Etiquette will mean a great deal to you. It has already opened the doors of social success to many, has shown hundreds of men and women the way to obtain the poise and charm their personalities lacked.

Let us send you the famous two-volume set of the Book of Etiquette free for 5 days' examination. Read a few of the chapters—you will enjoy particularly the chapter on "Games and Sports" and the chapter called "When the Bachelor Entertains." If you are not delighted with the books you may return them within the 5-day period without the least obligation. If you are delighted—as everyone is who examines the books—just send us $3.50 in full payment and the books are yours.

Don't make the mistake of putting it off. Here is your opportunity to examine the Book of Etiquette without cost or obligation. Mail the coupon now. Nelson Doubleday, Inc., Dept. 254, Garden City, N.Y.

- - - - - - - - - - - - - - - - -

NELSON DOUBLEDAY, Inc., Dept. 254, Garden City, New York.

You may send me the two-volume set of the Book of Etiquette for 5 days' free examination. I will either return them within the 5-day period or send you only $3.50 in full payment. This does not obligate me in any way, and I need not keep the books if I am not delighted with them.

Name...

Address..

☐ Check this square if you want these books with the **beautiful full-leather binding** at $5.00 with 5 days' examination privilege.
(Orders outside of the U. S. are payable cash with order.)

the Book of the Month Club, and he launched Arthur Murray in advertising correspondence-school dance courses.) Sackheim recalls that he himself made a number of mistakes in English in writing the Cody ad, but the school's proprietors fortunately managed to catch them. The ad has been running in essentially unchanged form for more than forty years. It is widely acclaimed in the trade as the most successful mail-order ad ever written, having pulled in literally millions of coupons over the years.

Worse than having said, "Leave them lay there" or "ave NOO" were the demoralizing terrors in a memorable series of mail-order ads that began in 1921. The ads, prepared by Ruthrauff & Ryan and written by a bright young copywriter named Lillian Eichler, were designed to sell a two-volume *Book of Etiquette* published by Nelson Doubleday. Miss Eichler had earlier produced an ad headlined "Has This Ever Happened

to You?" It showed a panicky guest upsetting his coffee over the napery. The ad was effective enough to clear out Doubleday's entire remainder stock of an earlier etiquette book, but since this volume was distinctly quaint, it had a high return rate on the money-back offer. So the publisher hired Miss Eichler to prepare a newer book and then to write the ads for it.

Early in the campaign, before she hit her full stride, the ads were content to peck away at the reader with nagging problems:

In the dining room we wonder whether celery may be taken up in the fingers or not, how asparagus should be eaten, the correct way to use the finger bowl. In the ballroom we are ill at ease when the music ceases and we do not know what to say to our partner. At the theater we are uncertain whether or not a woman may be left alone during the intermission . . .

If we do not know what to do or say, we hesitate —and blunder. Often it is very embarrassing—espe-

Again She Orders —
"A Chicken Salad, Please"

FOR him she is wearing her new frock. For him she is trying to look her prettiest. If only she can impress him—make him like her—just a little.

Across the table he smiles at her, proud of her prettiness, glad to notice that others admire. And she smiles back, a bit timidly, a bit self-consciously.

What wonderful poise he has! What complete self-possession! If only *she* could be so thoroughly at ease.

She pats the folds of her new frock nervously, hoping that he will not notice how embarrassed she is, how uncomfortable. He doesn't —until the waiter comes to their table and stands, with pencil poised, to take the order.

"A chicken salad, please." She hears herself give the order as in a daze. She hears him repeat the order to the waiter, in a rather surprised tone. Why *had* she ordered that again! This was the third time she had ordered chicken salad while dining with him.

He would think she didn't know how to order a dinner. Well, did she? No. She didn't know how to pronounce those French words on the menu. And she didn't know how to use the table appointment as gracefully as she would have liked; found that she

cially when we realize just a moment too late that we have done or said something that is not correct.

In an ad appearing a few months later, Miss Eichler sharpened up her aim on the reader's sense of inadequacy:

ARE YOU EVER TONGUE-TIED AT A PARTY? ARE YOU EVER "ALONE" IN A CROWD?

It is humiliating to sit next to a young lady or a young man at a dinner table and not be able to converse in a calm well-bred manner. It is awkward to leave one's dance partner without a word—or to murmur some senseless phrase that you regret the moment it leaves your lips.

But it was only when the *Book of Etiquette* campaign turned to narrative ads that the fullest toe-curling horror was achieved. Miss Eichler produced three or four masterpieces of infectious embarrassment. In one a man and a woman are shown at a table in a tony restaurant studded with ferns and suave guests. An elaborate setting is on the table; an urbane waiter hovers nearby with hooded eye. The man and woman at the table have constrained expressions; their hands flutter uncertainly over the tableware. The ad begins:

BOTH ARE EMBARRASSED—YET BOTH COULD BE AT EASE

They started out happily enough at the beginning of the evening. He was sure he had found ideal companionship at last. She was sure that she was going to impress him with her charm, with her cultured personality.

But everything seemed to go wrong after they entered the restaurant . . . Instead of allowing her to follow the head waiter to their places, he preceded —and when he realized his mistake he tried to make up for it by being extremely polite. But he made another humiliating blunder that made even the dignified waiter conceal a smile!

Once these ads began to open with little horror stories, the *Book of Etiquette* began to sell almost uncontrollably. More than three million copies were bought before the market approached saturation. In one effective ad, over the headline "Why I Cried After the Ceremony," a distracted and perspiring bride is attempting desperately to

Everything about a good mail-order ad was tested, including the shape, size, and phrasing of the coupon.

New Kind of Hat
Worn 10 Minutes a Day
Grows Hair in 30 Days — or No Cost

No matter how thin your hair may be this remarkable new scientific invention is absolutely guaranteed to give you a brand new growth of hair in 30 days—or it costs you nothing. Don't send a cent. Just mail coupon below.

By ALOIS MERKE
Founder of Famous Merke Institute, Fifth Ave., N. Y.

Touch a man's vanity and there is almost nothing that he won't try in the privacy of his bathroom. The copy explained that this "new kind of hat is worn on the head just 10 minutes a day. No unnecessary fuss of any kind."

march down the church aisle with a passing usher rather than with her father. In another, a panicky girl, her fingers tangled in a string of imitation pearls and a look of anguish on her simple face, is abjectly ordering "A chicken salad, please," in a restaurant for the third time in succession with the same escort—because she can't risk trying to pronounce those terrible French words in the menu. In time the Chicken Salad girl joined Addison Sims of Seattle as a kind of national comic figure. But she also had the result of making American women by the thousands resolve not to brave the humiliating implications of ordering chicken salad in public.

DURING the twenties it was often claimed that advertising was in transition from a primitive, imperfectly understood, and often wasteful gamble to an exact and predictable discipline.

Mail-order advertising, with its unassailable arithmetical verdicts, was hailed as a major cause of this break-through. Other techniques were also being developed to measure advertising effectiveness: sample offers, miniature campaigns in test cities or test regions, hidden offers buried deep in copy. Another valuable new tool was something called "split runs." These were special arrangements made by printers so that pairs of ads could be pitted against each other for comparison in the same edition of a magazine or newspaper.

But the more testing was done, the more disquieting the lessons of "scientific" advertising became. These could be summed up in a series of earthy admonitions. Slogans weren't important. Repetition wasn't important, and sometimes could even hurt. Long copy was often better than short, bearing out the old door-to-door maxim: "The more you tell the more you sell." Since

157

"He Wanted the Woman I Love!"

"I heard a shot—I saw him run — and then I saw her fall — the woman I loved. My leg was broken—and my gun was gone! I had only one thought — his strange, astounding plots must be revenged — he must die for a coward at my hand! He had the courage of a lion and the cunning of a rat. He came running toward me when — suddenly, I —"

But the story is too thrilling, too fascinating, as he tells it, for us to spoil it for you here, for it is told by the man who knows how to make a story the most breathless thing in the world —

Robert Louis STEVENSON

Pure cliff-hanging, with a light sprinkling of sex and violence, was found necessary to sell 25-volume sets of Stevenson by mail. In 1920, this did it.

large type faces took up more space, they were severely penalized on the vital cost-per-coupon-pulled measurement. Fancy art work and decorative borders were a waste of money. So were wit, grace, and charm in the copy. Such client-pleasing traditions as institutional copy about how the manufacturer was obsessed with a sense of service and duty, or aerial views of the plant with chimneys a-belch, or ancestor worship of the industrious and whiskered founders—all were poison, not worth the paper they were printed on.

Certain other findings were less displeasing; most advertising men felt that they had known them all along anyhow. Never knock the competition; simply pretend it doesn't exist. Use a positive approach; show happy people rendered radiant by The Product. Never use a negative approach; never say anything like "Why neglect this valuable offer?" Be affirmative always; show beauty but not wrinkles; your customers know

all about wrinkles. Always build copy around the purchaser's self-interest. Always sprinkle in specifics, because they add plausibility. Don't assume that the reader knows *anything*. And no printable word in English is more powerful than "FREE!"

As mail-order lore built up over thousands of tests, it became evident that the most crucial part of an ad was its headline. This had to be a powerful, lapel-grabbing phrase or none of the rest of the copy would have a chance. Identical ads differing only in headlines could vary by a factor of ten in the coupons they pulled. Some words and phrases were found to have almost magical strength, including How to, Which, At Last, New, Amazing, This, Who Else Wants? Certain other common phrases proved to be almost worthless: Extra Value, Finer Flavor, Beauty and Utility.

Much study was devoted to finding a generalized theory of headlines. It was not always desirable to write something that would arrest the maximum number of readers. For one thing, such heads would tend to be of such sensationalism as to annoy the reader after he discovered that he was being sold, say, a course in meat cutting. With most products, furthermore, the maximum number of readers was not the objective, but the maximum number of potential buyers. Men don't buy lipsticks, nor women shaving cream, nor children corsets. An ideal headline, it was theorized, had to select the maximum number of potential prospects. It had to catch their indifferent gaze and, in a fraction of a second, promise them something called a Reward for Reading.

Schwab & Beatty, an agency that specialized in mail order, periodically collected lists of successful headlines; and these winners were poked over, probed, and studied as thoroughly as were the outcrops of gold-bearing rock by Sutter's Mill. Some of the classics:

THE SECRET OF MAKING PEOPLE LIKE YOU

WHO ELSE WANTS A SCREEN STAR FIGURE?

HOW A NEW DISCOVERY MADE A PLAIN GIRL BEAUTIFUL

EVERYWHERE WOMEN ARE RAVING ABOUT THIS AMAZING NEW SHAMPOO!

TO MEN WHO WANT TO QUIT WORK SOME DAY

"I LOST MY BULGES . . . AND SAVED MONEY TOO"

It should be noted, parenthetically, that headlines are crucially important in general ads, too. Duane Jones tells in his memoirs of a crisis that assailed Heinz once when his agency had the account. "We had been running a Heinz Ketchup ad on the back cover of *The Saturday Evening Post,* and decided to try it in *Maclean's Magazine,* in Canada. It showed a very pretty waitress balancing a tray at shoulder height, smiling down at a businessman, who was presumably at lunch.

Courageous comeback after humiliating defeat, and the winning of fair ladies, were themes that paid off by mail.

159

The headline was 'What She Knows About Your Husband.'

"Then Maclean's ad manager phoned us from Toronto. 'Look, old chap,' he told me, 'you cawn't run that ad in Canada!'

"'Why not?'

"'It implies that the waitress is having an affair with the husband.'

"This floored me. After considerable discussion I told him to write a headline that he liked, and then to phone me. He called the next day, all enthusiasm. 'I've got it!' he announced, and read with great pride: 'He Gets It Downtown—So Why Not Let Him Have It At Home?' That was the way the ad ran, too. Except that the first 'it' was replaced with 'Heinz Ketchup.'"

MAIL-ORDER advertising has come to occupy a respected, if not honored, place within the larger body of general advertising. It is a small enclave within the parent body, tolerated and tolerant, though with occasional sallies of waspishness from both sides. The early dream of leading all advertising into scientific exactitude became tarnished after it was discovered that mail-order indicators could be "jimmied." Make the coupon

The vendor of this course in the home study of fingerprinting was clearly a believer in the maxim that no printable word in English is better than "FREE!"

FREE!

Actual Reports of Secret Service Operator 38

To men who want to

Quit Work some day

Mail-order ads weren't always bushy-tailed. This picture and headline proved to be an outstanding coupon-puller for Phoenix Mutual Life Insurance Co.

bigger and the return rate goes up, even with weaker headlines; blazon the word *free* and the return rate skyrockets even on an inferior ad.

As a means of distribution, mail order has proved to have natural limitations. It is unsuited for many products, notably the very cheap, the very expensive, and big-volume items. It has, moreover, a curious tendency toward diminishing returns. With some exceptions, notably correspondence courses and self-improvement books, typical mail-order products show a tendency to find a dwindling market after a few rich years. Helen Woodward, looking back on her greatest book-selling triumphs, wrote: "The mail-order book business grew more and more difficult, until it became necessary to use headlines like 'Battling Against a Human Vampire' or ' "Sold, She's Yours, Master," Muttered the Trembling Slave-Dealer.' "

To dignified and status-sensitive leaders of general advertising, mail order tends to be looked down on as a shabby relative with a tendency to eat peas with a knife. The crowded, noisy, "buck-eye" advertisements offend ad men who wish to view their trade as a profession. Yet any slighting references toward mail order can be

relied on to inflame its advocates into vigorous, if confidential, counterattack. Mail-order men whisper that a large percentage of general advertising is a total waste of the client's money, that results are lacking not because they can't be measured, but because they don't exist. A trend toward big-picture-small-copy ads in recent years is particularly annoying to mail-order partisans. They point out venomously that such ads never have worked in mail order, and that they are common in general advertising only because they are cheap and easy to produce. Mail-order men like to quote something that Claude Hopkins wrote back in 1923:

What real difference is there between inducing a customer to order by mail or order from his dealer? Why should the methods of salesmanship differ?

They should not. When they do, it is for one of two reasons. Either the advertiser does not know what the mail-order advertiser does. Or he is deliberately sacrificing a percentage of his returns to gratify some desire.

There is some apology for that, just as there is for fine offices and buildings. Most of us can afford to do something for pride and opinion. But let us know what we are doing. Let us know the cost of our pride.

Chapter 11

Advertising and the Outside World

Advertising ministers to the spiritual side of trade. It is a great power which has been entrusted to your keeping, which charges you with the high responsibility of inspiring and ennobling the commercial world. It is all part of the greater work of the regeneration and redemption of mankind.

—President Calvin Coolidge, to an advertising convention

"MUMMY, THEY HAVE A LOVELY HOUSE, BUT THEIR BATHROOM PAPER HURTS!"

—headline in a national ad

THERE has been much more to the history of advertising than the perfection of technique by inventive, hard-driving men. The fantasy world of advertising has repeatedly come into glancing contact with the real, or outside, world. One by-product of the first world war, for example, was sharply improved status for advertising in the eyes of those most conservative members of the commercial community, bankers. Previously the money guardians had tended to regard advertising as a wasteful frill, indicative of light-minded and possibly irresponsible management. But the notable success of the Red Cross and Liberty bond drives (the latter employing basic Barnum techniques, and pounding home the slogan "Buy till it hurts!"), proved that advertising could actually sell charity and low-interest securities. And nothing impresses a banker more than the ready sale of bonds. It also became evident that advertising was in considerable degree responsible for the astonishing growth of the auto industry. As Frank Presbrey triumphantly noted in 1928: "The banker . . . slowest as a class to come to an appreciation of the value of a large expenditure on so intangible a thing as advertising, has since 1920 become one of the strongest advocates of advertising. Thus advertising broke down the last great redoubt."

162

FROM A LITHOGRAPH, DRAWN ON THE STONE BY GEORGE BELLOWS

That Monstrous Thing Called Kultur

You haven't believed. Because your mind is clean, because you have been surrounded from childhood by an atmosphere of uprightness, and decency, and kindliness, because you hate to see even a dumb brute suffer—you haven't believed.

You have listened, with a doubting shrug, to the tales of German atrocity—doubting because these tales were so bestial, so revolting that to you they were unthinkable. But you, but we, must believe, because they are the truth.

The official documents of England, of France and of Belgium confirm them—absolutely. More—the half, the worst half has never been told in this clean land of ours, has never been told because unprintable.

There's a fester spot on this fair world—a spot that has spread from Berlin until it has poisoned all of Germany. And there's just one cure—the knife. The poison cannot be dammed up, it must be cut out else this monstrous thing called Kultur will fasten its hideous self on all the world.

Our boys over there have learned to believe. They are seeing the horror and the pity of it all. *They know*, and knowing, they set their jaws and go over the top with a righteous wrath, a holy anger that carries all before it. We have got to feel this war as they feel it. Have got to believe, and believing, set our jaws and do our part whatever that part may be. Right now it's money, money, money.

BUY U. S. GOVT. BONDS *of the* FOURTH LIBERTY LOAN

When advertising turned its emotive skills to fighting a world war, the results could be rather dismaying. But the sheltering roof of government policy kept off any questions of accuracy or even truth.

Elgin—
"Guiding Star of the Service"

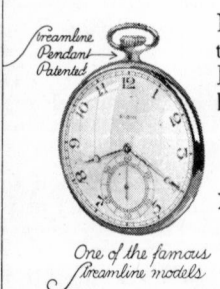TONIGHT in No Man's Land! Through all that wild inferno—shrieking shells and spewing shrapnel and stuttering machine guns and clanking, crunching tanks—on the tiniest and cheeriest of mechanisms hangs the destiny of the world.

Never before, in all history's wars, has Time played so appallingly vital a part. The grim significance of "zero hour" has burned this deep into the minds of our boys over there: unless their watches are in step with those of the fire-control, they will be wiped out by their own guns. Desperate, blood bought raids over the top, useless if delivered out of unison, become irresistible when timed to the tick of an Elgin.

Elgins! Guiding stars to our Emergency Fleet—trusted companions of a great Polar explorer—pathfinders for intrepid government scientists—official chronometers of our destroyers and torpedo boats!

Thousands of Elgins are used by the Government in our Navy—tens of thousands by our Signal Corps—and along that surging battle-line in France hundreds of thousands of Elgins are in hourly use by the fighting men of America and her gallant Allies—

—a war essential of the first rank.

ELGIN NATIONAL WATCH CO., ELGIN, U.S.A.

Streamline Pendant Patented

One of the famous Streamline models

The first, almost irresistible instinct of the wartime copywriter was to work up the theme that The Product, ably assisted by heroes, was busily winning the war.

War profits, the sharp postwar scramble for new markets as well as bigger slices of existing ones, and the inflation-deflation cycle of 1919–1921 all had the effect of giving advertising a potent shot in the arm. National advertising expenditures *doubled* between 1918 and 1920, and doubled again in the next few years. By greatly increasing the number of working women, the war poured hundreds of millions of new dollars into women's purses, from which it could be coaxed out by new ads for silk stockings, cosmetics, toilet goods, and dozens of other tempting products.

Even shortages that developed during the war helped advertising, because they gave a boost to the spreading idea of institutional campaigns. This was a vast and rich new territory where the objectives were wonderfully diffuse, and where companies never before thought of as advertisers became prized clients. The early wartime institutional ads did carry a kind of selling message (The Product or its materials are now going to beat the Hun, but hang on); later they became far less explicit. To most ad men institutional campaigns were a delightful development. It was in many ways easier to produce advertisements informing readers that a public utility, say, was a sort of folksy old codger among corporations, made up of persons virtually obsessed by ideals of service, than it was to try to drum up sales in some hotly competitive field.

There was also a tremendous postwar expansion in cooperative advertising. This is the term for national advertising purchased by groups of entrepreneurs too small to buy it individually. The idea had begun in England early in the century with a joint campaign by tea growers; in this country ads for Sunkist Oranges first appeared in 1907, and for Florida Citrus Fruits in 1909. By the twenties there was a torrent of cooperative campaigns. Ads appeared for (among many others) growers of apples, raisins, walnuts, and pecans; for makers of paint, cement, and brick, and of copper, brass, and iron pipe; for oak, pine, gum, and cypress lumbermen; for portrait photographers, candymakers, garagemen,

and laundrymen; and for scores of different cities, regions, and states, each of which beckoned seductively to tourists and new industries. There were also defensive cooperative campaigns: the coal industry brandished a grimy fist at the oil burner, and ice dealers inveighed with touching defiance against the pernicious and unhealthy electric refrigerator. One group, the florists, did so brilliantly with "Say It With Flowers" as to evoke this admiring bravo from a contemporary ad man:

Here was a pleasing and gracious habit that had been confined to a very small part of the popu-

IVORY SOAP follows the flag. Wherever America goes, it is "among those present." Ivory's use is as unchangeable a part of American life as the practice of cleanliness. Ivory Soap is, in fact, the very joy of living to Our Boys when they are relieved from the front lines for rest, recreation, clean clothes and a bath.

A NAME YOU CAN TRUST

E · R · SQUIBB & SONS

Besides seals and factories, Squibb sometimes ran a parable on Hakeem, the Wise One, that made dandy bathroom reading. It was in favor of Integrity.

lation, or to one or two days of the year. It was a notable example of underconsumption. The florists' oft-repeated suggestion has resulted in a diffusion of the flower-giving habit among a vast number of people who did not formerly think of flowers.

In the twenties the most exciting interaction between advertising and the outside world came in the sudden boom of highly advertisable products—some of them old but previously quiescent, like cigarettes and phonographs, and some new, like radios and trimotored planes. Mechanical refrigerators were advertised with such vigor that they became a kind of badge of middle-class respectability. And no home could be truly cultured until it had its Victrola with sets of Caruso and Harry Lauder records.

Radio came marching in with astonishing speed. In 1921 and 1922 there were only a few technically minded boys toying with this hobby in lonely attic rooms, but by 1923 the suppliers of sets—and headphones, tubes, and parts—found

that the market had grown big enough to call for national ads. (And to advertise on radio, too: one of the earliest commercial programs, the Eveready Hour, operated on the premise that a fine way to sell radio batteries was to encourage people to use up their existing ones in listening.) Then the dam broke: in 1928, just five years later, more than half a *billion* dollars were being spent annually on radio receivers. Not only had Americans by the million begun to listen in glazed-eye unison to Amos 'n' Andy and the A & P Gypsies, but radio itself was growing to be an advertising competitor. Already radio was begining to show its strange capacity for reaching masses of people who are inaccessible by the written word, and with abrasive iteration, drilling directly into their hitherto impenetrable skulls.

The biggest single success achieved by advertising in the twenties was with cigarettes, though social historians are careful to credit a major assist to changes in attitude arising from the war. Before the war cigarettes had unfortunate associations, reflected not only in such opprobrious epithets as "coffin nails" and "gaspers," but also in blasts from keepers of the public morals like Ford and Edison. (In a 1914 pamphlet Ford opined that cigarette smokers were unemployable, and he pointed out that criminals were almost always smokers. Edison's theory was that burning cigarette paper caused irreversible brain degeneration.) The cigarette smoker was widely held to be a dubious fellow—neurotic, of questionable masculinity and Americanism, possibly a dope fiend on the side.

Then, by the war's end, the pendulum swung. Cigarettes were found to be convenient, cheap, and more acceptable to most tastes than chewing tobacco or cigars. More important, the overtones changed. Images of uncertain masculinity and patriotism were demolished by news photos of fatigued doughboys, or nonchalant aviators, each with a cigarette negligently a-dangle. The step from the risk of depravity to the suggestion of

The Great Imitator

HIDING behind a mask, man's most dangerous enemy strikes in the dark and adds two out of every thirteen deaths to his score. Just so long as men and women, and boys and girls approaching maturity, are not taught to recognize the cruelest of all foes to health and happiness—just so long will many lives be wrecked, lives which could have been saved or made decently livable.

Strange as it may seem, tens of thousands of victims of this insidious disease (syphilis) are utterly unaware of the fact that they have it.

No other disease takes so many forms. As it progresses, it may mask as rheumatism, arthritis, physical exhaustion and nervous breakdown. It may appear to be a form of eye, heart, lung, throat or kidney trouble. There is practically no organic disease which it does not simulate.

Syphilis is responsible for more misery of body and mind than any other disease. It destroys flesh and bone. Its ulcers leave terrible scars. It attacks heart, blood vessels, abdominal organs—and most tragic of all are its attacks upon brain and spinal cord, the great nerve centers, resulting commonly in blindness, deafness, locomotor ataxia, paralysis, paresis and insanity—a life-long tragedy.

Countless millions of victims have been wickedly imposed upon and hoodwinked by quacks, charlatans and worse—insidious blackmailers pretending to practice medicine.

The United States Government took a brave step forward during the Great War and told our soldiers and sailors the truth about this dread disease.

It can be cured by competent physicians if detected in time and if the patient faithfully follows the scientific treatment prescribed by his doctor. After the disease has progressed beyond the first stages, cures are less certain, but a great deal can often be done to help chronic sufferers.

Men and women should learn the truth and tell it to those dependent upon them. It is a helpful sign that the best educators deplore the old habit of secrecy and urge wide-spread knowledge and frank instruction.

It is estimated that more than 12,000,000 persons in the United States have or at some time have had syphilis.

From 5% to 40% of all the cases in the general hospitals of this country are found to be suffering—directly or indirectly—from this disease. The variance in the figures depends upon the character and location of the hospital.

According to Government statistics, the deaths of 200,000 Americans, each year, are directly caused by syphilis and associated diseases. But thousands of deaths charged to other causes are actually due to this disease.

Hospital and clinic records show that early infant mortality can be reduced one-half by prenatal treatment of syphilitic infection.

The Metropolitan Life Insurance Company will gladly mail, free of charge, its booklet, "The Great Imitator". You are urged to send for it.

HALEY FISKE, *President.*

Published by

METROPOLITAN LIFE INSURANCE COMPANY~NEW YORK
Biggest in the World, More Assets, More Policyholders, More Insurance in force, More new Insurance each year

It took courage to mention syphilis in family magazines in 1927. But the Metropolitan's public-health ads have long been distinguished.

On the Veranda of the Country Club

WHERE Radio apparatus, like a professional entertainer, must meet the test of satisfying really discriminating people, Magnavox is certain to be installed.

The first requisites — tone clearness, pitch and quality — are fulfilled by the Magnavox Reproducer; the addition of a Magnavox Power Amplifier supplies the other requisite, volume.

Magnavox Products can be had from good dealers everywhere. Our interesting new booklet will be sent on request.

The Magnavox Co., Oakland, California
New York: 370 Seventh Avenue

MAGNAVOX Radio
The Reproducer Supreme

168

sophistication was a small but crucial one, and advertising did its multimillion-dollar bit to help.

One highly useful function of cigarettes—serving as something to fiddle with in times of awkwardness—was dinned into the public consciousness by a memorable campaign for Murads. Here characters faced with ludicrous embarrassment were shown emerging unruffled and unscathed, over the slogan, "Be Nonchalant—Light a Murad."

The cigarette wars—a series of savage struggles for dominance between the established leading brands, Camels and Chesterfields, and the upstart Lucky Strikes—raged from 1917 all through the twenties and thirties. In scale advertising had never seen anything like it. George Washington Hill of the American Tobacco Company, for example, spent more than a quarter of a billion dollars in pushing Luckies, ably assisted for much of the time in this task by Albert Lasker of Lord & Thomas.

Hill was, to put it temperately, an overpowering personality, and even the denatured language of an official company history has described him as "raw, brash, and impatient." His habits of wearing his hat constantly and spitting on the desk for emphasis were memorialized years later by a character in the novel, *The Hucksters.* Lasker once loosened his mask of imperturbability long enough to observe privately that "Hill was a particular pain in the neck." But personality aside, Hill pioneered in the development of advertising by attrition—a mass crassness that beat against the eyes and ears of every citizen of the republic—except perhaps a few souls immured in monasteries and mental hospitals. Hill generaled the great Lucky Strike campaigns of the twenties, fought under the slogans "Nature in The Raw Is Seldom Mild" and, later, "Reach for a Lucky Instead of a Sweet." The latter ad-

Even before radio outgrew its horn-and-wires stage, the advertising had started to mention "really discriminating people."

monition, coming with the force of millions of dollars behind it, quite naturally enraged the candy industry, and for a time Luckies had difficulty in getting distribution in small neighborhood candy stores.

Hill was alertly opportunistic. In 1926 Chesterfield came out with the celebrated headline, "Blow Some My Way," which delicately implied that women, too, might like to smoke in public. Hill, urged on by Lasker at his elbow, jumped at this chance to double the potential market. He burst out with a campaign laden with testimonials from actresses, society leaders, and female opera stars—all of them pleased with the beneficent effect of Luckies on their voices. So intense was the campaign, and so ripe the times, that in the space of a year or two Hill and Lasker managed to change the image of a woman who smoked in public from that of a scarlet sister to that of a woman who was stylishly advanced but nonetheless respectable.

The blatancy with which Hill used masses of testimonials distressed many people, including some advertising men. Earnest Elmo Calkins once fired off a blast at him in the relatively private pages of *Advertising and Selling*: "But testimonials like these, which reveal even to the gullible, unthinking public that they are not unsolicited, spontaneous tributes, but written and paid for by the advertiser, are undermining the belief of the public in all advertising." Calkins was referring to Lucky ads in which the heroes of a dramatic ocean rescue, Captain Fried and

The Best of Picnic Pals

Chief Officer Manning of the liner *America*, were quoted as expressing an almost irrational fondness for Lucky Strikes. This was a piece of Hill-Lasker enterprise that also incensed Sinclair Lewis, then at his prime of irritability. Writing in the *Nation* and emitting loud cries of "Mad—gone mad!" and "incredible spectacle," Lewis wound up with a characteristic roundhouse swing: "God help these romantic and free States when, after paying the bills of the bootlegger and the Men's League of the Methodist Church, we can get the thrill that our pioneer grandfathers had daily only by reading of Chief Officer Manning's almost sacerdotal passion for Lucky Strike cigarettes."

But perhaps the most perfect distillation of the Hill-Lasker essence came some years later. Lasker was casting about for a new refrain, and a copywriter showed him the line: "So round, so firm, so fully packed, so free and easy on the draw." According to the lore of the trade, these fourteen words seemed themselves so round and firm, so gloriously evocative of oral satisfaction and the Song of Solomon, that Lasker immediately paid

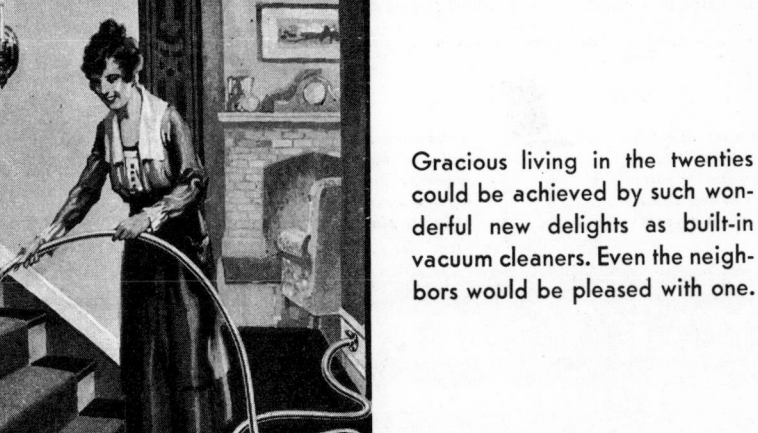

Gracious living in the twenties could be achieved by such wonderful new delights as built-in vacuum cleaners. Even the neighbors would be pleased with one.

No more dragging the stair carpet out on the porch and laboriously beating it to the disgust of the neighbors and in defiance of the law.

Getting the dust and dirt out of the stair carpet and from all corners and cracks is no work at all with the easy stroking of the ARCO WAND Cleaning Tool.

"It's a General Electric!"

LUXURIOUS CONVENIENCE that makes kitchen routine easier—new desserts and dainty dishes to add sparkle to daily menus—thrifty savings in the household budget every month for the years to come! That's what a Christmas gift of a G-E will mean. And added to this will be the thrill of having the finest refrigerator in the world.

The G-E Monitor Top is universally recognized as the standard of excellence. It carries 5 years protection against failure of its famous sealed-in-steel mechanism for only $1 a year—yet it costs no more than others having comparable capacity.

You will of course find all the modern convenience features in G-E refrigerators. Prices and terms were never lower. And the G-E will pay for itself both *winter* and summer in the food savings it makes possible. Remember, it is always summertime in the kitchen! For nearest General Electric dealer see "Refrigeration Electric" in classified pages of your phone book.

General Electric Co., Specialty Appliance Sales Dept., Section M-12, Nela Park, Cleveland, Ohio

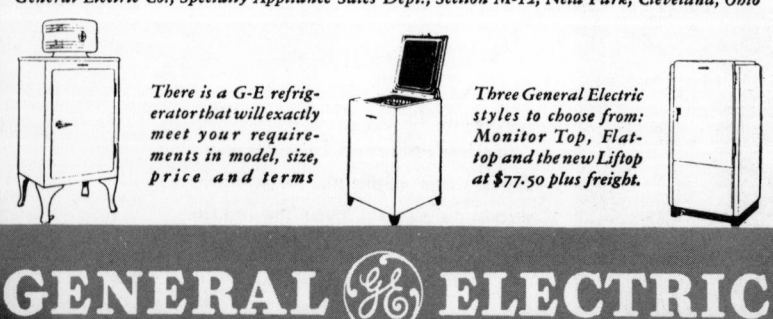

There is a G-E refrigerator that will exactly meet your requirements in model, size, price and terms

Three General Electric styles to choose from: Monitor Top, Flat-top and the new Liftop at $77.50 plus freight.

the fellow a bonus of $10,000. It figures out at $714.28 a word, including each of the four "so's."

THE GREAT DEPRESSION brought a shattering collision between the outside world and advertising's pink-flecked cosmos. In the decade ending in 1929, the volume of print advertising had set new records each year, spurting up to a glittering peak of $1,120,240,000 in the year of the crash. Then the climate changed as drastically as though a new ice age were on the way. Gone were the fine fat institutional accounts; gone were the breathless lyrics for the Jordan Playboy (and the Playboy itself). Each year set a nightmarish record in reverse: 1931 was worse than 1930, 1932 worse than 1931, and 1933 the worst of all. National advertisers by the score first slashed their budgets and then dropped out completely. Agencies retrenched, pruned staffs, cut salaries, fought savagely for possession of surviving accounts, made secret rate concessions, and then often went bankrupt. Agencies and accounts that remained took on a different look. The times were pictured this way by Ralph M. Hower, the official historian of N. W. Ayer & Son:

The urgent need for rigid economy, plus a natural desire to exploit every available means of stimulating sales, ultimately led to more efficient advertising techniques, but the first result was a nationwide rash of cheap and nasty copy. Expensive art work yielded place to cheaper (though often more effective) photographic illustrations. The tabloid or display type of layout almost crowded out other copy arrangements, and the comic-strip technique was adopted with a vengeance. The use of testimonials of all kinds increased, while premiums were recklessly offered and prize contests swept the country as swiftly as the craze for jigsaw puzzles. The shrieking headlines, gross exaggeration, and downright deceit which appeared had no parallel except the patent-medicine advertising of the nineteenth century, while the use of pseudo-scientific arguments and appeals to emotion and appetite surpassed all

Advertising has often labored under the curious misapprehension that Mom could be transfixed on Christmas by a new kitchen appliance.

"I have treated thousands of cases of CONSTIPATION—" declares *Dr. Antoine of Paris*

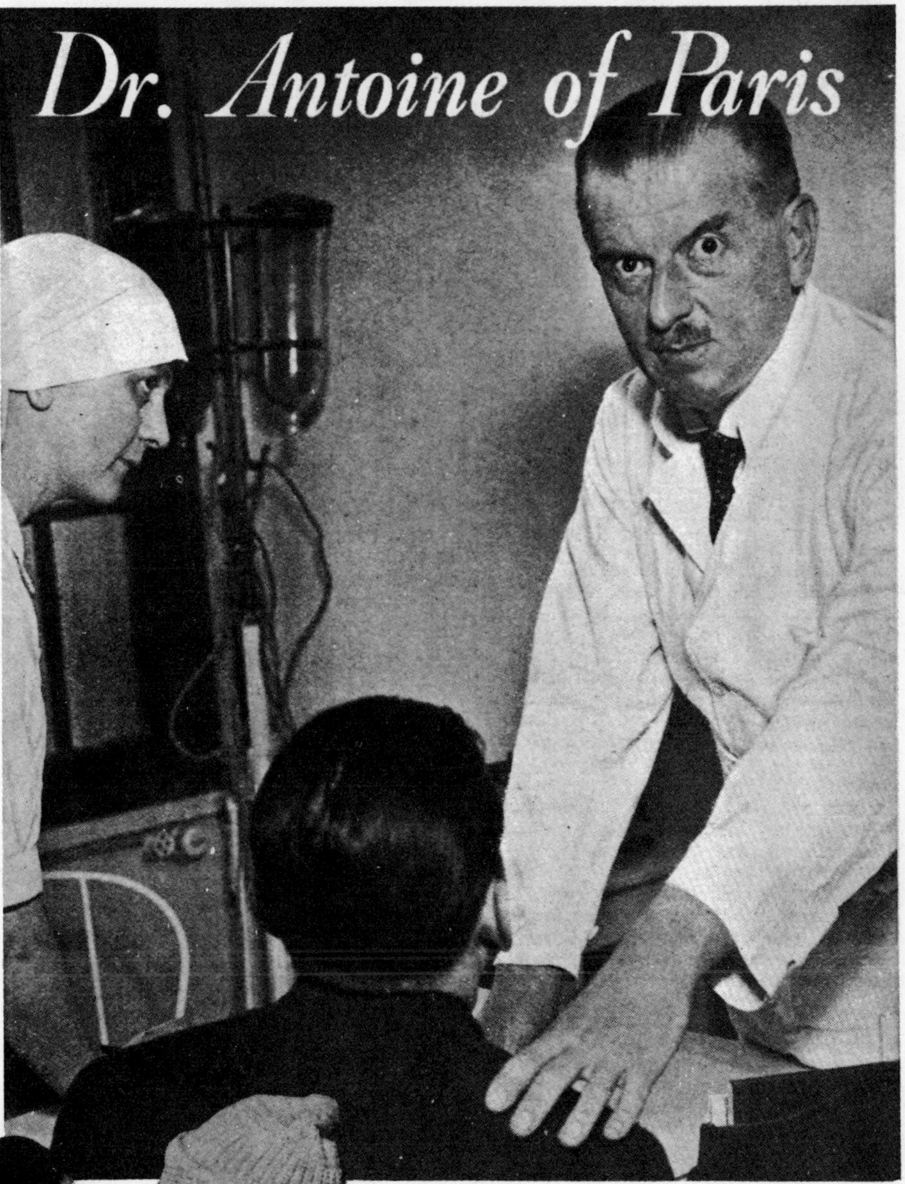

"The best way to correct this evil," he states, *"is to eat fresh yeast."* Try it now!

DR. ANTOINE is the physician to a European king. He is a specialist on the stomach and intestines. He is one of the most famous diagnosticians in France. *He states:—*

"I have treated thousands of cases of intestinal and stomach disorders. The majority were directly traceable to constipation.

"Unfortunately, the first act of the patient who is constipated is usually to take a laxative. But this helps only temporarily. Next time he needs a still stronger dose.

"In my opinion, the most effective means of correcting constipation is the eating of fresh yeast."

Fleischmann's Yeast is a food. It has the remarkable power to stimulate and literally *strengthen* your intestines. At the same time, it attacks and softens the intestinal wastes so they can be easily cleared away.

In this way yeast brings about regular, *natural* evacuations. And as it gently rids your body of harmful poisons, your "pep" comes back. Headaches go. Breath sweetens. Ugly skin blemishes in most cases very quickly disappear.

And — don't forget — yeast is entirely harmless. It's not a drug in any sense. It's not a medicine. It's richer than any other food in the group of three health-building vitamins—B, G, D.

So add Fleischmann's Yeast to your diet now—just plain, or dissolved in water (about a third of a glass). Eat 3 cakes every day, before meals, or between meals and at bedtime.

You can get Fleischmann's Yeast at grocers, restaurants and soda fountains. For free booklet write Dept. Y-H-2 Standard Brands Inc., 691 Washington St., New York City.

"Yes, the doctors are right in what they say about yeast"*

"I have a job that calls for one long smile," *writes* Miss Ruth Clarey, *of New York* (at left), "at the reception desk of a big company. But it's hard to be cheerful when you have a headache.

"I had let myself get run-down. Felt 'loggy.' I tried pills to correct my sluggishness, but results were only temporary.

"I took a friend's example—tried Fleischmann's Yeast. In 2 weeks—improvement. Sluggishness left. No more headaches. And back came the smile."

*IMPORTANT

Fleischmann's Yeast for health comes only in the foil-wrapped cake with the yellow label. It's yeast in its fresh, effective form—the kind doctors advise. Ask for it by name!

previous efforts and violated previously accepted standards of decency.

Among the worst offenders, Hower observed in a fastidious footnote, were makers of cigarettes, soap, sanitary napkins, disinfectants, deodorants, and yeast. The list, though incomplete, does verify the impression that strikes contemporary eyes when one leafs through magazines of the early thirties: much of the advertising that survived then had an extraordinary preoccupation with bodily flaws and functions. Cracked and fungus-rotted toes, hairy and noisome armpits, pimpled, blotchy, and blackheaded skins, baldness and dandruff, and such subclinical forms of obesity ("ugly fat") as Middle-Aged Spread or Office Hips all came under the most detailed scrutiny. The human intestine, always one of advertising's happiest hunting grounds, was flaunted as never before; and proprietary products for the achievement of felicitous bowel movements were described in the most glowing language.

Even products not directly related to the body took on the same rancid flavor, as when photographs of poor hulking unfortunates whose trousers buttoned up were contrasted pitilessly with those of prosperous moderns whose zipper-closed flies were sleek, streamlined, and gap-free. In part as a result of Listerine's success with the corrosive concept that even your best friends won't tell you, a preoccupation with horrid smells distinguished the ads of the period. Countless soaps, tooth pastes, and deodorants were offered to the poor malodorous reader who, even after doing all that was personally possible to stop smelling so bad, might still offend with something called "Undie Odor." Other bodily perils contrived to be both bizarre and unnerving, notably the tales recounted in comic-strip ads about the romances blasted and the careers cut off by the needless use of Harsh Toilet Tissue.

The hard sell, as ad men kept telling each other in the privacy of their trade press, was the way to move The Product off the shelves. But it was not a means of enhancing advertising's reputation, which sank low in the thirties. (It has never entirely regained the professional, almost priestly

172

ASHAMED TO GET OUT ON THE BEACH

status that it achieved by 1929.) In the depression years an attitude of skepticism about, and distaste for, advertising spread from being the province of a small intellectual group to a far wider public. To the dismay of many in the trade, several sharply antiadvertising books, notably *Your Money's Worth, 100,000,000 Guinea Pigs,* and *Skin Deep,* became best sellers. Subscription consumer services sprang up, dedicated to the premise that virtually all advertising was uninformative and much of it dishonest. Federal legislation that strengthened the food and drug laws and the Federal Trade Commission was passed with enthusiasm; even more stringent New Deal bills were headed off only by frenzied efforts. And it was in the thirties, for about a year and a half, that a curious antiadvertising magazine, *Ballyhoo,* flared into sudden national popularity. (It later degenerated into routine barbershop japery.) At its most successful, *Ballyhoo* leveled the dangerous weapon of derision at advertising, as in this glossary preserved by the British connoisseur, E. S. Turner:

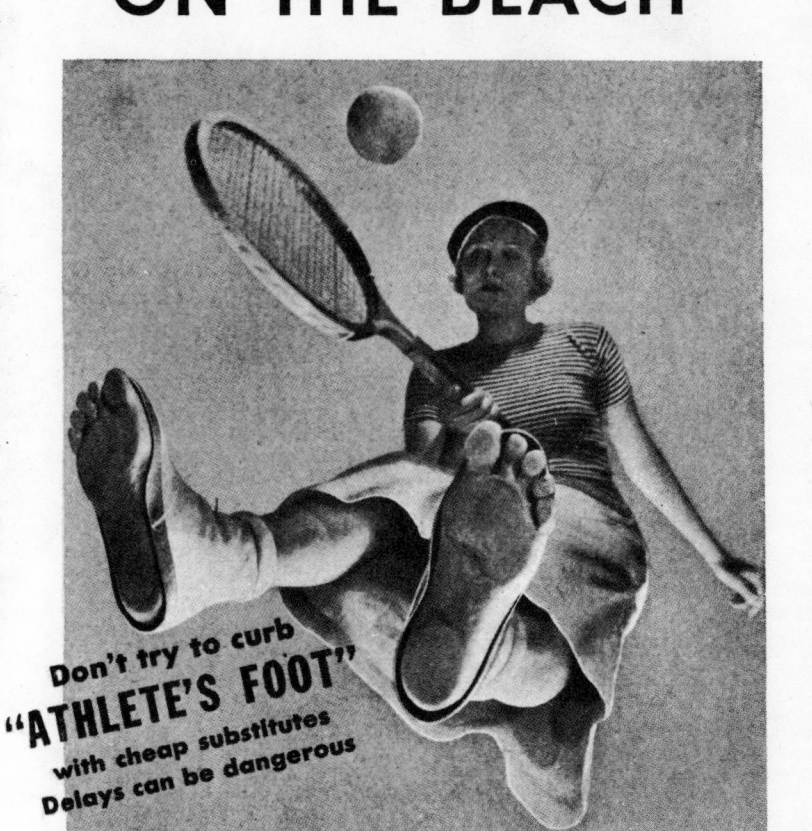

Don't try to curb "ATHLETE'S FOOT" with cheap substitutes Delays can be dangerous

"There's something shocking to romance," this ad asserted ". . . about that unpleasant moistness between her toes. . . ." Girls in ads should be nice to nibble on.

Delicate membrane	any part of the body
Lubricate the skin texture	put on grease
Pore-deep cleansing	washing the face
Harsh irritants	ingredients of competitor's product
Great scientist	anyone who signs an endorsement
Lifetime	until the new model comes out

By the middle of the decade the worst of the storm had been ridden out. The reviving economy, together with a salutary elimination of the uglier excesses, set magazine advertising moving along what the late C. W. Post would have called the Road to Wellville.

As ad pages and expenditures crept up to old high-water marks, it became evident that even sharply increasing magazine circulations were unable to match newspaper groups and radio in bulk of audience. Most magazines were destined to become special game preserves where advertisers could stalk comparatively prosperous, comparatively literate audiences—and newspapers and radio were media of choice where all that an advertiser required were people, people by the millions, most of them with, say, no more than a torpid intestine and twenty-five cents.

The transition of magazines into suppliers of selected rather than mass audiences continued despite a countertrend in 1936. This was the appearance of picture magazines like *Life* and *Look,* which, with their minimal literacy requirements, seemed an answer to the looming cloud of electronic advertising. Space salesmen for the new magazines could point out that it takes virtually no academic training to enjoy a magazine that regularly includes large photos of criminals, accidents, disasters, sports, strange

You wouldn't care to meet Marvin

Winning new users by thousands. Listerine Tooth Paste. The large tube 25¢

Money. Charm. Ability. In all New York there was no abler man in his field. Yet people called him "the prince of pariahs."

Men thought him a great fellow—for a little while. Women grew romantic about him—until they *knew*. People welcomed him at first—then dropped him as though he were an outcast.

Poor Marvin, yearning so for companionship and always denied it. Poor Marvin, ignorant of his nickname and ignorant, likewise, of the foundation for it.

Halitosis (unpleasant breath) is the damning, unforgivable, social fault. It doesn't announce its presence to its victims. Consequently it is the last thing people suspect themselves of having—*but it ought to be the first.*

For halitosis is a definite daily threat to all. And for very obvious reasons, physicians explain. So slight a matter as a decaying tooth may cause it. Or an abnormal condition of the gums. Or fermenting food particles skipped by the tooth brush. Or minor nose and throat infections. Or excesses of eating, drinking and smoking.

Intelligent people recognize the risk and minimize it by the regular use of full strength Listerine as a mouth wash and gargle. Night and morning. And between times before meeting others.

Listerine quickly checks halitosis because Listerine is an effective antiseptic and germicide★ which immediately strikes at the cause of odors. Furthermore, it is a powerful deodorant, capable of overcoming even the scent of onion and fish..

Keep Listerine handy in home and office. Carry it when you travel. Take it with you on your vacation. It is better to be safe than snubbed. Lambert Pharmacal Company, St. Louis, Mo., U. S. A.

, , ,

★Full strength Listerine is so safe it may be used in any body cavity, yet so powerful it kills even the stubborn Bacillus Typhosus (typhoid) and Staphylococcus Aureus (pus) germs in 15 seconds. We could not make this statement unless we were prepared to prove it to the entire satisfaction of the medical profession and the U. S. Government.

LISTERINE

animals, cute children, busts, and behinds.

Magazine men also hastened to point out that a magazine has multiple readership, and lasts from a week to a month—whereas a newspaper dies overnight, and a commercial on the air expires in seconds. Such arguments proved effective with many conservative advertisers, notably auto and appliance makers, utilities and insurance companies, food and soft-drink manufacturers. The Coca-Cola Company, for example, has long been an advertising man's dream: big, prosperous, and thoroughly convinced of the wisdom of lavish advertising expenditure in *all* media. (Coke is the most heavily advertised single product in the country.) Serenely disdaining competitive or quarrelsome claims, the company assigns $15 or $20 million a year to the intensive communication of such innocuous but profitable messages as "The Pause That Refreshes." Asked to analyze its success, a president of the company once put it down to an "accumulation of advertising."

By the time of Pearl Harbor, magazine advertising had fully recovered from the depression and was pressing on with new techniques. Many of the old ways were dead or dying—the leisurely parable, the mass of reasons-why, the mnemonic jingle (except over the air), the sonorous essays about the workers who find fulfillment in aggravated craftsmanship. Even testimonials and before-and-after-taking, as well as that third heritage from patent medicine, the bogus news story, were growing a little out of favor. In their stead were new themes, such as gracious living, and new methods—notably the big-picture, short-copy ad, which was calculated to get in its licks in just a flash of attention.

Wartime themes of conservation, patience, and dedication to the cause were quickly transmuted by advertising into product-identifying themes. Not only had Lucky Strike green gone to war, but it became a patriotic duty for women to load up on perfumes and creams so that they would be nice to come home to. The great bulk of wartime ads were devoted to explaining how The Product was now a vital part of a B-17 or a Sherman tank. Occasionally, . though, under the stimulus of emotional salesmanship fermented in patriotism, wartime ads managed to echo the old fruity days. Here is one for the New Haven Railroad (actually it is less than half of the full copy block):

THE KID IN UPPER 4

It is 3:42 a.m. on a troop train.
Men wrapped in blankets are breathing heavily.
Two in every lower berth. One in every upper.
This is no ordinary trip. It may be their last in the U.S.A. until the end of the war. Tomorrow they will be on the high seas.
One is wide awake . . . listening . . . staring into the blackness.
It is the kid in Upper 4.

Tonight, he knows, he is leaving behind a lot of little things—and big ones.
The taste of hamburgers and pop . . . the feel of driving a roadster over a six-lane highway . . . a dog named Shucks, or Spot, or Barnacle Bill. The pretty girl who writes so often . . . that grey-haired man, so proud and awkward at the station . . . the mother who knit the socks he'll wear soon.
Tonight he's thinking them over.
There's a lump in his throat. And maybe—a tear fills his eye. *It doesn't matter, Kid.* Nobody will see . . . it's too dark.

FOR FULLY fifty years advertising men have been building an elaborate rationale for their works. Rather like artisans building a cathedral, they have erected an edifice complete with spires, towers, and onion domes, a monument to the social utility of advertising from whose rose windows can be heard anthems in praise of the 15 per cent commission. This tendency to justify their works extends far beyond the normal self-appreciation of, say, accountants, dentists, or veterinarians—people who may be delighted to unfold the social value of their labors, but who rarely confuse it with the search for the Holy Grail.

This self-justifying tendency is perplexing; no glib explanation really seems to fit. It isn't purely vanity, for ad men by natural selection are people who generally prefer money to glory. It certainly isn't guilt, an emotion totally alien to the trade's mentality. And it can't be defensiveness, for the

"Ethics be hanged!

women are entitled to these vital beauty facts"

SYNOPSIS OF THE NATION·WIDE HALF·FACE TEST

WHO TOOK PART . . . 612 women, aged 17 to 55, from all walks of life—society women, housewives, clerks, factory workers, actresses, nurses.

THE TEST . . . For 30 days, under scientific supervision, each woman cleansed one-half her face by her accustomed method, and washed the other side with Woodbury's Facial Soap.

SUPERVISED BY 15 eminent dermatologists and their staffs. Reports checked and certified by one of the country's leading dermatological authorities.*

RESULTS . . . Woodbury's was more effective than other beauty methods in 106 cases of pimples; 83 cases of large pores; 103 cases of blackheads; 81 cases of dry skin; 115 cases of oily skin; 66 cases of dull "uninteresting" skin.

"Advertising is essential to the capitalist system of manufacturing and distributing goods. It is particularly important in a growing economy, for it helps fight business stagnation. It works to eliminate the economic evil of underconsumption. Furthermore, it can actually enhance the value to the consumer of the things advertised. It aids in selling virtually any product—including immensely expensive, or one-of-a-kind, objects. But it is best at selling things that can be manufactured in quantity, and that cost less when made in volume. Thus advertising more than pays its way: it stimulates production and cuts costs. If some evil djinn were to extinguish all advertising, everything from cigarettes to Chevrolets would soon cost much more, because fewer people would buy them. Manufacturing would grow less efficient and more costly, and pretty soon we'd be back in a kind of cottage-industry civilization. Even if you could afford it, which you couldn't, would you really want a Chevrolet built by cottage industry?

"And advertising does something besides selling: it communicates. It transmits news of new products, ideas, viewpoints. Through advertising people learn of the world around them, new styles and customs, new labor-saving devices and conveniences, what's going on in art, literature, and music. Advertising has enormous capacity to educate. It has taught people to wash, brush their teeth, eat and sleep in more healthful ways, wear more sensible clothes, learn new skills, and better themselves in a hundred ways.

"Sure, advertising has had its shabby moments. But advertising has done—and continues to do—a remarkable job of policing itself. It helped found the Better Business Bureaus and the Audit Bureau of Circulation; for the last forty years advertising men have been the force behind such things as truth-in-advertising drives and the Printers' Ink laws to make misstatements a crime. They are constantly working behind the scenes to control the sharpy and crook. In short, take a good look at people who are always yakking

phenomenon was evident long before criticism of advertising grew commonplace. Possibly the habit has arisen from some subtle interaction of these elements, perhaps enhanced by an awareness within the trade of the impermanence of its work. Few intensive labors of man are as perishable as an advertisement. Whatever the reason, there has arisen a body of dogma that might be hypothetically summed up this way:

about advertising, and you'll probably find that what they really don't like is free enterprise."

So runs, in highly condensed form, the standard body of belief. Elaborations can be found in innumerable convention speeches, where ad men indulge in the familiar foible of convincing the already convinced. It is not necessary to match this with a similar synopsis of the commonest criticisms of advertising; millions of words have been spilled on the topic since 1933. But there are generally three basic indictments: that much advertising is deceptive or dishonest; that still more of it reflects a crass debasement of language and logic; and that almost all of it is founded on the questionable premise that the good life can be attained by the ceaseless acquisition of material objects.

Deliberately deceptive ads were not uncommon in the past—especially during the heyday of the medicine man and the electric-belt promoter.

"I didn't get the job"

"He'd counted on landing the job—but he missed out. Again he'd have to 'stall' the landlord, the grocer, and all the rest." A depression ad for Gillette blades.

They are not, in fact, unknown today, though rarer in magazines than in most other media. This is not necessarily due to the overpowering probity of magazine publishers—although most have seen advantage as well as morality in not dirtying up the property. But magazines are forced to be exceptionally respectful of the postal authorities. When it comes to comparing the varying bite of government agencies, the Federal Trade Commission is usually considered about as savage as a hippopotamus, able to win an occasional point by leaning ponderously on some wretch over a twenty-four-month period. But the Post Office is a saber-toothed tiger at enforcement, able to work its will in twenty-four hours or less. As a result, radio, TV, and newspapers are far more likely than magazines to carry ads transparently designed to deceive. Typical of such booby-trap ads are those in which a low price is announced in a

shout and the words "as low as" passed off in a whisper, or where there is a childlike attempt to persuade the public that the down payment is the total price.

Some deceptions, nevertheless, are an inherent part of much advertising, in all of its media. They have become hallowed by time, so familiar that they go unseen. There are all the little artifices intended to make The Product look better than life: the drawing showing a car occupied by modish microcephalics, or the refrigerator retouched until its brightwork is a mass of sunbursts. Here also belongs that contortion of language, the floating comparison: The Product is 18 per cent milder, or uses 18 per cent less fuel, or contains 18 per cent less tar, fat, starch, or undissolved solids—or has 18 per cent more lanolin, a preferred term for sheep grease. The floating comparison, incidentally, is often found bobbing placidly alongside the silly syllogism, a contortion of logic where imperfect premises are marshaled to masquerade as convincing proof. (Most dogs are lovable; dogs need dog food; hence you really owe it to Towser to stock up on Fidelis Kibbled T-Bones, the Best Food for Man's Best Friend.) Here too is that wonder-working gray magic of association, with its hidden spirit voices that whisper: Just buy The Product and you too will join the mystic circle of the wise and discerning, all happy, handsome, loved, and sweet-smelling.

The third typical indictment—that we are led down the path to crass materialism—is the hardest to evaluate objectively. Certainly advertising has played a part in speeding acceptance of such civilizing practices as bathing, using inside plumbing, and brushing teeth. It has unquestionably accelerated the use of labor-saving devices like vacuum cleaners and washing machines. But whether advertising has also made us a nation emulating the families shown on the advertising pages of *Life*—all bunched in mindless togetherness between the chrome-plated Thundermobile and the split-level ranch house, joshing Dad's funny chef cap as he barbecues the steaks on the motor-driven rotisserie—is

During the depression, scare themes could even sell woolen underwear.

This wartime classic, by Nelson C. Metcalf, Jr., was reprinted and distributed by the government, read on radio by Eddie Cantor, and set to music.

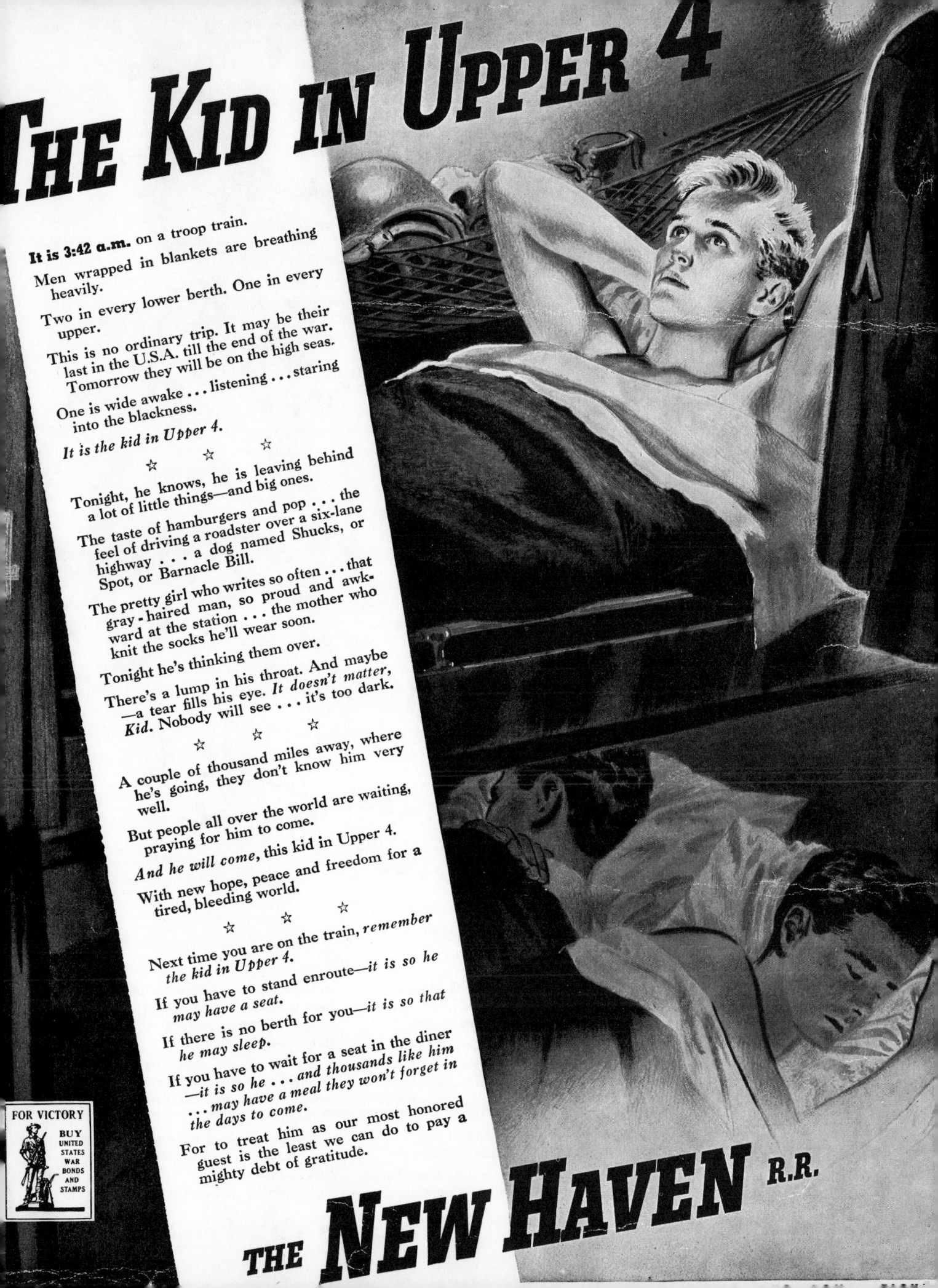

THE KID IN UPPER 4

It is 3:42 a.m. on a troop train.

Men wrapped in blankets are breathing heavily.

Two in every lower berth. One in every upper.

This is no ordinary trip. It may be their last in the U.S.A. till the end of the war. Tomorrow they will be on the high seas.

One is wide awake . . . listening . . . staring into the blackness.

It is the kid in Upper 4.

☆ ☆ ☆

Tonight, he knows, he is leaving behind a lot of little things—and big ones.

The taste of hamburgers and pop . . . the feel of driving a roadster over a six-lane highway . . . a dog named Shucks, or Spot, or Barnacle Bill.

The pretty girl who writes so often . . . that gray-haired man, so proud and awkward at the station . . . the mother who knit the socks he'll wear soon.

Tonight he's thinking them over.

There's a lump in his throat. And maybe —a tear fills his eye. *It doesn't matter, Kid.* Nobody will see . . . it's too dark.

☆ ☆ ☆

A couple of thousand miles away, where he's going, they don't know him very well.

But people all over the world are waiting, praying for him to come.

And he will come, this kid in Upper 4.

With new hope, peace and freedom for a tired, bleeding world.

☆ ☆ ☆

Next time you are on the train, *remember the kid in Upper 4.*

If you have to stand enroute—*it is so he may have a seat.*

If there is no berth for you—*it is so that he may sleep.*

If you have to wait for a seat in the diner —*it is so he . . . and thousands like him . . . may have a meal* they won't forget in the days to come.

For to treat him as our most honored guest is the least we can do to pay a mighty debt of gratitude.

THE NEW HAVEN R.R.

and remember those swell picnics in Birch Grove?

"Remember the picnic we took Mary on?.... How is the garden doing this year? . . . Sure could go for one of Mom's apple pies."

Yes, he has weightier matters on his mind... battles to be fought and a war to be won. But where there's time ... he writes a letter home— to ask about the small, familiar things that he remembers. These are the things that he'll be coming back to when the war is over . . . the *little* things that remind him of home.

It happens that to many of us these important little things include the right to enjoy a refreshing glass of beer. Cool, sparkling, friendly, beer is a sigh of satisfaction . . . a forehead wrinkle erased . . . a firm-set mouth relaxing into a friendly smile.

Wholesome and satisfying—how good it is as a beverage of moderation after a hard day's work . . . with good friends . . . with a home-cooked meal.

A glass of beer or ale—not of crucial importance, surely . . . yet it is little things like this that help mean home to all of us, that do so much to build morale—ours and his.

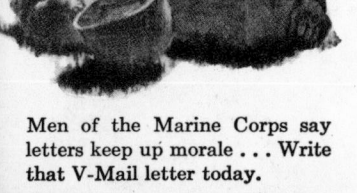

Men of the Marine Corps say letters keep up morale ... Write that V-Mail letter today.

Morale is a lot of <u>little</u> things

BREWING INDUSTRY FOUNDATION

almost impossible to gauge. The difficulty is, of course, that we are in the midst of it. It would have been as easy to know, in 1775, whether James Watt's wheezy steam pumps were going to be socially influential.

Most attacks on advertising have so strong an emotional content that they tend to be self-discrediting. They fail to recognize that advertising is a major point of contact between man and the commercial world he lives in—in fact, except perhaps for his employment, the most important one. Some of the friction arises from the basic requirements of commerce (selling, despite disclaimers to the contrary, is almost never a spiritual pursuit). To succeed, advertising has to reach out and scratch through a customer's protective skin of indifference. If it doesn't, it is a pure waste. Of course, if it scratches hard enough to raise an angry red weal, the customer will be antagonized away. The problem that advertising men face is achievement of just the right degree of irritation; and their judgment is often harried by sidelong glances at the competition, which can be seen to be rubbing none too delicately on the customer at the same time.

Magazine advertising has clearly settled down into a sedate middle age, far removed from its wild-oats youth. The extent to which this is true can be demonstrated at the flip of a switch. Television advertising, complete with hound's-tooth vest and rhinestone stickpin, as well as 20 per cent higher volume-level on the commercials, has taken over unquestioned leadership in outrageous crassness. See any 90-second commercial where an actor, festooned with stethoscope and head mirror, and armed with a shadowbox to show The Product's timely arrival in the intestine, delivers a message of unexampled fatuity. Radio and TV, with their special capacity for reaching audiences of immense size, including masses of customers scarcely able to fog over a chilled mirror, have inevitably shouldered magazine advertising into a comparatively select category.

Possibly the best thing about radio and TV advertising is that it ordinarily disappears with the speed of electromagnetic waves. It has nothing of the relative durability of advertising in print, which not only can be scanned or ignored by several readers at their own time and pace, but also is preserved in libraries the world over for subsequent examination. Earnest Elmo Calkins, writing in retirement as a gray eminence of magazine advertising, put it this way:

The advertising [of past years], both newspaper and magazine, is a revealing record of social history. The changing habits of a people can be learned from what it buys as surely as the history of the earth can be learned from the fossils buried in its strata. . . . In this we may trace our sociological history, the rise and fall of fads and crazes, changing interests and tastes, in foods, clothes, amusements, and vices, a panorama of life as it was lived, more informing than old diaries or crumbling tombstones.

ABOUT THE AUTHOR

A New Englander by birth and magazine editor by trade, Frank Rowsome, Jr., has never worked for an advertising agency. He notes, however, that "I have been nourished by advertising all my working life, thanks to its support of magazines I've worked for. Such support has been very warming, too, considering that in the early days some of them were distinctly odd periodicals. One was the Official Organ for a group of Fur, Fin, and Feather Clubs; another, devoted to building maintenance, was subtitled 'A Journal for Janitors'; a third was preoccupied with describing the newest and most stainless surgical instruments. In recent years I've worked for *Popular Science*, lately as managing editor, where I have grudgingly learned to accept such improbabilities as electrons, atoms, and other figments of the long-hair imagination."

Mr. Rowsome traces his fascination with the advertising craft back to earliest childhood. "I recall, as a small, damp bundle of credulity, being persuaded by an ad to sell cartons full of perfume bottles to my elders in order to get a hand-cranked movie projector that could display 36 jerky feet of William S. Hart defending the bunkhouse against the Sioux. Equally memorable was an enchanting ad headlined 'Boys, Throw Your Voice!' that showed a flabbergasted porter carrying a trunk from which emerged the plaintive cry 'Help, Help, Let Me Out!' From the same advertiser there was also an offer of an 'X-Ray Device, 49 Cents, No Stamps' with which it was reportedly possible to see if girls were *really* made of sugar and spice."

Even though much of his early credulity has since been leached away, Mr. Rowsome describes himself as "essentially amiable and harmless, a genuine enthusiast for the fine foolish advertisements of yesterday. The trouble with today's ads is that they often replace that old lusty goofiness with a kind of crafty rancidity. The voice of the cuckoo is silent; no more does a muted 'Help, Help, Let Me Out!' emerge from the trunk. Instead, we have tested and inexpressible fatuities about the thinking man's cigarette, capable less of charming the eye and ear than of producing involuntary spasms of distaste."

This forty-five-year-old ex-Harvard man, tall and with less sandy hair than in former years, is known as "Red" by both friends and enemies. "The latter will increase immeasurably after a perusal of this volume," he remarks dryly.

Q

Rowsome, Frank

They laughed when I sat
                down